# Numerical Techniques in Finance

# Numerical Techniques in Finance

Simon Benninga

The MIT Press
Cambridge, Massachusetts
London, England

Second Printing, 1990

This book was set in Times Roman by Asco Trade Typesetting Ltd. in Hong Kong and printed and bound by Halliday Lithograph in the United States of America.

The programs provided in this book are for instructional purposes only and are intended solely as examples of how a particular problem might be solved. Neither the author nor The MIT Press makes any implied or express warranty or representation that the programs are correct or free of error. In particular, we do not guarantee that the programs meet any standard of merchantability or utility. Neither the author nor The MIT Press is responsible for any damages, direct or indirect, arising out of the use of the materials in this book.

Library of Congress Cataloging-in-Publication Data

Benninga, Simon.
   Numerical techniques in finance.

   Includes index.
   1. Finance—Mathematical models.   I.  Title.
HG174.B38   1989      658.1'5'02855369      88-27147
ISBN 0-262-02286-9
ISBN 0-262-52141-5 (pbk.)

# Contents

## IV  DURATION AND IMMUNIZATION

## V  THE TECHNICAL BACKGROUND

# Preface

The aim of this book is to present some important models in finance and to show how they can be solved numerically and/or simulated. In this sense, this is a finance "cookbook." Like any cookbook, it gives recipes with a list of ingredients and instructions for making and baking. A recipe, however, is just a starting point; having followed it a number of times, you can think of variations of your own and make the results suit your own tastes and needs.

The minimum background you will need for this book is a good introductory course in finance. For some of the more advanced applications, it will help to have some knowledge of portfolio theory and/or speculative markets.

In addition to this theoretical background, it is necessary to know enough Lotus 1-2-3 to be able to set up a simple spreadsheet. Advanced Lotus techniques, such as Lotus functions, macros, and the use of data tables, are explained in the text. The models in the book are solved, and the programs written, in Lotus spreadsheets; where necessary, the Lotus Version 2 macro language is used.

The first four of the book's five parts address various areas of finance. The parts are largely independent, though chapters within the same part are likely to draw heavily on one another. The last part of the book focuses on technical topics. Some of these topics are mathematical (the Gauss-Seidel and Newton-Raphson methods, matrices, and random-number generators), and some deal with advanced aspects of Lotus. This part is meant to be used as a reference when you encounter an unfamiliar concept or a Lotus technique in one of the finance chapters.

I owe thanks to a great many people (colleagues and students alike) for comments on various portions of the book. Among those who have given me their time are Rami Amir, Lew Asimow, Ilan Ben Melech, Elizabeth Caulk, Yoav Dothan, Mike Fink, Terry Garden, Don Keim, Haim Levy, Ofra Lustigman, Batia Mintz, Vikas Nath, Lillian Ng, Marshall Sarnat, Meir Schneller, George Szpiro, and Frans Tempelaar. Students at Ben-Gurion University in Beer Sheva, the Hebrew University of Jerusalem, Tel Aviv University, the Wharton School of the University of Pennsylvania, and the University of Groningen in the Netherlands have been guinea pigs for portions of the book. I want to thank the Krueger Center for Finance and the Recanati Fund (both of the Hebrew University) and the Anderson Graduate School of Management at the University of California at Los Angeles for financial support.

Finally, Paul Bethge and Terry Vaughn of The MIT Press have been especially helpful in guiding the editing process. My special thanks for extraordinary editorial assistance go to Brian Maizlish.

**Note**

Computer input and output have been photographed from computer-generated hard copy.

# I CORPORATE FINANCE

# Overview

Chapters 1–5 present some models of corporate finance that require extensive numerical computation.

The first is a model of financial-statement prediction. Such models are extremely important in that they allow the simulation of financial performance over time with the standard accounting constraints. This does not mean, however, that the models are merely technical. Indeed, the accounting constraints are broad enough to incorporate a variety of modes of corporate behavior. Because a corporation's balance sheet and its income statement must be solved simultaneously, this kind of model is ideal for a spreadsheet that allows circular arguments (as Lotus's does).

The second chapter uses the financial-statement-prediction model in valuing mergers and acquisitions. Valuation of this type requires that discount rates be related to the leverage of the company. The appendix of the chapter discusses the current state of the finance theory that relates the calculation of rates of return and leverage.

Chapter 3 shows how to derive debt capacity from riskless cash flows. This intrinsically important topic has applications in real-estate finance and in leasing.

Leasing is the topic of chapters 4 and 5. Chapter 4 discusses lease analysis using the equivalent-loan method. Chapter 5 discusses the lessor's analysis of leveraged leases and compares the internal-rate-of-return method of analyzing these leases with the accounting profession's multiple-phases method.

# 1 Simulating Financial Statements

## 1.1 Introduction

The usefulness of financial-statement projections for corporate financial management is undisputed. By examining *pro forma* financial statements, we can predict how much financing a firm will need in future years. We can play the usual "what if" games of simulation models, and we can ask what strains on the firm may be caused by changes in financial and sales parameters.

The use of spreadsheet models for the prediction of balance sheets is usually limited, however, to models in which all the items in the financial statement follow in a straightforward manner from sales or from other financial-statement items. To use a spreadsheet in this way—worthwhile though it is—is to fail to consider two other major types of financial-statement-prediction models that have been widely discussed in the literature:

• *Models in which it is assumed that the firm wishes to maintain a given ratio of debt to equity in its balance sheet* (see, for example, Warren and Shelton 1971). As will be shown further on, this assumption means that certain balance-sheet relations are determined from the simultaneous solution of several linear equations. In the Warren-Shelton model the firm solves a problem that involves some twenty simultaneous equations in as many unknowns.

• *Models in which the firm maximizes its value subject to a set of financing constraints* (see Myers and Pogue 1974 and further references in Brealey and Myers 1984).[1]

The latter models are theoretically preferable to the former, but the Warren-Shelton conception of financial planning is much more widespread in practice.

The Warren-Shelton model proceeds on two assumptions: that most balance-sheet items are directly or indirectly related to sales, and that the firm's primary financing concern is to maintain an appropriate balance between the value of debt and the value of equity in the balance sheet. Given these two assumptions, the firm predicts its sales for the coming year (or years) and predicts the interest rates it will have to pay on its long-term debt over the planning period. The model is solved by finding the solution to a set of simultaneous linear equations predicting both the balance sheets and the income statements for the coming years.

The introduction of simultaneity of financial relationships is usually thought to be beyond standard spreadsheet programs, and thus the Warren-Shelton-type financial-planning models are generally solved on larger computer systems. In fact, despite the simultaneity, these types of models can easily be set up and solved using commonly available microcomputer spreadsheet programs.

The next section presents a simple example that embodies all the essential features of the Warren-Shelton-type financial-planning model; the following section shows how this example may be solved using Lotus 1-2-3.

## 1.2   How Financial Models Work: Theory and Examples

Almost all financial-statement models are sales-driven; that is, most financial-statement variables are assumed to be functions of the sales level of the firm. For example, accounts receivable may be taken to be a direct percentage of the sales of the firm. A slightly more complicated example would postulate that the net-fixed-assets account is a step function of the level of sales:

$$\text{Net fixed assets} = \begin{cases} a & \text{if sales} < A \\ b & \text{if sales } A \leqslant \text{sales} < B \\ \text{and so on.} \end{cases}$$

In order to solve a financial-planning model, one must distinguish between those financial-statement items that are functional relationships of sales and perhaps of other financial-statement items and those items that involve policy decisions. The asset side of the balance sheet is usually assumed to be dependent only on functional relationships. The current liabilities may also be taken to involve functional relationships only, leaving the mix between long-term debt and equity as a policy decision.

A simple example of this is the following. We wish to predict the financial statements for a firm whose current (year 0) level of sales is 1,000. The firm expects its sales to grow at a rate of 10 percent per year. In addition, the firm anticipates the following financial-statement relations:

CA/sales (ratio of current assets to sales):   15%

CL/sales (ratio of current liabilities to sales):   8%

NFA/sales (ratio of net fixed assets to sales):   77%

Expenses, excluding interest and depreciation = 80% of sales.

## Depreciation

Fixed assets and depreciation are troublesome to model. For the moment, we shall employ the following model of depreciation of fixed assets (at the end of the chapter, we shall return to this topic, and explore some alternative models).

• The firm's depreciation policy is to depreciate all fixed assets over a ten-year life span, using straight-line depreciation.

• New assets are purchased at the end of the year.

• The accumulated depreciation in any given year is calculated as follows:

Accumulated depr($t$)

$$= \text{Accumulated depr}(t - 1) + \frac{\text{Assets at cost } (t - 1)}{\text{Average depreciable life}}.$$

## Long-Term Debt

The firm has a long-term debt of 280 in year 0, on which it pays interest of 10.5 percent. The debt is to be repaid in annual equal installments over 5 years. The firm estimates that interest on any new long-term debt will be 9.5 percent. The common-stock account in the balance sheet shows an initial balance of 450, and the firm has retained earnings in year 0 of 110. The firm has a 47 percent tax rate.

## Financial Statement

The firm's balance sheet and its profit-and-loss statement look as follows.

**Balance sheet**

| *Assets* | *Liabilities* |
|---|---|
| CURRENT ASSETS | CURRENT LIABILITIES |
| FIXED ASSETS | LONG-TERM DEBT |
|    at cost | STOCK |
|    depreciation | RETAINED EARNINGS |
|    net | |
| TOTAL ASSETS | TOTAL LIABILITIES |

**Profit-and-loss statement**

Sales
— Expenses
— Interest payments
— Depreciation

Profit before tax
— Taxes

Profit after tax
— Dividend

Addition to Retained Earnings

The facts given thus far suffice to determine the asset side of the balance sheet as well as the current liabilities. Three variables remain to be determined: NEW STOCK (which the firm will sell), NEW LONG-TERM DEBT, and the ADDITIONAL RETAINED EARNINGS for the year. To determine these, we have to examine the firm's financial policies.

As a matter of policy, the firm wishes to reduce its current 50 percent ratio of the book value of debt to the book value of equity to 40 percent over the next 5 years. This decision imposes a constraint on the financing, which the model must solve.

## 1.3   Setting Up and Solving the Model using Lotus

A schematic of the financial statements for year 1 follows. (Usually the numbers refer to the year. Thus, RET1 is year 1's retained earnings. The dollar signs indicate, loosely, which items you will want to copy absolutely to the next years.)

```
CURRENT ASSETS              ($SALES*(1+$SALES GROWTH)^YEAR1*$CA/SALES)
FIXED ASSETS
  at cost                   +NET FIXED ASSETS1+ACCUMULATED DEPR1
  accumulated depreciation  +FIXED ASSETS AT COST0*0.1+ACCUMULATED DEPR0
  net                       +SALES1*$NFA/SALES
TOTAL ASSETS                (CURRENT ASSETS1+NET FIXED ASSETS1)
```

(We have assumed that all new assets are purchased at the end of year 1, so that these assets will first be depreciated in year 2.)

```
CURRENT LIABILITIES    ($SALES*(1+$SALES GROWTH)^YEAR1)*$CL/SALES
LONG TERM DEBT         +DEBT/EQUITY1*(STOCK1+RETAINED EARNINGS1)
STOCK                  (STOCK0+NEW STOCK1)
RETAINED EARNINGS      (RETAINED0+RETENTION1)
TOTAL LIABILITIES      @SUM(CL1,LTD1,STOCK1,RETAINED1)


determination of unknowns
NEW STOCK              (TOTAL ASSETS1-CURRENT LIAB1-LTDEBT1-STOCK0-RETAINED EARNINGS1)
NEW DEBT               +TOTALNEWDBT1-TOTALNEWDBT0
TOTAL NEW DEBT         +LTDEBT-$LTDEBT0*(1-0.2*YEAR1)
```

Long-term debt is determined by the desired debt/equity ratio for year 1. Since 20 percent of the long-term debt on the books in year 0 has to be repaid in year 1, total new debt is determined by the expression given above. In each year $t$,

NEW DEBT = TOTALNEWDEBT(t) − TOTALNEWDEBT(t1).

The variable TOTALNEWDEBT0 (which is, of course, zero) has been put in only for consistency in copying the formula.

```
income statement
SALES              ($SALES*(1+$SALES GROWTH)^YEAR1)
EXPENSES           +SALES1*$EXPENSES/SALES
INTEREST PAYMENTS  +$LTDEBT0*(1-0.2*YEAR1)*$CURRENT%+TOTALNEWDBT1*$NEW INTEREST
DEPRECIATION       +ACCUMULATED DEPR1-ACCUMULATED DEPR0
PROFIT BEFORE TAX  +SALES1-EXPENSES1-INTEREST1-DEPR1
PROFIT AFTER TAX   +PBT1*(1-$TAX)
DIVIDENDS          (PAT1*$PAYOUT)
RETENTION          +PAT1-DIV1
```

The additional retained earnings are derived from the firm's income statement. The net profits after taxes depend on the firm's total debt, which depends on the new debt raised, which depends on the firm's desired debt/

equity ratio. In Lotus, none of these circularities is material. (As soon as Lotus detects a circularity in the argument, you will see a CIRC at the bottom of the screen. This does not prevent a solution, however.)

One way to solve this model is to write out the equations for the various balance-sheet items explicitly and to solve them as a system of simultaneous linear equations. This is the approach taken by Warren and Shelton (1971). Another way to solve the model is to use recursion. A recursive solution looks like the schematic spreadsheet solution above: Each unknown in the model is written as a function of other unknowns, and the unknowns are substituted one into the other. At any stage, the current value of an unknown depends on the previous values of the other unknowns on which it is dependent.

As an example of recursion, take our equation for STOCK. Stock in any year is the sum of the STOCK in the previous year plus the NEW STOCK. NEW STOCK is defined in terms of other balance-sheet items (RETAINED EARNINGS for the current year, the LONG TERM DEBT for the current year, and so on). These items, in turn, are functions of balance-sheet and income-statement items. Ultimately, our model involves extensive circularity of argument: STOCK depends on NEW STOCK, which depends on RETAINED EARNINGS, which depends on RETEN-TION, which depends on PROFIT AFTER TAX, which depends on INTEREST PAYMENTS, which depends on LONG TERM DEBT, which depends on STOCK. This is only one example of the kinds of circularities involved.

Recursive methods involve taking an initial solution for the variables and successively "plugging this solution into" the model. Every time we do this, we get an imprecise approximation to a solution, since the current value of any variable depends on the previous values of the other variables. At some point the approximations will converge; that is, the current value of STOCK based on the previous values of all the other variables will be the same as the current value of these variables based on the previous value of STOCK.[2]

Because the solution involves a circularity of arguments, the model will not converge immediately to the correct solution. Several presses of the F9 ("calc") button usually suffice to cause the model to converge.[3]

The finished product looks like this (all numbers have been rounded off to the nearest whole number, so there may be some rounding errors):

|                    |        |                     | 0    | 1    | 2    | 3    | 4    | 5    |
|--------------------|--------|---------------------|------|------|------|------|------|------|
| INITIAL SALES      | 1000   | balance sheet       |      |      |      |      |      |      |
| SALES GROWTH       | 0.10   | CURRENT ASSETS      | 150  | 165  | 182  | 200  | 220  | 242  |
|                    |        | FIXED ASSETS        |      |      |      |      |      |      |
| CA/SALES           | 0.15   |   at cost           | 1100 | 1287 | 1500 | 1744 | 2020 | 2335 |
| CL/SALES           | 0.08   |   depreciation      | 330  | 440  | 569  | 719  | 893  | 1095 |
| NFA/SALES          | 0.77   |   net               | 770  | 847  | 932  | 1025 | 1127 | 1240 |
| EXPENSES/SALES     | 0.80   | TOTAL ASSETS        | 920  | 1012 | 1113 | 1225 | 1347 | 1482 |
| INITIAL DEBT       | 280    | CURRENT LIABILITIES | 80   | 88   | 97   | 106  | 117  | 129  |
| CURRENT INTEREST   | 0.105  | LONG TERM DEBT      | 280  | 300  | 320  | 342  | 364  | 387  |
| NEW INTEREST       | 0.095  | STOCK               | 450  | 502  | 561  | 628  | 704  | 791  |
| INITIAL STOCK      | 450    | RETAINED EARNINGS   | 110  | 123  | 136  | 149  | 162  | 175  |
| INITIAL RETAINED   | 110    | TOTAL LIABILITIES   | 920  | 1012 | 1113 | 1225 | 1347 | 1482 |
| TAX RATE           | 0.47   | determination of unknowns |   |      |      |      |      |      |
| DIVIDEND PAYOUT    | 0.70   | NEW STOCK           |      | 52   | 59   | 67   | 76   | 87   |
|                    |        | NEW DEBT            |      | 76   | 77   | 77   | 78   | 79   |
|                    |        | TOTAL NEW DEBT      | 0    | 76   | 152  | 230  | 308  | 387  |
|                    |        | RATIO OF DEBT/EQUITY |     | 0.48 | 0.46 | 0.44 | 0.42 | 0.40 |
|                    |        | income statement    |      |      |      |      |      |      |
|                    |        | SALES               | 1000 | 1100 | 1210 | 1331 | 1464 | 1611 |
|                    |        | EXPENSES            | 800  | 880  | 968  | 1065 | 1171 | 1288 |
|                    |        | INTEREST PAYMENTS   | 29   | 31   | 32   | 34   | 35   | 37   |
|                    |        | DEPRECIATION        | 110  | 110  | 129  | 150  | 174  | 202  |
|                    |        | PROFIT BEFORE TAX   | 61   | 79   | 81   | 83   | 83   | 83   |
|                    |        | PROFIT AFTER TAX    | 32   | 42   | 43   | 44   | 44   | 44   |
|                    |        | DIVIDENDS           | 22   | 29   | 30   | 31   | 31   | 31   |
|                    |        | RETENTION           | 10   | 13   | 13   | 13   | 13   | 13   |

## 1.4   Where Do We Go From Here?

The model presented above is a highly simplified representation of what really goes on in the firm. Specific applications of the model require more knowledge of how the firm works. This section suggests some ways to extend the basic model.

A word of warning: The more detail you put into your model, the more guesses you are going to have to make, and thus the more opportunities there will be for mistakes. You are often better off using a simple model all of whose faults and inaccuracies you understand than with a complicated model in which the big picture gets lost in a welter of details. This "can't see the forest for the trees" phenomenon is a well-known modeling problem.

Here are some ways to make the model realistic:

• The firm may not be able to raise new equity in the coming years. In this case, all of the firm's new financing will come from additional debt. In terms of the model, this involves a simplification, since there are fewer simultaneous equations to be solved.

• The model we have used assumes that you pay no interest on your current liabilities. In a more detailed model, you might break down current liabilities into payables (which bear no explicit interest, though an interest charge is implicit in the extension of trade credit) and bank loans (which bear an explicit interest charge).

• You might want to break down the current assets into their various items—for example, a line for accounts receivable, one for inventories, and one for cash and marketable securities. You would then want to model the relation of each of these items to the activities of the firm. A reasonable set of assumptions is the following.

*Accounts receivable*: Directly and linearly related to sales (i.e., a percentage of sales).

*Inventories*: If operations-research models are to be believed, the optimal inventories rise as the square root of sales (see Baumol 1972, chapter 1). The result is that the optimal (cost-minimizing) inventory $I$ is given by

$$I = \sqrt{2aQk},$$

where $a$ is the fixed cost of reordering, $k$ is the unit carrying cost of inventory, and $Q$ is the level of sales. We can easily insert this into our models.

*Cash and marketable securities*: We can distinguish two primary motives for holding these items. The firm must hold some cash (we will use this term loosely to include marketable securities) to complete the day-to-day transactions associated with the business. Such cash items are clearly related to sales, though the connection may be complex. For a survey of models (of varying degrees of implementibility), see chapter 29 of Brealey and Myers 1984. However, many firms use marketable securities to "park" excess cash. This use of cash should not be directly related to sales. See problem 5 at the end of this chapter for an example.

• You may want to break down the fixed assets of the firm and build a separate model in which the classes of assets, their relation to sales, and their depreciation schedules are detailed.

• You may want to break down the firm's current liabilities into their components.

• You may want to improve the modeling of the fixed-asset accounts. This is such a big subject that a separate section has been reserved for it below.

## 1.5   Modeling Fixed Assets

The model we have employed so far assumes that assets do not die and consequently have to be removed from the depreciable base. This is a troubling assumption. To see why, consider the following example.

A certain firm's NFA is equal to 100 percent of its sales. Suppose the depreciable life of the assets is 5 years, and suppose that initially the firm has assets that cost 1,000 and have been depreciated for 4 years. (For purposes of illustration we assume that no new assets have been purchased during the last 4 years. This story itself is internally consistent only if the firm's sales have been declining for the last 4 years.) The state of affairs in year 0 is thus

```
assets at cost       1000
accumulated depr.     800
net fixed assets      200
```

Suppose the anticipated sales are as follows:

| year | 1 | 2 | 3 |
|------|-----|-----|-----|
| sales | 250 | 300 | 400 |

What level of assets will be needed? If we use the model above, we will get the following:

| year | 0 | 1 | 2 | 3 |
|------|------|------|------|------|
| assets at cost | 1000 | 1250 | 1550 | 1960 |
| accumulated depr. | 800 | 1000 | 1250 | 1560 |
| net fixed assets | 200 | 250 | 300 | 400 |
| annual depreciation | | 200 | 250 | 310 |

This is clearly not true, however, since after year 1 the old assets (which cost 1,000) have been fully depreciated and are "dead." They should thus be removed from the books. Taking this into account, we get the following:

"ACTUAL FIXED ASSETS ACCOUNT"

| year | 0 | 1 | 2 | 3 |
|------|------|------|------|------|
| assets at cost | 1000 | 250 | 350 | 520 |
| accumulated depr. | 800 | 0 | 50 | 120 |
| net fixed assets | 200 | 250 | 300 | 400 |
| annual depreciation | | 200 | 50 | 70 |

("Actual Fixed Assets Account" is put in quotation marks here because the subject as a whole is so iffy. Nobody really believes that depreciation reflects the actual economic use of the assets. Thus, what we are calling actual should really be called a better version of the model. The real question is whether the model can give us some insight into what is happening in the firm. Experience indicates that the answer is Yes, provided you use the model judiciously and understand its limitations.)

Now the real problems start: If you knew the exact ages of all of the assets, and you knew their depreciation schedules, you could implement these ideas in a more correct model. However, this is not only unrealistic; it also negates the whole purpose of financial-statement modeling, which is to get a snapshot of the firm at different stages in the future. There are two ways out of this conundrum:

- Stick with the old model. As long as you don't stretch it too far into the future, and as long as your initial asset base isn't too old, this model will give you a pretty good feel for what's going on.

- If your assets have a constant, depreciable life, then in the long run the assets at cost will be equal to

$$\frac{\text{Net fixed assets}}{1 - 1/\text{Depreciable asset life}}.$$

Thus, if the depreciable life of assets is 10 years, we would expect that in the long run the assets at cost will be equal to

$$\frac{\text{Net fixed assets}}{0.9}.$$

If you like this story better than the previous one, use it.

## Exercises

1. Generate the model described in the chapter. Assume that current liabilities bear no interest.

2. Now consider a different problem. The firm feels that it will not be able to sell any new stock in the next five years.
a. If it pays no dividends, what will happen to its debt/equity ratio? Assume the same growth rate of sales as in the previous problem.
b. What is the maximum annual growth rate of sales so that the firm's debt/equity ratio will not exceed 0.6?

3. The model described in the chapter assumes that all new debt is raised at the beginning of the year and that rapayments of the old debt are made at the beginning of the year. (Somewhat inconsistently, it assumes that new assets are acquired only at the end of each year—this is a didactic compromise.) Set out a model in which debt repayment is made at the end of the year and in which new debt is likewise raised at the end of the year.
4. Consider the following variation of the model of exercise 2: Let "current assets" denote only current assets needed to support sales, and add another

current account called "cash." Make the following additional assumptions: The firm does not repay any debt, the interest on old debt and new debt is the same (9.5 percent), the ratio of net fixed assets to sales is 0.65, the firm puts retained earnings not needed to support sales into its cash accounts, and cash earns 8.7 percent interest. Build an appropriate model.

5. Find a firm whose financial statements are available for the past 10 years. Go back to the last 5 years and try to figure out how the various financial-statement items are related to the sales of the firm. Then build a financial-statement model for the firm based on what you have learned. Finally, compare the output of your model with the actual results for the last 5 years.

## Notes

1. These models correspond to the constrained-maximization models of linear programming. The solution of these models makes use of the Kuhn-Tucker constraints.

2. This recursive method of solving simultaneous linear equations, called the Gauss-Seidel method, involves the iterative substitution of solutions in simultaneous linear equations. For further explanation of the Gauss-Seidel method, see chapter 20. Although convergence of the Gauss-Seidel method is not always guaranteed, almost all financial simulation models of the kind set out here converge. For sufficient conditions under which recursive solutions of linear equations in several unknowns converge, see pp. 561–567 of Hildebrand 1974.

3. Once you have the model set up and running, you may want to do two things: First, use /Worksheet Global Recalculation Manual to prevent updating of the spreadsheet unless you use the CALC function key (F9). Second, use /Worksheet Global Recalculation Iteration to set the model for twenty iterations every time you hit CALC.

## References

Baumol, W. J. 1972. *Economic Theory and Operations Analysis*. Englewood Cliffs, N.J.: Prentice-Hall.

Brealey, R., and S. C. Myers. 1984. *Principles of Corporate Finance*. New York: McGraw-Hill.

Hildebrand, F. B. 1974. *Introduction to Numerical Analysis*. New York: McGraw-Hill.

Myers, S. C., and G. A. Pogue. 1974. "A Programming Approach to Corporate Financial Management." *Journal of Finance* 29 (May): 579–599.

Warren, J. M., and J. P. Shelton. 1971. "A Simultaneous Equation Approach to Financial Planning." *Journal of Finance* 26 (December): 1123–1142.

# 2 Analyzing Mergers and Acquisitions

## 2.1 Introduction

The financial model introduced in chapter 1 can be a useful tool for analyzing a merger or an acquisition, as this chapter will illustrate.

Suppose that Scrooge, Inc., is considering purchasing Waif, Inc. Waif looks like a good purchase because of its strong management team, its good product line, its stable earnings, and its growth potential. The only question remaining is the price.

To figure the price, Scrooge puts its best financial analyst to work: Simple Simon, a recent MBA from one of the best business schools in the country. Simon's plan is simple: He is going to make a five-year financial projection for Waif, and discount the projected dividends and terminal value to Scrooge at a risk-adjusted discount rate. This is what he learned at business school.

## 2.2 Simon's Assumptions

• After the merger Scrooge will own 100 percent of Waif's equity, but Waif will continue to operate as an independent company. Scrooge's ownership will allow it to determine Waif's financial policy.

• The following are critical values for Waif for the next 5 years.

b.1. Current assets/Sales = 32%

b.2. Current liabilities/Sales = 10%

b.3. Net fixed assets/Sales = 60%

b.4. Expenses (excluding depreciation and interest)/Sales = 80%

b.5. Tax rate = 40%

• Scrooge will take over Waif with its existing long-term debt, which is $4,522. This debt bears interest of 10 percent. The current market interest rate on long-term debt is likewise 10 percent, and Simon expects this rate to continue for the next 5 years. (If you believe in efficient markets, there is not much reason to assume anything else.)

• Any new financing Waif needs will have to come from debt. Scrooge is too tight-fisted to contribute any equity to Waif.

• Any new assets purchased will be depreciated over a 10-year life. New assets are purchased at the beginning of the year, so that incremental depreciation is based on the full balance-sheet value of at-cost assets of the same year. (This is somewhat different from the assumption of the model in chapter 1.)

• Scrooge will own Waif for 5 years, and will sell it at the end of year 5 after taking the year-5 dividend from Waif. A major problem is to calculate some kind of reasonable number for the value of Waif at this time (see below).

• Cash flows accruing to Scrooge from its ownership of Waif will be discounted at *Waif's cost of equity*. This rate reflects the riskiness of owning shares in Waif, and it has to reflect both the underlying business risk of Waif and any additional risks that accrue to shareholders in Waif because of Waif's leverage.

The next section discusses the method used to adjust the cost of Waif's equity to reflect the leverage.

## 2.3  Adjusting the Cost of Equity to Reflect Leverage

Simon uses the Modigliani-Miller theorem to adjust the cost of equity to reflect leverage. Were Waif completely unlevered, its cost of equity would be 10 percent. The Modigliani-Miller formulation says that the cost of equity adjusted for leverage is given by

$$k_e(L) = k_e(U) + [k_e(U) - i]\frac{D}{E}(1 - T),$$

where $k_e(U)$ is the cost of equity capital were the firm unlevered, $k_e(L)$ is the cost of equity capital adjusted for leverage, $i$ is the current market interest rate on the firm's debt, $D$ is the market value of the firm's debt, $E$ is the market value of the firm's equity, and $T$ is the firm's tax rate.

After reading the textbooks, Simon is sure that this formula represents the best approach, even though he is aware that in using it he is making a lot of compromises. (For example, the Modigliani-Miller analysis assumes infinite-lived cash flows, no growth, and no personal taxes. For the relevance of the current formula as an approximation, see chapter 19 of Brealey and Myers 1984.)

Even before he starts, Simon makes another compromise: Although the theory says that $D$ and $E$ in the formula should be the *market values* of the debt and the equity of the firm, Simon decides to substitute the *book values*. The reason he gives is that Waif's stock is not listed on any market. In any case, he thinks the balance-sheet numbers are a fair approximation.

## 2.4 Calculating the Residual Value of Waif, Inc.

One of the biggest problems for Simon is to calculate a reasonable value for Waif at the end of the five-year period. Simon assumes that Waif's terminal market value (debt and equity) will be the discounted value of its net operating cash flows. (This is not the only plausible way in which the terminal value of the firm might be calculated. Three additional alternatives are given in the exercises at the end of this chapter.) Simon's method gives the following formula for the terminal value of Waif, Inc.:

$$\frac{(1 - T)[\text{Sales}(5) - \text{Expenses}(5) - \text{Depreciation}(5)](1 + g)}{k_a - g},$$

where $T$ is Waif's marginal tax rate, $k_a$ is its weighted average cost of capital in year 5, and $g$ is the rate of growth of sales.

This calculation assumes that Scrooge sells Waif after collecting the year-5 dividend, and that the market value of the firm at this point in time is equal to

$$\sum_{t=1}^{\infty} \frac{(1 - T)[\text{Sales}(5) - \text{Expenses}(5) - \text{Depreciation}(5)](1 + g)^t}{(1 + k_a)^t}.$$

This calculation of the firm's terminal value is an appropriate extension of the Modigliani-Miller theorem. Under the Modigliani-Miller assumptions (infinite-lived cash flows, no growth, etc.), the market value of the firm is the discounted value of the firm's after-tax operating cash flows, discounted at the firm's weighted-average cost of capital (WACC). When we take growth into account, we assume that the firm's year-5 after-tax operating cash flows will grow by the rate of sales growth. In the no-growth Modigliani-Miller model, depreciation is reinvested in the assets of the firm to maintain their productive capacity. The difficult implicit assumption made here is that when the deduction made for depreciation grows at the rate of sales growth, this suffices to ensure that the productive capacity of these assets also grows at this rate. The formula used here assumes that the

WACC in year 5 is the appropriate discount rate for the firm's operating cash flows, and that these cash flows grow at the growth rate of sales.

Given this total anticipated market value of the firm, the value of the firm's equity in year 5 is equal to

Value of firm(5) − Total debt of firm(5).

This number must be discounted at Waif's year-5 cost of equity to give the present value to Scrooge of selling its equity in Waif in year 5. In the spreadsheet below, this number has been calculated to be 31,569—which, when discounted, gives 13,474.

The last problem is to calculate $k_a$, Waif's weighted-average cost of capital. Simon uses the standard formula:

$$k_a = \frac{E}{E + D} k_e + \frac{D}{E + D} k_d (1 - T),$$

where $E$ and $D$ are the values of the firm's equity and debt and where $k_e$ and $k_d$ are the firm's cost of equity and cost of debt. The cost of equity reflects both Waif's underlying business risks and any riskiness caused by Waif's financing. It should be changed year by year to reflect these factors, although Simon's adjustment assumes a constant business risk and uses the Modigliani-Miller formula to adjust for financial risk. ($E$ and $D$ should be the *market values* of the firm's equity and debt. In this chapter we shall use the balance-sheet values as proxies for the market values. This is very bad practice and should be avoided. Often, however, there is no alternative; for example, a firm's equity may not be publicly traded, or one may be trying to predict a firm's WACC several years in the future.)

## 2.5 The Results

When Simple Simon got through with his analysis, he had a spreadsheet that was like the one below. The particular spreadsheet says that at a dividend payout ratio of 60 percent and a 8 percent annual growth rate of sales, Waif is worth $14.41 million.

| INITIAL SALES | 10000 | |
|---|---|---|
| DIVIDEND PAYOUT | 0.6 | assumptions: |
| SALES GROWTH | 0.08 | 1. All new assets purchased at beginning of year |
| EQUITY RATE(U) | 0.14 | 2. Roll-overs of existing debt at same interest rate |
| CA/SALES | 0.32 | |
| CL/SALES | 0.1 | |
| NFA/SALES | 0.6 | |
| EXPENSES/SALES | 0.8 | |
| DEPRECIATION | 0.1 | |
| INITIAL DEBT | 4522 | |
| CURRENT INTEREST | 0.1 | |
| INITIAL STOCK | 2000 | |
| INITIAL RETAINED | 1678 | |
| INITIAL DEPR | 500 | |
| TAX RATE | 0.4 | |

| balance sheet | 0 | 1 | 2 | 3 | 4 | 5 | terminal value (year 5) |
|---|---|---|---|---|---|---|---|
| CURRENT ASSETS | 3200.00 | 3456.00 | 3732.48 | 4031.08 | 4353.56 | 4701.85 | |
| FIXED ASSETS | | | | | | | |
| at cost | 6500.00 | 7755.56 | 9193.28 | 10836.84 | 12712.78 | 14850.90 | |
| depreciation | 500.00 | 1275.56 | 2194.88 | 3278.57 | 4549.85 | 6034.94 | |
| net | 6000.00 | 6480.00 | 6998.40 | 7558.27 | 8162.93 | 8815.97 | |
| TOTAL ASSETS | 9200.00 | 9936.00 | 10730.88 | 11589.35 | 12516.50 | 13517.82 | |
| | | | | | | | |
| CURRENT LIABILITIES | 1000.00 | 1080.00 | 1166.40 | 1259.71 | 1360.49 | 1469.33 | |
| LONG TERM DEBT | 4522.00 | 4964.89 | 5465.30 | 6030.62 | 6669.12 | 7390.11 | |
| STOCK | 2000.00 | 2000.00 | 2000.00 | 2000.00 | 2000.00 | 2000.00 | |
| RETAINED EARNINGS | 1678.00 | 1891.11 | 2099.18 | 2299.02 | 2486.89 | 2658.38 | |
| TOTAL LIABILITIES | 9200.00 | 9936.00 | 10730.88 | 11589.35 | 12516.50 | 13517.82 | |

| income statement | | | | | | | |
|---|---|---|---|---|---|---|---|
| SALES | 10000.00 | 10800.00 | 11664.00 | 12597.12 | 13604.89 | 14693.28 | |
| EXPENSES | 8000.00 | 8640.00 | 9331.20 | 10077.70 | 10883.91 | 11754.62 | |
| INTEREST PAYMENTS | 452.20 | 496.49 | 546.53 | 603.06 | 666.91 | 739.01 | |
| DEPRECIATION | 500.00 | 775.56 | 919.33 | 1083.68 | 1271.28 | 1485.09 | |
| PROFIT BEFORE TAX | 1047.80 | 887.96 | 866.94 | 832.68 | 782.79 | 714.55 | |
| PROFIT AFTER TAX | 628.68 | 532.77 | 520.16 | 499.61 | 469.67 | 428.73 | |
| DIVIDENDS | 377.21 | 319.66 | 312.10 | 299.76 | 281.80 | 257.24 | 31569.07 |
| RETENTION | 251.47 | 213.11 | 208.07 | 199.84 | 187.87 | 171.49 | |

| check on debt/equity | | | | | | | |
|---|---|---|---|---|---|---|---|
| total debt/equity | 1.50 | 1.55 | 1.62 | 1.70 | 1.79 | 1.90 | |
| ltd/equity | 1.23 | 1.28 | 1.33 | 1.40 | 1.49 | 1.59 | |

| | | | | | | | |
|---|---|---|---|---|---|---|---|
| equity rate(L) | 0.176032 | 0.177284 | 0.178827 | 0.180699 | 0.182949 | 0.185643 | |
| WACC | 0.106387 | 0.105930 | 0.105391 | 0.104772 | 0.104074 | 0.103298 | |
| pres.value(t) | | 271.53 | 224.59 | 182.12 | 143.91 | 109.79 | 13473.81 |

PV of acquisition 14405.74 this is the value of the equity we're willing to pay today

## 2.6   Sensitivity

Mr. Scrooge of Scrooge, Inc., wanted to know how sensitive the results
would be to differences in the payout ratio. Simon used /Data Table 1 to
produce the following table:

| payout ratio | value of Waif |
|---|---|
| 0 | 10935.94 |
| 0.1 | 11485.27 |
| 0.2 | 12047.28 |
| 0.3 | 12621.31 |
| 0.4 | 13206.52 |
| 0.5 | 13801.79 |
| 0.6 | 14405.74 |
| 0.7 | 15016.62 |
| 0.8 | 15632.25 |
| 0.9 | 16249.99 |
| 1 | 16866.55 |

Why do the values go up as we go down the columns in this table? The
Modigliani-Miller model assumes that the tax shields on debt increase the
firm's value. Given a particular growth rate for sales, as the firm's payout
ratio increases, its debt increases, and hence its capitalized tax shields
increase—which, in turn, increases the firm's value.

**A Note on Techniques**

The /Data Table commands recalculate the spreadsheet for each payout
ratio. Because the spreadsheet itself is recursive, one must carry out each
recalculation several times to guarantee accuracy. Thus, before you implement the /Data Table command, make sure you set the spreadsheet for
multiple recalculation. The way to do this is to use the /Worksheet Global
Recalculation Iteration. Choosing Iteration = 20 should do the trick. (This
means that it will take relatively long to implement the /Data Table
command.)

## Exercises

1. Suppose Simon assumes that Scrooge can sell Waif in year 6 for whatever he buys it for today. Given the assumptions of the spreadsheet in section 2.4, what is the price of Waif?

2. The model in this chapter assumes that the terminal value of Waif is based on the explicit discounting of future cash flows. This is, of course, the assumption that is best suited (theoretically) to the standard financial model. Here are two more alternatives for calculating the terminal value of the firm, neither of which makes an explicit assumption about discounting future cash flows. For each alternative, calculate the value of acquiring Waif.
a. Assume that the firm's terminal equity value is the value of its net worth (STOCK plus RETAINED EARNINGS).
b. Assume that the terminal value of Waif is its year-5 earnings times a multiplier. This might be suitable if you believed that markets calculate stock values by multiplying earnings per share by a multiple. Calculate the terminal value using a multipliers of 10, 15, and 20.

3. Calculate the value of Waif to Scrooge for payout ratios of 0, 0.1, ..., 1 and for growth rates of 0, 1, ..., 10 percent. You have to use /Data Table 2 to do this. (While your computer is doing the calculations, you can go out and get a cup of coffee—this calculation will take a while.)

4. In many cases when a firm is sold for more than its book value, the excess of the acquisition price over the book value is attributed to the firm's fixed assets. (Some of the excess may also be attributed to goodwill.) The merger model in this chapter ignores asset writeups, which are important because they generated higher depreciation writeoffs. Write a model of the Scrooge-Waif merger that incorporates the asset writeups.

## References

Brealey, R., and S. Myers. 1984. *Principles of Corporate Finance*. New York: McGraw-Hill.

Levy, H., and M. Sarnat. 1986. *Capital Investment and Financial Decisions*. London: Prentice-Hall.

## Appendix:    Leverage and the Cost of Capital

### The Issue

At issue are the proper discount rates to be used for the cash flows derived from the financing of a project or on the firm. This issue has received a tremendous amount of attention in the finance literature. In this appendix an attempt will be made to summarize the relevant facts, insofar as they are known and agreed upon, and to indicate some of the areas of disagreement.

### Additivity in Perfect Capital Markets

First some notation should be defined. A cash flow for $N$ periods will be denoted by $A = \{A_0, A_1, \ldots, A_N\}$; we shall take $A_k$ to be the *expected cash flow* at the end of period $k$. If $A$ is a cash flow, we shall mean by NPV($A$) "the discounted value of the cash flows in A *at a discount rate that reflects their riskiness.*" (NPV stands for *net present value.*) Thus, the notation NPV( ) implies a discount rate dependent on the riskiness of the cash flows under consideration.

The starting point of our discussion is the *principle of additivity*: If $A$ and $B$ are cash flows, then

$$\text{NPV}(A + B) = \text{NPV}(A) + \text{NPV}(B).$$

This looks more innocuous than it really is. NPV($A + B$) is the net present value of the sum of two cash flows (at the discount rate reflecting the riskiness of this sum). By the principle of additivity, this is equal to the sum of the NPVs of the two cash flows.

The proof of the principle of additivity depends on the kinds of assumptions that are summarized in introductory economics courses under the heading "competitive markets." Suppose individuals in the market can costlessly combine and split up cash flows. Now consider a violation of the principle of additivity of the type

$$\text{NPV}(A + B) > \text{NPV}(A) + \text{NPV}(B).$$

In this case individuals could profit by buying cash flows $A$ and $B$ separately, combining them, and selling them at a profit. This would drive up the prices of $A$ and $B$ until the profit opportunity disappeared. The opposite inequality would disappear when individuals bought the combined cash flow, $A + B$, and split it up into its component parts.

## The Application of Additivity to Capital Structure: An Example

Here the use of the principle of additivity will be illustrated in a simple example. In the first part of the example we will consider the budgeting of capital for replacing an old machine with a new machine (no financing questions arise in this case). In the second part of the example, we will consider whether the financing of the replacement can affect the decision to replace the machine.

### The Replacement Problem

We start with a simple example of capital budgeting: The XYZ Corporation is using a machine that originally cost $100,000 ten years ago. The machine can be sold today for $30,000. It is being depreciated on a straight-line basis over a twenty-year life to a salvage value of zero. XYZ is considering replacing the old machine with a new model. The new model costs $200,000 and has a ten-year anticipated economic life. Over this period it will be depreciated using straight-line depreciation to a salvage value of zero.

The reason for the replacement is that the company anticipates that it will save $38,000 per year in pre-tax costs if it purchases the new machine. XYZ's tax rate is 45 percent.

XYZ's financial analysts come up with the following cash flows: The initial (period 0) cost of replacing the machine is $161,000. This number is arrived at by subtracting from the $200,000 price of the new machine the $30,000 received for the old machine and the $9,000 *tax shield* on the loss over book value on the sale of the old machine, for a net of $161,000. The tax shield arises from the fact that the current book value (i.e., original cost minus accumulated depreciation) of the old machine is $50,000. Yet XYZ can get only $30,000 for the machine. The $20,000 loss incurred, though not a cash expense, is an expense for tax purposes, and thus reduces the company's taxes by $0.45 \times \$20,000 = \$9,000$.

The change in the annual cash flows resulting from the purchase of the new machine is the sum of two cash flows. In each of the next ten years, the company will, if it purchases the new machine, save $38,000 in costs. After taxes, this results in a net cash flow of $(1 - 0.45) \times \$38,000 = \$20,900$. The second cash flow relates to the depreciation tax shields generated when XYZ buys the new machine. The new machine will be depreciated at

$20,000 per year, whereas the old machine was depreciated at $5,000 per year. The difference, $15,000, generates an additional tax shield of 0.45 × $15,000 = $6,750 per year.

Thus, if XYZ purchases the machine, its annual cash flows in years 1–10 will increase by $20,900 + $6,750 = $27,650.

This annual cash flow is not riskless. The depreciation tax shield component is nearly riskless (its realization depends only on XYZ's continued profitability and the anticipation that its tax rate will not change), but the $20,900 is definitely risky.

XYZ's analysts perceive a current riskless interest rate for 10-year loans of 10 percent. This, they feel, is an appropriate rate at which to discount the incremental depreciation tax shields from replacing the machine. These tax shields thus have a value of

$$\sum_{t=1}^{10} \frac{\$6,750}{(1.10)^t} = \$41,476.$$

After much discussion and argument, the analysts decide that the riskiness of the $20,900 annual savings warrants a discount rate of 17 percent. This gives the NPV of the cost savings as

$$\sum_{t=1}^{10} \frac{20,900}{(1.17)^t} = \$97,365.$$

The NPV of the replacement (we are using the principle of additivity) is thus

$$-\$161,000 + \$41,476 + \$97,365 = -\$22,159.$$

The project has a negative NPV and should not be undertaken.

There is an alternative—theoretically inferior, but perhaps intuitively more attractive—way of doing the NPV calculation. The annual cash flows of $27,650 are 24.4 percent depreciation tax shields and 75.6 percent after-tax savings. This gives a *weighted-average discount rate* of 0.244 × 10% + 0.756 × 17% = 15.29% for the total annual cash flows. Taking the present value of the total cash flows ($27,650) at this rate and subtracting out the initial cost gives a net present value of −$23,757. In theory this answer is less accurate than our previous answer (the additivity principle always gives the theoretically correct answer). However, given the amount of "noise" in the numbers (are the savings from the new machine ten years hence really known?), one would, in realistic situations, expect to take enough margin for error so that the two answers are, for practical purposes, indistinguishable.

### Financing the replacement

After doing the above calculations, the XYZ Corporation informed the manufacturer of the machine that it had decided that the replacement was not worthwhile. The manufacturer then made an additional offer: He was willing to finance XYZ's purchase of the new machine by giving a 10-year, 9 percent loan of $150,000 to XYZ. The conditions of the loan were to be these: In years 1–9, XYZ would pay only the interest on the loan ($13,500). In year 10, XYZ would pay the interest and repay the loan's principal.

The ball was back in the analysts' court. They reasoned as follows. By the principle of additivity,

NPV(replacement + loan) = NPV(replacement) + NPV(loan).

$$= -\$22,159 + \text{NPV(loan)}.$$

Thus it only remained for the analysts to calculate the NPV of the loan cash flows. Since interest is an expense for tax purposes, the after-tax cash flows from the loan were $+\$150,000$ in year 0, $-\$7,425$ in each of years $1, \ldots, 9$, and $-\$157,425$ in year 10.

The analysts perceived these cash flows as essentially riskless, reasoning that XYZ would almost surely have pre-tax profits in each of the next 10 years, so that it would in fact have earnings from which to deduct the loan interest. They also felt that XYZ's tax rate wasn't likely to change. So they came to the conclusion that the proper risk-adjusted discount rate for the loan's cash flows was 10 percent—the risk-free rate in the market. Thus, the NPV of the loan was calculated to be

$$\$150,000 - \sum_{t=1}^{9} \frac{\$7,425}{(1.10)^t} - \frac{\$157,425}{(1.10)^{10}} = \$46,545.$$

Thus the *package* of the machine and the loan has a net present value of $-\$22,159 + \$46,545 = \$24,386$.

(The loan's interest rate is subsidized. Thus, 9 percent represents the cost of the loan, but not the loan's risk. Individuals can set prices, but the market determines the risks. In this case, the market interest rate of 10 percent on 10-year loans determines the riskiness of the loan.)

The analysts concluded that the XYZ Corporation should replace the machine and take the loan.

### Further Analysis

Further analysis of the loan in the XYZ case reveals some interesting facts. Rewrite the NPV(loan) as follows:

$$\$150,000 - \sum_{t=1}^{10} \frac{\$13,500}{(1.10)^t} - \frac{\$150,000}{(1.10)^{10}} + \sum_{t=1}^{10} \frac{0.45(\$13,500)}{(1.10)^t}.$$

The first three terms of the above equation give the net present value of the loan, ignoring taxes. Were the loan given at market interest rates, the sum of these three terms would be zero. In this case, the loan is subsidized, and the NPV of this subsidy is given by

$$\$150,000 - \sum_{t=1}^{10} \frac{\$13,500}{(1.10)^t} - \frac{\$150,000}{(1.10)^{10}} = \$9,217.$$

The last item is the NPV of the *interest tax shield* on the loan. Its value is

$$\sum_{t=1}^{10} \frac{0.45(\$13,500)}{(1.10)^t}.$$

This tax shield would be there even if the loan were not subsidized.

### The Modigliani-Miller Theorem

The results proved above can be stated more generally: If we assume that firms generally borrow at unsubsidized rates (i.e., market rates of interest), then the difference that leverage makes to a firm's market value is the *net present value of the tax shields on the interest from the debt.*

Modigliani and Miller (1985, 1963) were the first to set out this proposition formally. To Modigliani and Miller we also owe a framework which gives a simple equation for the effect of debt on the firm's capital structure.

### The Modigliani-Miller Model

Consider a firm U (short for *unlevered*) that has no debt whatsoever. Suppose that U is expected to produced cash flows forever. Also suppose that U produces an annual pre-tax cash flow whose mean is expected to remain constant, and denote this cash flow by EBIT (*earnings before interest and taxes*). Finally, assume that U pays out all of its after-tax earnings to its shareholders.

Let $k_e(U)$ denote U's *equity cost of capital* (i.e., the risk-adjusted discount rate at which U's shareholders discount their future anticipated earnings). Then the *market value of U*, denoted $V_U$, is equal to

$$\sum_{t=1}^{\infty} \frac{(1-T)\text{EBIT}}{[1+k_e(U)]^t} = \frac{(1-T)\text{EBIT}}{k_e(U)}.$$

Now assume that U's management decides to issue some debt and use the proceeds to repurchase some of the firm's equity. Furthermore, suppose that the debt issue has value $D$ and bears the market rate of interest $k_d$ ("the cost of debt").

It follows from the logic of the previous sections that issuing the debt changes the market value of U only by the net present value of the tax shields on the debt. (Firms usually issue debt to undertake investment in productive capital. Such an investment will surely change the firm's EBIT. It may also change the firm's business risk and thus the risk-adjusted discount rate appropriate to the firm's EBIT. In the example of this section, we have assumed away all these complications by assuming that the proceeds from the sale of the debt are used to repurchase equity. Thus the firm's EBIT doesn't change, and neither does the discount rate appropriate to the riskiness of the EBIT.) To make life really simple, assume that the debt is infinite-lived. By this we mean that the principal need never be repaid, so that the firm has to pay only an annual interest charge of $k_d D$. The present value of the interest tax shields is thus

$$\sum_{t=1}^{\infty} \frac{Tk_d D}{(1+k_d)^t} = \frac{Tk_d D}{k_d} = TD.$$

The Modigliani-Miller theorem says: If we let $V_L$ denote the market value of the firm after the above-described financial manipulation, and let $V_U$ denote the firm's market value before it issued the debt, then, assuming that all cash flows are infinite-lived and constant in the mean, we have

$$V_L = V_U + DT.$$

## Some Consequences of the Modigliani-Miller Theorem: Three Useful Facts

A formulation that assumes that all cash flows are infinite-lived and unchanging (in the sense that their means are constant) is obviously unrealistic. This formulation can, however, provide us with some useful insights into the economics of leverage. It can also provide us with some formulas that can be used as approximations to more realistic situations. In this subsection we will state (and, where necessary, prove) some of the corollaries of the Modiagliani-Miller theorem.

Throughout, we shall refer to the "unlevered firm U" and the "levered firm L." This is shorthand for referring to the story of the previous subsection, in which the same firm makes a change that affects only its capital structure.

*Fact 1:* One immediate consequence of the theorem is that the value of the levered firm L's equity is given by

$$E(L) = E(U) - D(1 - T),$$

where $E(U)$ and $E(L)$ are the values of firm U's and firm L's equity. To see this, note that the market value of a firm is always the sum of the values of its debt and equity. Thus,

$$V_L = E(L) + D$$

$$= V_U + DT$$

$$= E(U) + DT,$$

where the last equality follows from the fact that firm U is *only equity.*

*Fact 2:* The market value of the firm (levered or unlevered) is the after-tax value of its EBIT discounted at its weighted-average cost of capital:

$$E(L) + D = \frac{(1 - T)\text{EBIT}}{k_a}.$$

To see this, note that

$$k_e E = (1 - T)(\text{EBIT} - I)$$

and

$$(1 - T)k_d D = (1 - T)I,$$

where I represents interest. Adding these two together and dividing by $V_L$ gives

$$k_e \frac{E}{V_L} + (1 - T)k_d \frac{D}{V_L} = \frac{(1 - T)\text{EBIT}}{V_L}.$$

Since the left-hand side is $k_a$, we have proved fact 2.

*Fact 3:* The relation of the cost of equity capital to the firm's leverage.

From the preceding subsection we know that when the leverage of the firm increases, its cost of equity capital increases. By how much, though? The following equation relates the cost of equity capital to the leverage of the firm:

$$k_e(L) = k_e(U) + [k_e(U) - k_d]\frac{D}{E(L)}(1 - T).$$

*Proof of the formula:* First we rewrite the formula; we shall prove that

$$k_e(L) = k_e(U)\left(1 + \frac{D}{E(L)}(1 - T)\right) - k_d\frac{D}{E(L)}(1 - T).$$

To see this, multiply through by $E(L)$:

$$k_e(L)E(L) \stackrel{?}{=} k_e(U)[E(L) + D(1 - T)] - k_dD(1 - T).$$

Now,

$$V_L = E(L) + D \qquad \text{(by definition)}$$

$$= V_U + DT \qquad \text{(by the M-M theorem)}$$

$$= E(U) + DT \quad \text{(since firm U is all equity).}$$

Therefore, $E(U) = E(L) + D(1 - T)$. We use this result to simplify the expression with the question mark. This expression now becomes

$$k_e(L)E(L) \stackrel{?}{=} k_e(U)E(U) - k_dD(1 - T).$$

Expanding the left-hand side of this gives

$$k_e(L)E(L) = (1 - T)(\text{EBIT} - k_dD);$$

expanding the right-hand side gives

$$k_e(U)E(U) - k_dD(1 - T) = (1 - T)\text{EBIT} - k_dD(1 - T)$$

$$= (1 - T)(\text{EBIT} - k_dD).$$

This proves the formula.

### Personal Taxes: Miller's "Debt and Taxes"

The analysis above considers only taxation of corporate incomes; it ignores the taxation of personal incomes. In this section we consider personal taxation. The basic propositions were developed by Merton Miller in a paper entitled "Debt and Taxes," which appeared in the *Journal of Finance* in 1977. We consider only enough of the topic to make sense of the corporate valuation models in chapters 1 and 2. The subject is much broader, however, and an interested reader should refer to an introductory textbook and to some of the references given at the end of this chapter. A good starting place is Miller's 1977 article.

### Segmentation in the Bond Market

Consider the situation in the United States. While the interest from most kinds of riskless securities (bank deposits, corporate bonds, money-market funds, etc.) is subject to state and local taxes, the interest on bonds issued by municipalities is not subject to federal income taxation. In some places, interest on municipal bonds is also exempt from local and state taxes.) The interest paid by these tax-exempt securities is, of course, lower than that paid by fully taxable securities.

What is the optimal strategy of an investor, given the differing tax treatment of interest from assets whose risk profiles are essentially the same? It is not hard to see that highly taxed investors will prefer tax-exempt (but low-interest-paying) municipal bonds, whereas low-taxed investors will prefer tax-liable (but high-interest-paying) bank deposits, corporate bonds, and so on.

To see this, suppose that a one-year municipal bond pays interest of 6 percent and a one-year note issued by a corporation pays interest of 10 percent. Consider three investors: one in a 20 percent marginal tax bracket, the second in a 40 percent marginal tax bracket, and the third in a 50 percent tax bracket. The returns to the investors from the two kinds of bonds are as follows:

| Tax bracket | Municipal bond | | Corporate note | |
|---|---|---|---|---|
|  | Before taxes | After taxes | Before taxes | After taxes |
| 20% | 6% | 6% | 10% | 8% |
| 40% | 6% | 6% | 10% | 6% |
| 50% | 6% | 6% | 10% | 5% |

Note that the investor in the 40 percent bracket is indifferent between the two bonds. (According to Ayanian [1983], the difference between yields on one-year municipal notes and on one-year U.S. Treasury bills corre-

sponds roughly to a 40 percent tax bracket. The evidence for longer-term
securities is different, but in these securities it is not always clear that the
risks are the same; see Gordon and Malkiel 1981, Mussa and Kormendi
1979, and Trczinka 1982.)

The differing tax treatments of the two kinds of securities thus leads
to *market segmentation of ownership.* (There is another possibility: tax
arbitrage. This occurs when highly taxed investors short-sell the taxable
bonds—i.e., borrow money at high, though tax-deductible, rates—in order
to buy more municipal bonds. It also occurs when low-tax investors short-
sell municipals in order to buy more taxable bonds. The spirit of the tax
code, and occasionally the letter, forbids such financial shenanigans. Miller's
analysis explicitly rules out short-selling.)

**Ownership of Corporate Equity**

With regard to the ownership of corporate equity, Miller stresses that
equity payouts are subject to preferential tax treatment. This applies especially to the realization of capital gains from shares, which in most countries
are subject to much lower rates of taxation than ordinary income. The
tendency seems to be either to exempt capital gains from income taxation
altogether, or to credit the taxpayer with the corporate income taxes paid
by the corporation on the dividend payout (this is done in Canada and
Australia). The 1986 tax reform in the United States abolished the capital-
gains preference.

If returns from shares are subject to preferential tax treatment, then
according to our analysis in the preceding subsection the purchasers of
shares should be investors in the high tax bracket. If some shares have high
dividend payouts (taxable at ordinary rates) and other shares have low
dividend payouts, so that shareholders have to realize capital gains in order
to "earn" money from their shares, then the Miller analysis indicates that
low-taxed shareholders should prefer the dividend-paying stocks and that
highly taxed shareholders should prefer the capital-gains stocks. (The
evidence on this point is less conclusive than Ayanian's [1983] evidence
describing the interest-rate differentials. See Kim, Lewellen, and Mc-
Connell 1979.)

**Maximizing Firm Value**

Suppose we accept for the moment that it is primarily highly taxed investors
who own equity in firms. Denote by $r$ the interest paid on tax-exempt securities, by $i$ the interest on corporate bonds, and by $T$ the corporate tax rate.

It is easily shown that if $i(1 - T) < r$, it is profitable for corporations to issue bonds. To see this, suppose that a corporation issued \$1 of a perpetual bond at interest rate $i$. The present value of this bond to the corporation's shareholders (who, after all, own the corporation and have to pay the interest) is

$$1 - \sum_{t=1}^{\infty} \frac{i(1 - T)}{(1 + r)^t} = 1 - \frac{i(1 - T)}{r},$$

and this expression is positive when $i(1 - T) < r$. (The assumption that the bond is perpetual is made for simplicity only. The critical assumption is that the relevant discount rate is $r$, the interest rate on the municipal bonds. This assumption stems from the conclusion that the marginal owner of equity is also the marginal purchaser of tax-exempt municipal bonds.)

If $i(1 - T) < r$, it would be profitable for corporations to issue more and more debt. On the other hand, if $i(1 - T) > r$, it would not be profitable for corporations to issue any debt. Miller concludes from this that the only equilibrium relation of $i$ and $r$ is that $i(1 - T) = r$.

**Putting It All Together**

If the Miller analysis holds, the following statements are true:

• Corporations do not profit by issuing debt. That is, $V_U = V_L$.

• The proper discount rate for riskless cash flows generated by corporations is the interest rate on riskless, tax-exempt securities.

• The weighted-average cost of capital, $k_a$, is not affected by corporate leverage.

• The relation of $k_e(L)$ and $k_e(U)$ is given by

$$k_e(L) = k_e(U) + [k_e(U) - r]\frac{D}{E(L)}(1 - T).$$

(The proof of this last fact is similar to the proof given in the preceding subsection.)

**What to Do? What to Use?**

In this appendix we have considered a basic principle (additivity) and two different approaches to the evaluation of the effects of leverage on corporate valuation and discount rates.

The evidence is not yet in on which of the two approaches is most correct. Each approach captures some relevant aspects of capital markets. The Modigliani-Miller approach stresses that interest tax shields are often important in valuing a project or a firm; the Miller approach stresses that *in equilibrium* there are forces that negate (and may even cancel) the tax advantages of debt.

## A Warning

The models used in this chapter are based on the assumption that the owners of a firm (shareholders and bondholders) have full information about the way the firm works. Under this assumption, financial structure and dividends matter only insofar as they affect the cash flows of the firm or of its owners. However, it has become increasingly clear that when a firm's owners have imperfect information, financial structure and dividends may be interpreted as having informational content, and hence may influence owners' perceptions of the firm. (The literature in which these questions are explored is quite large; a few of the references are Ambarish et al. 1987, Franke 1987, Jensen and Meckling 1976, Kalay 1982, Miller and Rock 1985, Myers 1977, Myers and Majluf 1984, Ofer and Thakor 1987, Ross 1987, Talmor 1981, and Williams 1987.) The major problem with this literature is that it is difficult to operationalize these theoretical insights.

## References

Aivazian, V. A., and J. L. Callen (1987). "Miller's Irrelevance Theorem: A Note." *Journal of Finance* 42 (March): 169–180.

Ambarish, R., K. John, and J. Williams. 1987. "Efficient Signalling with Dividends and Investments." *Journal of Finance* 42 (June): 321–344.

Auerbach, A. J. 1983. "Taxation, Corporate Financial Policy and the Cost of Capital." *Journal of Economic Literature* 21: 905–940.

Auerbach, A. J., and M. King. 1983. "Taxation, Portfolio Choice, and Debt-Equity Ratios: A General Equilibrium Model." *Quarterly Journal of Economics* 98: 587–609.

Ayanian, R. A. 1983. "Expectations, Taxes and Interest: The Search for the Darby Effect." *American Economic Review* 73 (September): 762–765.

Barnea, A., R. A. Haugen, and E. Talmor. 1987. "Debt and Taxes: A Multiperiod Investigation." *Journal of Banking and Finance* 11 (March): 79–97.

Benninga, S., and E. Talmor. 1988. "Financing the Government with Corporate and Personal Income Taxes: A General Equilibrium Analysis." *Journal of Business* 61 (April): 233–258.

Cooper, I., and J. R. Franks. 1983. "The Interaction of Financing and Investment Decisions When the Firm Has Unused Tax Credits." *Journal of Finance* 38: 571–583.

Cordes, J. J., and S. M. Sheffrin. 1981. "Taxation and the Sectoral Allocation of Capital in the U.S." *National Tax Journal* 34: 419–432.

Cordes, J. J. and S. M. Sheffrin. 1983. "Estimating the Tax Advantage of Corporate Debt." *Journal of Finance* 38: 95–105.

DeAngelo, H., and R. W. Masulis. 1980. "Optimal Capital Structure under Corporate and Personal Taxation." *Journal of Financial Economics* 8: 3–29.

DeAngelo, H., and R. W. Masulis. 1980. "Leverage and Dividend Irrelevance under Corporate and Personal Taxation." *Journal of Finance* 35: 453–464.

Feldstein, M., and L. Summers. 1979. "Inflation and the Taxation of Capital Income in the Corporate Sector." *National Tax Journal* 32: 445–470.

Franke, G. 1987. "Costless Signalling in Financial Markets." *Journal of Finance* 42: 809–822.

Gordon, R. H. 1985. "Taxation of Corporate Capital Income: Tax Revenues versus Tax Distortions." *Quarterly Journal of Economics* 100: 1–27.

Gordon, R. H. 1986. "Taxation of Investment and Savings in a World Economy." *American Economic Review* 76 (December): 1086–1102.

Gordon, R. H., and B. G. Malkiel. 1981. "Corporation Finance." In H. J. Aaron and J. A. Pechman (eds.), *How Taxes Affect Economic Behavior* (Washington: Brookings Institution).

Jensen, M. C., and W. H. Meckling. 1976. "Theory of the Firm: Managerial Behavior, Agency Costs, and Ownership Structure." *Journal of Financial Economics* 3: 305–360.

Kalay, A. 1982. "Stockholder-Bondholder Conflict and Dividend Constraints." *Journal of Financial Economics* 10: 211–233.

Kim, E. H., W. Lewellen, and J. McConnell. 1979. "Financial Leverage Clienteles: Theory and Evidence." *Journal of Financial Economics* 7 (March): 97–113.

McDonald, R. 1983. "Government Debt and Private Leverage." *Journal of Public Economics* 22: 303–25.

Miller, M. H. 1977. "Debt and Taxes." *Journal of Finance* 32: 261–275.

Miller, M. H., and K. Rock. 1985. "Dividend Policy under Asymmetric Information." *Journal of Finance* 40: 1031–1051.

Modigliani, F., and M. H. Miller. 1958. "The Cost of Capital, Corporation Finance, and the Theory of Investment." *American Economic Review* 48: 261–297.

Modigliani, F., and M. H. Miller. 1963. "Taxes and the Cost of Capital: A Correction." *American Economic Review* 43: 433–443.

Mussa, M., and R. Kormendi. 1979. *The Taxation of Municipal Bonds.* Washington: American Enterprise Institute.

Myers, S. C. 1977. "Determinants of Corporate Borrowing." *Journal of Financial Economics* 5: 147–175.

Myers, S. C., and N. Majluf. 1984. "Corporate Financing and Investment Decisions When Firms Have Information That Investors Do Not." *Journal of Financial Economics* 13 (June): 187–221.

Ofer, A. R., and A. V. Thakor. 1987. "A Theory of Stock Price Responses to Alternative Corporate Cash Disbursement Methods." *Journal of Finance* 42: 365–394.

Protopapadakis, A. 1983. "Some Indirect Evidence on Effective Capital Gains Tax Rates." *Journal of Business* 56 (April): 127–138.

Roley, V. V. 1982. "The Effect of Federal Debt-Management Policy on Corporate Bond and Equity Yields." *Quarterly Journal of Economics* 97: 645–668.

Ross, S. 1977. "The Determination of Financial Structure: The Incentive Signalling Approach." *Bell Journal of Economics* 8 (spring): 23–40.

Ross, S. A. 1987. "Debt and Taxes and Uncertainty." *Journal of Finance* 40: 637–656.

Stiglitz, J. E. 1969. "A Re-Examination of the Modigliani-Miller Theorem." *American Economic Review* 59: 784–793.

Stiglitz, J.E. 1974. "On the Irrelevance of Corporate Financial Policy." *American Economic Review* 64: 851–866.

Taggart, R. A. 1981. "Taxes and Corporate Capital Structure in an Incomplete Market." *Journal of Finance* 35: 645–659.

Taggart, R. A. 1983. Secular Patterns in the Financing of U.S. Corporations. Working paper.

Talmor, E. 1981. "Asymmetric Information, Signalling and Optimal Corporate Financial Structure." *Journal of Financial and Quantitative Analysis* 16 (November): 413–435.

Trczinka, C. 1982. "The Pricing of Tax-Exempt Bonds and the Miller Hypothesis." *Journal of Finance* 37 (September): 907–924.

Warren, A. C., and Auerbach, A. J. 1982. "Transferability of Tax Incentives and the Fiction of Safe Harbor Leasing." *Harvard Law Review* 95: 1752–1786.

Williams, J. 1987. "Perquisites, Risk, and Capital Structure." *Journal of Finance* 42 (March): 29–48.

# 3 Debt Capacity and Riskless Cash Flows

## 3.1 Introduction

The effects of debt on corporate valuation have long perplexed finance theorists. Whether it makes any difference to corporate value how much debt a firm has, what the effect of additional debt is upon the cost of equity, whether corporate and personal taxes make a difference—these and other questions are by no means settled. (See the appendix to chapter 2 for a discussion of some of these issues.)

One way to duck (initially, at least) these tricky questions is to concentrate on how much a firm should be able to borrow under certain circumstances.

## 3.2 Example

Suppose you know for certain that one year from now your Aunt Mabel is going to give you $11,000. If banks are lending money at a rate of 10 percent, you should be able to go to your local loan officer and borrow $10,000 now. After all, if he lends you $10,000 today, you will be able to repay it and the interest next year with the proceeds of Aunt Mabel's present. (As usual, it is easy to get bogged down in technicalities: You go to the loan officer and show him Aunt Mabel's letter, hoping he doesn't get to the part where she says: "Of course this promise depends on both your and your father's continued good behavior." Since markets are competitive in our story, the loan officer will recognize that Aunt Mabel is going to give you $11,000 with certainty next year, and therefore he will lend you $10,000 today.)

## 3.3 A Slightly More Realistic Example

Reliable Builders has just signed a contract to put up a building in downtown Jefferson. The owner of the building has agreed to pay Reliable $100,000 now and $100,000 next year, upon the completion of the building.

The owner of Reliable goes to her local bank and discusses the financing of this project with her loan officer. The current interest rate is 8 percent. Reliable is a profitable firm, and can therefore deduct any interest costs from its taxable income. Its tax rate is 40 percent. The loan officer examines the contract and says: We'll lend you $95,419.85 today, for one year, at 8 percent.

Why $95,419.85? Next year, Reliable will owe the bank $95,419.85 ×
1.08 = $103,053.44. The interest charge on this loan, $103,053.44 −
$95,419.85 = 7,633.59, is a recognized expense for tax purposes, and Reli-
able will therefore get a tax shield on this interest of 0.4 × 7,633.59 =
$3,053.44. Net of taxes, therefore, Reliable will be able to repay its loan to
the bank out of the proceeds from the contract. (Of course, there is more
to it than this: Reliable is well known to the bank, and so is the owner of
the new building, whose signature graces the contract. Reliable may have
to give some security to the bank—for example, it may have to sign a note
giving the bank first rights to the cash it receives from the owner of the
building.)

We will refer to the $95,419.85 as the *debt capacity created by the contract*,
or *debt capacity* for short.

The calculation we have just done is the following:

$$\text{Debt capacity} = \frac{\text{Promised future payment}}{1 + (1 - \text{Tax rate})\,\text{Interest rate}}.$$

Try it:

$$\$95,419.85 = \frac{\$100,000}{1 + (1 - 0.4)0.08} = \frac{\$100,000}{1.048}.$$

## 3.4   More Complications

What if Reliable had been promised two payments, the first of $300,000 and
the second (in two years, upon completion of the building) of $200,000?
What debt capacity is created by this contract?

The way to answer this question is to go backwards: One year from now,
having already received the first $300,000, Reliable should be able to
borrow against the $200,000 it will receive one year hence. Let us label this
sum DBT(2), to stand for the debt capacity created by the contrast at the
beginning of year 2. By the logic of the preceding section,

$$\text{DBT}(2) = \frac{\$200,000}{1.048} = \$190,839.69.$$

Reliable will be able to borrow $190,839.69 one year from now, on the
basis of its contract. But how much will it be able to borrow today? We can

label this amount DBT(1), meaning the debt capacity created by the contract at the beginning of year 1. (Remember that year 1 begins today.)

We calculate DBT(1) as follows: If Reliable borrows DBT(1) today, its net after-tax interest costs in one year will be 0.048 × DBT(1). At the end of year 1 the bank will want to reduce the principal of the outstanding loan to $190,839.69, so Reliable will have to repay DBT(1) − $190,839.69 in principal. Thus, its net after-tax cash outflow from the loan in one year will be

$$[DBT(1) - \$190,839.69] + (1 - 0.4)0.08\,DBT(1).$$

(Remember that repayment of principal is not a recognized expense for tax purposes, whereas payment of interest is.)

To finance this cash flow, Reliable has the promised payment of $300,000. Thus, the calculation of DBT(1) involves the solution of

$$[DBT(1) - \$190,839.69] + (1 - 0.4)0.08\,DBT(1) = \$300,000.$$

This gives

$$DBT(1) = \frac{\$300,000 + \$190,839.69}{1.048}$$

$$= \$468,358.49.$$

Let us check this. Today, Reliable borrows $468,358.49. One year from now, Reliable has the following cash flow from this loan.

Interest: $468,358.49 ∗ .08 = $37,468.68
Tax shield on interest: −$37,468.67 ∗ 0.4 = −14,987.47
Repayment of principal: $468,358.49 − $190,839.69 = $277,518.80
Net after-tax payment, beginning of year 1: $300,000.01

Except for the rounding error of $0.01, this is what we wanted! Thus, the contract creates debt capacity of $468,358.49 today and $190,839.69 next year.

## 3.5 A Spreadsheet Implementation

The above procedure cries out for a spreadsheet. Before we do one, however, we need to know how we calculated DBT(1) in the example above.

Reexamining the equation, we see that

$$DBT(1) = \frac{\text{Payment in year 1} + DBT(2)}{1 + (1 - \text{Tax rate}) \times \text{Interest rate}}$$

$$= \frac{\text{Payment in year 1} + DBT(2)}{1 + (1 - T)i}$$

$$= \frac{\text{Payment in year 1}}{1 + (1 - T)i} + \frac{\text{Payment in year 2}}{[1 + (1 - T)i]^2}.$$

We can obviously implement this procedure for any number of years. Given $N$ payments, we find that

$$DBT(t) = \frac{\text{Payment in year } t + 1}{1 + (1 - T)i} + \frac{\text{Payment in year } t + 2}{[1 + (1 - T)i]^2} \cdots$$

$$+ \frac{\text{Payment in year } N}{[1 + (1 - T)i]^N}.$$

As an illustration, consider the following example: A company has promised after-tax payments of \$14,720 at the end of each of the next 10 years. What is the debt capacity created by these payments if the interest rate is 8 percent and the company's tax rate is 33 percent?

Using Lotus, we can calculate the following spreadsheet:

```
interest rate    0.08
tax rate         0.33
```

| year | DBT(t) | rDBT(t) | TrDBT(t) | payments |
|------|--------|---------|----------|----------|
| 1 | 111702.74 | 8936.22 | 2948.95 | 14720 |
| 2 | 102970.01 | 8237.60 | 2718.41 | 14720 |
| 3 | 93769.20 | 7501.54 | 2475.51 | 14720 |
| 4 | 84075.23 | 6726.02 | 2219.59 | 14720 |
| 5 | 73861.66 | 5908.93 | 1949.95 | 14720 |
| 6 | 63100.64 | 5048.05 | 1665.86 | 14720 |
| 7 | 51762.84 | 4141.03 | 1366.54 | 14720 |
| 8 | 39817.33 | 3185.39 | 1051.18 | 14720 |
| 9 | 27231.54 | 2178.52 | 718.91 | 14720 |
| 10 | 13971.15 | 1117.69 | 368.84 | 14720 |

The spreadsheet that produced these numbers follows:

```
C1: 'CALCULATING DEBT CAPACITY
A3: [W15] 'interest rate
B3: 0.08
A4: [W15] 'tax rate
B4: 0.33
B5: 'year
C5: 'DBT(t)
D5: 'rDBT(t)
E5: 'TrDBT(t)
F5: 'payments
B6: 1
C6: +C7/(1+$INTEREST RATE*(1-$TAX RATE))+F6/(1+$INTEREST RATE*(1-$TAX RATE))
D6: +C6*$INTEREST RATE
E6: +D6*$TAX RATE
F6: 14720
B7: 2
C7: +C8/(1+$INTEREST RATE*(1-$TAX RATE))+F7/(1+$INTEREST RATE*(1-$TAX RATE))
D7: +C7*$INTEREST RATE
E7: +D7*$TAX RATE
F7: 14720
B8: 3
C8: +C9/(1+$INTEREST RATE*(1-$TAX RATE))+F8/(1+$INTEREST RATE*(1-$TAX RATE))
D8: +C8*$INTEREST RATE
E8: +D8*$TAX RATE
F8: 14720
B9: 4
C9: +C10/(1+$INTEREST RATE*(1-$TAX RATE))+F9/(1+$INTEREST RATE*(1-$TAX RATE))
D9: +C9*$INTEREST RATE
E9: +D9*$TAX RATE
F9: 14720
B10: 5
C10: +C11/(1+$INTEREST RATE*(1-$TAX RATE))+F10/(1+$INTEREST RATE*(1-$TAX RATE))
D10: +C10*$INTEREST RATE
E10: +D10*$TAX RATE
F10: 14720
B11: 6
C11: +C12/(1+$INTEREST RATE*(1-$TAX RATE))+F11/(1+$INTEREST RATE*(1-$TAX RATE))
D11: +C11*$INTEREST RATE
E11: +D11*$TAX RATE
F11: 14720
B12: 7
C12: +C13/(1+$INTEREST RATE*(1-$TAX RATE))+F12/(1+$INTEREST RATE*(1-$TAX RATE))
D12: +C12*$INTEREST RATE
E12: +D12*$TAX RATE
F12: 14720
B13: 8
C13: +C14/(1+$INTEREST RATE*(1-$TAX RATE))+F13/(1+$INTEREST RATE*(1-$TAX RATE))
D13: +C13*$INTEREST RATE
E13: +D13*$TAX RATE
F13: 14720
B14: 9
C14: +C15/(1+$INTEREST RATE*(1-$TAX RATE))+F14/(1+$INTEREST RATE*(1-$TAX RATE))
D14: +C14*$INTEREST RATE
E14: +D14*$TAX RATE
F14: 14720
B15: 10
C15: +F15/(1+$INTEREST RATE*(1-$TAX RATE))
D15: +C15*$INTEREST RATE
E15: +D15*$TAX RATE
F15: 14720
```

# 4 Leasing

## 4.1 Introduction

A lease is a contractual arrangement by which the owner of an asset (the *lessor*) rents the assets to a *lessee*. In this chapter we analyze leases, starting from the viewpoint of the lessee. The leases analyzed in this chapter are long-term leases, in which the asset spends most of its useful life with the lessee. Effectively, then, the leases considered in this chapter are alternatives to purchasing assets.

In the example below, we shall consider a company that is faced with the choice of either purchasing or leasing a piece of equipment. We shall assume that the net inflows from the equipment's operation are not affected by its ownership—in other words, that the company must bear the responsibility for maintaining the equipment whether or not it is leased and that the lease does not imply any other diminished operating costs. In the words of Statement 13 of the Financial Accounting Standards Board Statement, the lease we are considering is one that "transfers substantially all of the benefits and risks incident to the ownership of property" to the lessor.

The analysis in this chapter concentrates exclusively on *cash flow*. It is assumed that the lessor pays tax on the income from the lease rentals and gets a tax shield on the depreciation of the asset, and that the lessee can claim the rent as an expense. Thus, it is assumed that the tax authorities treat the lessor as the owner of the asset and the lessee as the user. As is explained in the appendix to the chapter, this assumption is not trivial. In addition to the cash-flow issues of leasing, there are heavy accounting issues. These are also touched on briefly in the appendix.

## 4.2 A Simple Example and a Simplistic Analysis

A company has decided to acquire the use of a machine costing $500,000. If purchased, the machine will be depreciated on a straight-line basis to a residual value of zero. The machine's estimated life is 6 years. The company's tax rate is 38 percent.

The company's alternative to purchasing the machine is to lease it for 6 years. A lessor has offered to lease the machine to the company for $125,077 annually, with the first payment to be made today and with five additional payments to be made at the start of each of the next five years.

One way (a misleading way, as it turns out) of analyzing this problem is to examine the cash flows to the company of leasing and of buying the asset.

The company feels that the lease payment and the tax shield from depreciation are riskless. Suppose, furthermore, that the risk-free rate is 12 percent. On the basis of the calculation below, the company should lease the asset. (Throughout this chapter and the next we will follow the convention of giving costs a positive sign and inflows a negative sign. This means that we will always be calculating the NPV of costs. It will thus follow that the alternative with the lowest NPV is preferable.)

$$\text{NPV(leasing)} = \sum_{t=0}^{5} \frac{0.62 \times 125,077}{(1.12)^t} = 357,090$$

$$\text{NPV(buying)} = 500,000 - \sum_{t=1}^{6} \frac{0.38 \times 83,333}{(1.12)^t} = 369,805$$

This method of analysis is misleading because it ignores the fact that leasing is very much like buying the asset with a loan. The financial risks are thus different when we compare a lease (implicitly a purchase with loan financing) against a straightforward purchase without loan financing. If the company is willing to lease the asset, then perhaps it should also be willing to borrow money to buy the asset. This borrowing will change the cash-flow patterns and could also produce tax benefits. Hence, our decision about the leasing decision could change if we were to take the loan potential into account.

The following method of analyzing leases deals with this problem by imagining what kind of a loan would produce cash flows (and hence financial risks) equivalent to those produced by the lease. Not surprisingly, it is called the *equivalent-loan method*.

### 4.3   Leasing and Firm Financing—the Equivalent-Loan Method

The idea behind the equivalent-loan method is to devise a hypothetical loan that is somehow equivalent to the lease. It then becomes easy to see whether the lease or the purchase of an asset is preferable.

The easiest way to understand the equivalent-loan method is with an example. We return to the previous example:

```
tax                       0.38
initial cost            500000
interest                  0.12
lease                   125077
annual depreciation   83333.33
```

Consider the *differential after-tax cash flows* attributable to the lease, i.e., the difference in cash flows between leasing the asset and purchasing it:

| year | 0 | 1 | 2 | 3 | 4 | 5 | 6 |
|---|---|---|---|---|---|---|---|
| lease rentals | 77547.7 | 77547.7 | 77547.7 | 77547.7 | 77547.7 | 77547.7 | |
| cost | -500000 | | | | | | |
| depr. tax shield | | 31666.6 | 31666.6 | 31666.6 | 31666.6 | 31666.6 | 31666.6 |
| salvage | | | | | | | 0 |
| TOTAL | -422452.2 | 109214. | 109214. | 109214. | 109214. | 109214. | 31666.6 |

Now suppose that we borrowed $463,161.73 at 12 percent for 6 years. The claim is that this loan principal (plus the accumulated interest) can be paid off by annual cash flows exactly equivalent to the differential after-tax cash flows attributable to the lease: $109,214, $109214, $109,214, $109,214, $109,214, and $31,666.60. This is easy to prove, by building a loan table:

| year | principal beginning of year | interest | repayment of principal | after-tax outflow |
|---|---|---|---|---|
| 1 | 463161.73 | 55579.41 | 74755.17 | 109214.41 |
| 2 | 388406.55 | 46608.79 | 80316.96 | 109214.41 |
| 3 | 308089.59 | 36970.75 | 86292.54 | 109214.41 |
| 4 | 221797.05 | 26615.65 | 92712.71 | 109214.41 |
| 5 | 129084.35 | 15490.12 | 99610.53 | 109214.41 |
| 6 | 29473.81 | 3536.86 | 29473.81 | 31666.67 |

The trick to this table is, of course, to construct the payments so that in each year

Repayment of Principal = After-tax outflow − (1 − tax) × Interest.

This means that we take the after-tax outflows as given and build the table accordingly.

The $463,171.73 is in fact the debt capacity lost by the stream of payments $109,214, $109,214, $109,214, $109,214, $109,214, $31,666.60. This means (see chapter 3) that the $463,171.70 is the present value, at the after-tax discount rate, of these cash flows:

$$463,171.73 = \sum_{t=1}^{5} \frac{109,214}{[1 + (1 - 0.38) \times 0.12]^t} + \frac{31,667}{[1 + (1 - 0.38) \times 0.12]^6}.$$

It is now easy to compare the lease against the purchase. The cash flows caused by purchasing the asset with a debt of $463,161.73 are equivalent to those of leasing the asset. To see this, we build another table:

CASH FLOWS OF LEASE VS BUY/EQUIVALENT LOAN

| year | 0 | 1 | 2 | 3 | 4 | 5 | 6 |
|---|---|---|---|---|---|---|---|
| LEASE CASH FLOWS | 77547.74 | 77547.74 | 77547.74 | 77547.74 | 77547.74 | 77547.74 | |
| BUY/EQUIVALENT LOAN | | | | | | | |
| cost | 500000 | | | | | | |
| depr. tax shield | | -31666.6 | -31666.6 | -31666.6 | -31666.6 | -31666.6 | -31666.6 |
| salvage | | | | | | | 0 |
| loan | -463161.73 | | | | | | |
| outstanding principal | | 463161.7 | 388406.5 | 308089.5 | 221797.0 | 129084.3 | 29473.81 |
| payment | | 130334.5 | 126925.7 | 123263.2 | 119328.3 | 115100.6 | 33010.67 |
| of which: | | | | | | | |
| interest | | 55579.40 | 46608.78 | 36970.75 | 26615.64 | 15490.12 | 3536.857 |
| principal | | 74755.17 | 80316.95 | 86292.54 | 92712.70 | 99610.53 | 29473.81 |
| after-tax loan payment | | 109214.4 | 109214.4 | 109214.4 | 109214.4 | 109214.4 | 31666.66 |
| TOTAL BUY/LOAN OUTFLOW | 36838.27 | 77547.74 | 77547.74 | 77547.74 | 77547.74 | 77547.74 | 0 |

From this table we see quite clearly that the buy/loan alternative has a smaller initial cost than the lease alternative, even though it has the same outflows in years 1–5.

Thus, the equivalent-loan method works as follows: Compare the equivalent-loan principal (in this case $463,161.73) and the differential year-0 cash flow from leasing ($422,452.20). If the equivalent loan is larger, then purchasing is preferable.

## 4.4   Adjusting the Simplistic Analysis to Account for Debt Capacity

An alternative way of doing the above analysis gives a better feel for the economics of the equivalent loan. When we lease the asset, we are giving the leasing company annual after-tax cash flows of $109,214 for the next five years and $31,667 in year 6. We have already seen that the debt capacity created by these cash flows is $463,162. Referring to our loan table (above), we see that this debt capacity creates interest tax shields:

| year | interest | interest tax shield |
|------|----------|---------------------|
| 1 | 55579.40 | 21120.17 |
| 2 | 46608.78 | 17711.33 |
| 3 | 36970.75 | 14048.88 |
| 4 | 26615.64 | 10113.94 |
| 5 | 15490.12 | 5886.246 |
| 6 | 3536.857 | 1344.005 |

The net present value of these interest tax shields at the borrowing rate of 12 percent is $53,425. This is an extra cost of leasing which the simplistic analysis of section 4.2 failed to recognize. Recognizing this cost, we get

| | |
|---|---|
| NPV((1-tax)*lease rental,12%) | 357090 |
| NPV(FOREGONE INTEREST TAX SHIELDS) | 53425 |
| NPV(LEASE) | 410515 |

| | |
|---|---|
| cost of asset | 500000 |
| NPV(tax*depreciation) | 130195 |
| NPV(PURCHASE) | 369805 |

Thus, the purchase is preferable to the lease.

To sum up: You can make a lease/buy decision by following one of the following rules.

• Use the equivalent-loan method. If you do this, you are implicitly assuming that all the cash flows involved have the same riskiness.

• Use the simplistic analysis, adding to the cost of the lease the present value of the tax shields on the debt capacity lost through the lease. An alternative is to subtract the present value of the tax shields on the foregone debt capacity from the cost of the purchase. In the example above, these two methods give the same answer. In a more general case, you might decide that not all the cash flows involved in a lease can be borrowed against at the riskless rate; this might be the case, for example, with the asset's salvage value.

The analysis presented thus far applies directly to those cases in which one is faced with the choice of either buying an asset or leasing it. In some cases, however, the alternative is posed as one of either leasing the asset or buying it with a loan. This might be the case, for example, if the manufacturer of the equipment were willing to give a loan to purchase the equipment. If this is the case, we can follow a variation of the rule above:

• If you are analyzing a lease versus a buy/borrow, use the simplistic analysis, and then subtract the present value of the tax shields on the debt used to purchase the asset from the simplistic cost of the purchase.

## 4.5 The Lessor's Problem: Calculating the Highest Acceptable Lease Rental

The lessor wants to charge the highest possible lease rental, but doesn't want to ask so much that the lessee would prefer to buy the asset. If the lessor and the lessee have the same tax rates, discount rates, and perceptions of the asset's salvage value, it follows that the only mutually acceptable rental rate is the rate at which the lessor is indifferent about renting out the asset and at which the lessee is indifferent between buying the asset and leasing it. Fortunately, in the real world there are usually differences in these vital parameters for the lessee and the lessor. We can use the logic above to calculate the maximum lease payment the lessor can charge. We know that, using the equivalent-loan method, we can ignore all future cash flows. Thus, we only have to calculate the cash flows at time 0. In the example above, these are the following.

| | |
|---|---:|
| after-tax lease cash flow, $(1 - \text{Tax}) \times$ Rental: | $77,548 |
| cost: | 500,000 |
| minus the equivalent loan: | 463,162 |
| after-tax buy/equivalent-loan cash flow: | 36,838 |

The maximal acceptable rental must equate the after-tax lease cash flow in year 0 with the after-tax buy/equivalent-loan cash flow in year 0. Thus, we must calculate

$$(1 - \text{Tax}) \times \text{Rental} = \text{Cost} - \text{Equivalent loan}.$$

Write $L$ for the rental, $D$ for the depreciation, $r$ for the discount rate, and $T$ for the tax rate. In the case at hand,

$$\text{Equivalent loan} = \sum_{t=1}^{5} \frac{(1 - T)L}{[1 + (1 - T)r]^t} + \sum_{t=1}^{6} \frac{TD}{[1 + (1 - T)r]^t}.$$

We thus have to solve

$$(1 - T)L + \sum_{t=1}^{5} \frac{(1 - T)L}{[1 + (1 - T)r]^t} = \text{Cost} - \sum_{t=1}^{6} \frac{TD}{[1 + (1 - T)r]^t}.$$

Since $r = 12\%$, $T = 38\%$, and $D = \$83,333$, the maximum acceptable rental is $L = \$112,081$.

## Exercises

1. Consider the example in the chapter with the following two changes:

• The lease rental is payable at the beginning of years $1, \ldots, 6$.

• The asset is depreciated on a straight-line basis to a salvage value of $50,000. The lessor and the lessee anticipate that the actual market value of the asset when sold at the beginning of year 7 will be $76,000. The difference between this value and the book value will be taxed at the firm's regular tax rate.

a. Suppose that the after-tax cash flow received from the salvage value is part of the cash flows that determine the equivalent loan. Should the firm buy or lease if the lease rate is $112,000?
b. What is the maximum acceptable lease payment?

2. Recalculate your answers to exercise 1 under the assumption that the salvage value is *not* part of the cash flows that determine the equivalent loan.

3. See exercise 1. Calculate the maximum acceptable lease payment for a range of lessee tax rates from 0 to 50 percent.

## References

Copeland, T. E., and J. F. Weston. 1982. "A Note on the Evaluation of Cancelable Operating Leases." *Financial Management* (summer): 68–72.

Financial Accounting Standards Board. 1976. Statement No. 13: Accounting For Leases. Stamford, Conn.

Franks, J. R., and S. D. Hodges. 1978. "Valuation of Financial Lease Contracts: A Note." *Journal of Finance* 33 (May): 647–669.

Franks, J. R., and S. D. Hodges. 1987. "Lease Valuation When Tasable Earnings Are a Scarce Resource." *Journal of Finance* 42 (September): 987–1006.

Levy, H., and M. Sarnat. 1979. "On Leasing, Borrowing and Financial Risk." *Financial Management* (winter).

Lewellen, W. G., M. S. Long, and J. J. McConnell. 1976. "Asset Leasing in Competitive Capital Markets." *Journal of Finance* 31 (June): 787–798.

McConnell, J. J., and J. S. Schallheim. 1983. "Valuation of Asset Leasing Contracts." *Journal of Financial Economics* 12 (August): 237–261.

Miller, M. H., and C. W. Upton. 1976. "Leasing, Buying, and the Cost of Capital Services." *Journal of Finance* 31 (June): 761–786.

Myers, S. C., D. A. Dill, and A. J. Bautista. 1976. "Valuation of Financial Lease Contracts." *Journal of Finance* 31 (June): 799–819.

Ofer, A. R. 1976. "The Evaluation of the Lease Versus Purchase Alternatives." *Financial Management* (summer): 67–74.

## Appendix:   The Tax and Accounting Treatment of Leases

The above chapter discusses the case where the lessor retains the tax benefits of ownership; that is, the lessor is able to take the depreciation on the leased asset, and the lessee deducts the lease payments from his income as an expanse. In order for this to happen, it is critical that the Internal Revenue Service be willing to recognize the lease as a *true lease*.

Although the specific IRS rules change from time to time (especially when, as in recent years, the tax laws change), the principle underlying the rules remains that the lessor should be accorded the benefits of ownership only if he bears some of the economic risks of ownership. This principle has led the IRS to develop a series of tests to determine whether or not the lessor has transferred essentially all of the ownership risks to the lessee. If he has, the IRS treats the "lease" arrangement as a sale of the asset from the "lessor" to the "lessee." If he has not, we have a true lease and the analysis of the chapter holds.

Revenue Ruling 55-540 sets out seven conditions under which a transaction will be found to be a sale rather than a lease for tax purposes:

• Portions of the rental payments are specifically applicable to an equity interest to be acquired by the lessee.

• The lessee will acquire title upon payment of a stated amount of rentals.

• A substantial proportion of the asset's purchase price is paid in rentals in a relatively short period of time from the inception of the lease.

• The rental payments exceed a "fair" rental value.

• There is a bargain-purchase option; the option price is nominal in relation to the fair market value of the asset at the time when the option can be exercised.

• Some part of the payments is designated as interest.

• The lease may be renewed at nominal rentals over the useful life of the asset.

In addition to the above conditions, Revenue Ruling 55-541 deals with the relation of the lease term to the useful life of the asset. The ruling would seem to suggest that the transaction will be classified as a conditional sale and not as a lease if the useful life of the asset is not in excess of the lease term.

One lease packager states that the IRS will generally classify a lease as a true lease if all of the following criteria are met:

• The estimated fair market value of the leased asset at the end of the lease term will equal at least 20 percent of the original cost of the leased property.

• The lease term does not exceed 80 percent of the estimated useful life of the asset.

• There is no bargain-purchase option.

• The lessor's equity in the leased asset is at least 20 percent.

**The Accounting Treatment of Leases**

Accountants have found leases troublesome. Before the advent of Financial Accounting Standards Board Statement 13, in 1976, it was common for firms to leave leases off their balance sheets altogether, and to record the fact that some assets were leased only in footnotes to the financial statement. This created an asymmetry between the accounting treatment of a lease and the accounting treatment of a purchase of an asset with debt. Since the economic similarity between these two transactions is great, this asymmetric treatment is illogical.

FASB 13 attempts to solve this problem. This statement is long and complex, and it is beyond the purview of this book to fully present the statement's solutions. This appendix will sketch the solution to the problem as outlined in FASB 13, and the next chapter will deal with FASB 13's solution of the leveraged-lease problem.

The basic idea behind the FASB 13 treatment of leases is that *in some cases the lessee should record a leased asset on his balance sheet, even though, legally, the asset belongs to someone else.* The cases in which this should happen are those in which the economic substance of the lease transaction (as opposed to the legal fiction) is that the lessee effectively owns the asset. An example would be a lease of an automobile which the lessee owns for 10 years. By the time the car is returned to the lessor, it is likely to be practically worthless; hence, FASB 13 would require the lessee to record the asset on his balance sheet.

Formally, FASB 13 requires the lessee to put the lease on his balance sheet (the terminology is that in this case we have a *capital lease*) if one of four criteria applies:

• The lease transfers ownership of the property to the lessee at the end of the lease term.

• The lease contains a bargain-purchase option, which allows the lessee to purchase the leased asset at a very low price at the end of the lease term.

• The lease term exceeds 75 percent of the life of the asset.

• The present value of the lease payments (at the lessee's incremental borrowing rate) exceeds 90 percent of the asset's fair value.

If a lease is a capital lease under the FASB 13 rules, then the lessee records the capital lease as an asset and records a corresponding liability on his balance sheet. The asset is then depreciated, and the liability is amortized, over the lease term. It is as if the asset in question had been bought with 100 percent loan financing.

What does the lessor do if the lessee has to record the lease on his balance sheet? If the lessee has (in an accounting sense) bought the asset with 100 percent loan financing, then the lessor must have (in the same sense) sold the asset with 100 percent loan financing. This is the essence of the FASB 13 treatment of the lessor.

### Reconciling the Tax and Accounting Treatments of Leases

The tax treatment and the accounting treatment of leases are very similar in spirt. It is therefore logical to expect that whenever a lease is classified under the FASB 13 rules as a capital lease, it should be classified by the IRS as a sale. Thus, if the world were a rational place, lessees would put leases on their books only if the IRS decided to treat the leases as sales.

However, the world is a funny place. It turns out to be fairly simple to keep a lease off the lessee's balance sheet, have the IRS treat it as a true lease, and still have all the parties involved feel as if they had transferred almost all of the economic benefits of ownership from the lessor to the lessee. The following references are relevant:

Abdel-Khalik, R. 1981. *Economic Effects on Lessees of FASB Statement No. 13, Accounting For Leases*. Stamford, Conn.: Financial Accounting Standards Board.

El-Gazzar, S., S. Lilien, and V. Pastena. 1986. "Accounting for Leases by Lessees." *Journal of Accounting and Economics* 8: 217–237.

Nakayama, M., S. Lilien, and M. Benis. 1981. "Due Process and FAS No. 13." *Management Accounting* 52: 49–53.

# 5 The Financial Analysis of Leveraged Leases

## 5.1 Introduction

In a *leveraged lease* the lessor finances the purchase of the asset to be leased with debt. From the point of view of the lessee, there is no change in the analysis of a leveraged or a nonleveraged lease. From the lessor's point of view, however, the cash flows of a leveraged lease present some interesting problems.

At least six parties are typically involved in a leveraged lease: the lessee, the equity partners in the lease, the lenders to the equity partners, an owner trustee, an indenture trustee, and the manufacturer of the asset. And in most cases a seventh party is involved: a lease packager (a broker or a leasing company).

Figure 5.1 illustrates the arrangements among the six parties of a typical leveraged lease.

The two major problems relative to leveraged leases are these:

• *The straightforward financial analysis of the lease from the point of view of the lessor.* This concerns the calculation of the cash flows obtained by the lessor, and a computation of these cash flows' net present value (NPV) or internal rate of return (IRR).

• *The accounting analysis of the lease.* Accountants use a method called the *multiple-phases method* (MPM) to calculate a rate of return on leveraged leases. The MPM rate of return is different from the internal rate of return (IRR). In an ordinary financial context this should be of no concern, since the efficient-markets hypothesis tells us that only cash flows matter. However, in a less than efficient world, people tend to get very concerned about how things look on their financial statements. Since the accountant's rate of return on the lease is difficult to compute, we will use Lotus to calculate it; then we will analyze the results.

## 5.2 Example

We can explore these issues by considering an example, roughly based on an example given in appendix E of FASB 13, the accounting profession's magnum opus on accounting for leases.

A leasing company is considering purchasing an asset whose cost is $1,000,000. The asset will be purchased with $200,000 of the company's equity and with $800,000 of debt. The interest on the debt is 9 percent, so

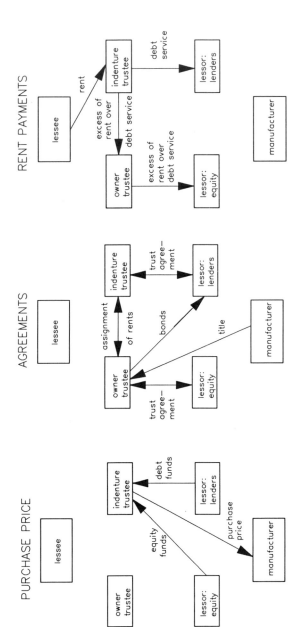

**Figure 5.1**
Leveraged leases.

the annual (interest and principal) over the 15-year term of the debt is $105,179.

The company will lease the asset out for $110,000 per year, payable at the end of each year. The lease term is 15 years. The asset will be depreciated over 5 years at the following annual depreciation rates: 15, 22, 21, 21, and 21 percent. The company anticipates that at the end of the lease term the asset will have a market value of $300,000. Because the asset will be fully depreciated at the time it is sold (in year 16), the whole residual value ($300,000) will be taxable.

The company's tax rate is 37 percent.

These facts are summarized in the table below, which also derives the cash flows of the lessor:

| cost of asset | 1000000 | |
|---|---|---|
| lease term | 15 | |
| lease rental | 110000 | |
| residual value | 300000 | |
| equity | 200000 | 15-year term loan, equal payments of interest & principal |
| debt | 800000 | |
| interest | 0.1 | |
| annual debt payment | 105179 | |
| tax | 0.37 | |

| year | equity invested | rental and/or salvage | after-tax rental/ salvage | depr. | T*depr | principal at start of year | loan payment | interest | repayment of principal | CASH FLOW |
|---|---|---|---|---|---|---|---|---|---|---|
| 0 | -200000 | | | | | | | | | -200000 |
| 1 | | 110000 | 69300 | 150000 | 55500 | 800000 | 105179 | 80000 | 25179 | 49221 |
| 2 | | 110000 | 69300 | 220000 | 81400 | 774821 | 105179 | 77482 | 27697 | 74189 |
| 3 | | 110000 | 69300 | 210000 | 77700 | 747124 | 105179 | 74712 | 30467 | 69465 |
| 4 | | 110000 | 69300 | 210000 | 77700 | 716657 | 105179 | 71666 | 33513 | 68337 |
| 5 | | 110000 | 69300 | 210000 | 77700 | 683144 | 105179 | 68314 | 36865 | 67097 |
| 6 | | 110000 | 69300 | | | 646280 | 105179 | 64628 | 40551 | -11967 |
| 7 | | 110000 | 69300 | | | 605728 | 105179 | 60573 | 44606 | -13467 |
| 8 | | 110000 | 69300 | | | 561122 | 105179 | 56112 | 49067 | -15117 |
| 9 | | 110000 | 69300 | | | 512056 | 105179 | 51206 | 53973 | -16933 |
| 10 | | 110000 | 69300 | | | 458082 | 105179 | 45808 | 59371 | -18930 |
| 11 | | 110000 | 69300 | | | 398711 | 105179 | 39871 | 65308 | -21127 |
| 12 | | 110000 | 69300 | | | 333403 | 105179 | 33340 | 71839 | -23543 |
| 13 | | 110000 | 69300 | | | 261565 | 105179 | 26156 | 79023 | -26201 |
| 14 | | 110000 | 69300 | | | 182542 | 105179 | 18254 | 86925 | -29125 |
| 15 | | 110000 | 69300 | | | 95617 | 105179 | 9562 | 95617 | -32341 |
| 16 | | 300000 | 189000 | | | | | | | 189000 |

A typical year's cash flow is calculated as follows:

$$\text{Cash flow}(t) = (1 - T)\text{Rent} + T\text{Depr}(T) - (1 - T)\text{Interest}(t)$$
$$- \text{Principal repayment}(t).$$

In the last year of the lease, the after-tax value of the residual is added.

The cash flows are positive at the beginning of the lease terms, and they decline over time, turning positive again at the end of the lease term. This is typical for a leveraged lease. There are two causes for this phenomenon:

• The cash flow caused by depreciation typically ends or falls off rapidly before the end of the lease term. The more accelerated the depreciation method, the larger will be the depreciation allowances (and hence the larger the depreciation tax shields) at the beginning of the asset's life.

• In the later years of the lease, the portion of the annual debt payments devoted to interest (tax-deductible) falls, while the portion of the annual debt payments that constitutes a repayment of principal (not tax-deductible) rises.

## 5.3    Analyzing the Example by NPV or IRR

What do we make of these cash flows? One way of viewing the problem (probably the best, in theory) is to take the net present value of the cash flows at some appropriate risk-adjusted discount rate. Since the riskiness of these cash flows is quite low, it is safe to discount them at the riskless interest rate. Assuming this rate to be the loan rate, we get a net present value of $38,206 (we discount at the lessor's after-tax riskless rate, since that is the relevant alternative). Thus, the lease appears to be a good deal for the lessor.

Lessors are often uncomfortable with net present value. They prefer internal rate of return as a measure of the acceptability of the project. Since the cash flows of the project have two changes in sign, in principle it is possible that they have two IRRs. A quick check using Lotus's @NPV function shows that there is only one IRR between −99 percent and 140 percent. This IRR is 12.95 percent. If we use this IRR, we can ascribe the following economic income pattern to the leveraged lease cash flows:

INTERNAL RATE OF RETURN
ATTRIBUTION OF CASH FLOWS

| year | investment, beginning of year | cash flow | income | reduction of investment |
|------|------|------|------|------|
| 1 | 200000 | 49221 | 25903 | 23318 |
| 2 | 176682 | 74189 | 22883 | 51306 |
| 3 | 125376 | 69465 | 16238 | 53227 |
| 4 | 72149 | 68337 | 9344 | 58993 |
| 5 | 13156 | 67097 | 1704 | 65393 |
| 6 | -52237 | -11967 | -6766 | -5201 |
| 7 | -47036 | -13467 | -6092 | -7375 |
| 8 | -39661 | -15117 | -5137 | -9981 |
| 9 | -29680 | -16933 | -3844 | -13089 |
| 10 | -16591 | -18930 | -2149 | -16781 |
| 11 | 190 | -21127 | 25 | -21151 |
| 12 | 21341 | -23543 | 2764 | -26307 |
| 13 | 47648 | -26201 | 6171 | -32372 |
| 14 | 80020 | -29125 | 10364 | -39489 |
| 15 | 119509 | -32341 | 15478 | -47819 |
| 16 | 167329 | 189000 | 21671 | 167329 |

The income attributed to the project in each year is calculated as the product of the IRR and the investment in the project at the beginning of the year. The remainder of the year's cash flow is the reduction of the project's investment. As in every such table, the final reduction of investment ($167,329) is exactly equal to the outstanding investment at the beginning of the last year. Thus, in economic terms, the investment repays itself at the IRR of 12.95 percent.

The interesting thing about this particular table is that five of the income figures are negative. There are two ways to understand this:

• In "mechanical" terms, the only way to make the table work is to have some negative income numbers. This, though true, is hardly an interesting interpretation.

• In economic terms, the negative income figures mean that in some years the project is not worth holding onto but cannot be given away. To see this, consider the lessor's position at the beginning of year 6. *Ten years* of negative cash flows lie ahead. Only in 11 years, in year 16, will the lessor again see a positive cash flow from the lease. A rational lessor would like to give away the lease contract at this point; the present value of the future cash flows at the beginning of year 6 at a 10 percent discount rate is $-\$51,493$. But of course no rational investor would take over the contract at the beginning of year 6 *unless he were paid to so* or unless his discount rate were very low. It is this fact—that the lessor would have to pay someone to take the contract off his hands in year 6—that makes us attribute negative income to the project at this point. In economic terms, the lease at this point is worse than valueless; it is a burden.

As we shall see in the next section, the negative income of leveraged leases caused the accounting profession a considerable headache.

### 5.4   Accounting for Leveraged Leases: The "Multiple-Phases Method"

Financial Accounting Standards Board Statement 13 mandates that the lessor in a leveraged lease allocate the cash flow from the lease between income and investment. The logical way to do this would be to use the internal rate of return of the lease's cash flows in the way illustrated in the preceding section. But here the promulgators of FASB 13 apparently ran up against the troublesome facet of human nature that hates to record a loss even if it is economically warranted. (The implausibility of the method for leveraged leases mandated in the statement is explained only by the assumption that lessors did not want, under any circumstances, to record economic losses that stemmed from the leases.)

The method that was devised to avoid the reporting of negative income is sometimes termed the "multiple-phases method" (MPM). A better term might have been "bastardized IRR method."

The fact that a somewhat silly method of recognizing income is used shouldn't bother us, since foolishness is rampant in this world. However, the complexity and the opaqueness of the method have lent it respectibility. (There must be a lesson in this!) A little debunking, in the form of an explanation, is in order.

Let the multiple-phases rate of return $Q$ (short for *quirky*) be defined as follows:

*MPM 1*   Define the lessor's investment in the lease at the beginning of year 1, Investment(1), to be equal to his initial ivnestment in lease's equity. In our example, Investment(1) = \$200,000.

*MPM 2*   Define the lessor's income from the lease at the end of any year
$t$ (we will use the notation Income($t$)) to be

$$\text{Income}(t) = \begin{cases} Q \times \text{Investment}(t) & \text{if this number is positive} \\ 0 & \text{otherwise.} \end{cases}$$

*MPM 3*   Define the lessor's investment in the lease at the beginning of any
year $t > 1$ to be

Investment($t$) = Investment($t - 1$)

$$- [\text{Cash flow}(t - 1) - \text{Income}(t - 1)].$$

*MPM 4*   Now find $Q$ so that

Investment(end of last year of lease) = 0.

This sounds somewhat complicated, and it is. To better understand it,
look at the second restriction, which says that the income cannot be
negative. If we eliminate the nonnegativity restriction, so that MPM 2
becomes MPM 2' ("Define the lessor's income from the lease at the end of
any year $t$ to be Income($t$) = $Q \times$ Investment($t$), then $Q$ will simply be the
internal rate of return of the lease's cash flows.

As FASB 13 correctly points out, the MPM rate of return can be found
only by trial and error. The Lotus macro that easily does this uses the
following variables (shown here with their final values):

| | |
|---|---:|
| phase rate | 0.106483 |
| LOW | 0.106475 |
| HIGH | 0.106491 |
| END | 0.170996 |
| RUNNUMBER | 17 |
| MAXRUN | 20 |

The key to the whole matter is the range called END. END is defined as

Reduction of investment in year 16 — Investment at beginning of year 16.

If END is positive, the trial phase rate is too low; if END is negative, the
trial rate is too high.

The macro \A starts by asking you to enter a HIGH rate (i.e., a rate
that should be *too* high) and then checks whether this rate is high enough

(i.e., if END is negative). If it is not, you go to \C, which repeatedly asks
you for a HIGH rate until you give one that is high enough.

```
\A                        starting
{let LOW,0}{getnumber Enter high guess for phase rate.   ,HIGH}~
{let PHASE RATE,HIGH}~
{if END>0}{branch \C}~
{for runnumber,1,maxrun,1,\B}~
```

The macro \B is the heart of the routine. The first time you run \B, the
LOW rate is 0 and trial PHASE RATE is the average of the LOW and the
HIGH rates. You then calculate the Multiple Phase worksheet (see the final
version, below the macros). If END is negative for this rate, then the rate
is too high, and it replaces the current HIGH rate. If END is positive, then
the rate is too low, and thus it replaces the current LOW rate. The process
repeats itself until \B has been run 20 times or until the absolute value of
END is less than 1.

```
\B                        calculating the MPM rate
{let phase rate,(HIGH+LOW)/2}~
{if @ABS(END)<1}{quit}~
{if END<0}{let HIGH,(HIGH+LOW)/2}~
{if END>0}{let LOW,(HIGH+LOW)/2}~
```

The macro \C is called only if your initial guess for a HIGH MPM
rate was too low. \C keeps at you until you guess a high enough HIGH
rate.

```
\C
{getnumber Your HIGH guess is too LOW.  Try again.   ,HIGH}~
{let PHASE RATE,HIGH}~
{if END>0}{branch \C}~
{for runnumber,1,maxrun,1,\B}~
```

Now create the following spreadsheet, making sure that the cells in the
INCOME column contain the formula

@MAX(Phase rate * Investment at beginning of year, 0).

The final result looks like this:

MULTIPLE PHASES METHOD
ATTRIBUTION OF INCOME

| year | investment, beginning of year | cash flow | income | reduction of investment |
|------|------|------|------|------|
| 1 | 200000 | 49221 | 21297 | 27924 |
| 2 | 172076 | 74189 | 18323 | 55866 |
| 3 | 116210 | 69465 | 12374 | 57090 |
| 4 | 59119 | 68337 | 6295 | 62042 |
| 5 | -2923 | 67097 | 0 | 67097 |
| 6 | -70020 | -11967 | 0 | -11967 |
| 7 | -58053 | -13467 | 0 | -13467 |
| 8 | -44586 | -15117 | 0 | -15117 |
| 9 | -29469 | -16933 | 0 | -16933 |
| 10 | -12536 | -18930 | 0 | -18930 |
| 11 | 6394 | -21127 | 681 | -21808 |
| 12 | 28202 | -23543 | 3003 | -26546 |
| 13 | 54748 | -26201 | 5830 | -32031 |
| 14 | 86779 | -29125 | 9241 | -38365 |
| 15 | 125144 | -32341 | 13326 | -45667 |
| 16 | 170811 | 189000 | 18189 | 170811 |

## 5.5   Comparing the MPM Rate of Return and the IRR

The MPM rate of return is widely used in the leveraged-leasing industry. How does it compare with the IRR?

• In general, MPMRR ≤ IRR. The two will be equal if all the lease's cash flows are positive. Otherwise, MPMRR < IRR.

• If MPMRR < IRR, then at some point the IRR will attribute negative income to the lease, whereas the MPMRR will attribute zero income to the lease.

Graphically, for the specific example of this chapter, we have the situation shown in figure 5.2.

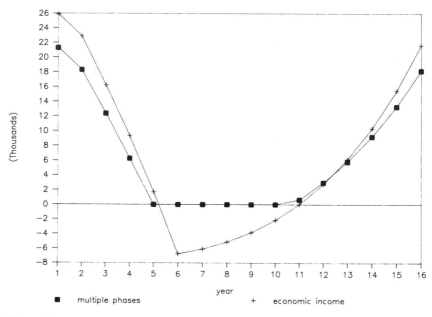

**Figure 5.2**
Economic income ( + ) versus multiple phases ( ■ ).

## Exercises

1. Reconsider the example in this chapter. Show that if the depreciation schedule follows a straight line over the whole life of the asset (i.e., 15 years), then MPMRR = IRR. Explain.

2. In the example of the section, find the lowest lease rental so that MPMRR = IRR.

# II PORTFOLIO PROBLEMS

# Overview

The portfolio approach to investment, pioneered by Harry Markowitz in 1952, was one of the major theoretical advances in modern financial theory. The main insight of the portfolio approach is that the characteristics of one's individual assets do not matter as much as the characteristics of one's entire portfolio of asserts. In a sense, this insight is not at all new; "Don't put all your eggs in one basket" is a fairly well-known aphorism. What makes the portfolio approach exciting is that it can be quantified. In principle, this enables us to make definitive statements about what is a "good" portfolio investment.

The structure of Part II is as follows.

*Chapter 6: Introduction and theory.* Portfolio theory assumes that individuals are concerned with the mean and the variance of the return from their investment (whether this is in fact plausible was, for a while, a hot theoretical issue). Given this assumption, the first concern of portfolio theory is to define how the mean and the variance of a portfolio of asserts are related to the attributes of the assets that make up the portfolio.

*Chapter 7: Calculating means, variances, and covariances.* In this chapter we shall be concerned with the derivation of the necessary statistics from empirical data. We shall spend considerable energy (and computer time) deriving the covariances of the returns of the various assets.

*Chapter 8: Calculating the efficient frontier.* This makes it possible to find mean-variance-efficient portfolios among a given set of assets.

*Chapter 9: Calculating betas and the security-market line.* Here we shall test equilibrium models of capital markets.

*Chaper 10: Entering means and covariances when data are known.* Entering portfolio data into a spreadsheet is a minor task that can be very irritating. This chapter gives a macro that makes it easier.

*Chapter 11: Bibliography.* The literature on portfolio models is huge, and the topic is well-covered in the major texts. This chapter offers a very limited selection of the major books and articles on the topic.

# 6 Portfolio Models—An Introduction

In this chapter we shall cover the basic mechanics of portfolio calculations. Our starting point is a set of $N$ risky assets. Each asset $i$ (they may be shares, bonds, real estate, or whatever, although our numerical examples will generally be confined to shares) is characterized by several statistics: $E(R_i)$, the expected return on asset $i$; $Var(R_i)$, the variance of asset $i$'s return; and $Cov(R_i, R_j)$, the covariance of asset $i$'s and asset $j$'s returns.

In our applications, it will often be convenient to write $Cov(R_i, R_j)$ as $\sigma_{ij}$ and $Var(R_i)$ as $\sigma_{ii}$ (instead of $\sigma_i^2$, as usual). Since the covariance of an asset's returns with itself, $Cov(R_i, R_i)$, is in fact the variance of the asset's returns, this notation is not only economical but also logical.

## 6.1 Example

We have monthly price data for twelve months on two shares: one of Stock A and one of Stock B. The data look as follows:

| month | Stock A price | Stock B price |
|-------|---------------|---------------|
| 0 | 25 | 45 |
| 1 | 24.125 | 44.875 |
| 2 | 23.375 | 46.875 |
| 3 | 24.75 | 45.25 |
| 4 | 26.625 | 50.875 |
| 5 | 26.5 | 58.5 |
| 6 | 28 | 57.25 |
| 7 | 28.875 | 62.75 |
| 8 | 29.75 | 65.5 |
| 9 | 31.375 | 74.375 |
| 10 | 36.25 | 78.5 |
| 11 | 37.125 | 78 |
| 12 | 36.875 | 78.125 |

These data give the closing price at the end of each month for each stock. The month-0 price is the initial price of the stock (i.e., the closing price at the end of the month preceding month 1). We wish to calculate the relevant return statistics for each stock.

First we calculate the *monthly return* for each stock. This is the percentage return that would be earned by an investor who bought the stock at the end of a particular month $t - 1$ and sold it at the end of the following month. For month $t$ and Stock A, the monthly return $R_{At}$ is defined as

$$R_{At} = \frac{P_{At} - P_{At-1}}{P_{At-1}}.$$

(Strictly speaking, we are calculating the price return of the stock. Had the stock paid a dividend in month $t$, the total return would have been

$$\frac{P_{At} - P_{At-1} + \text{Div}_t}{P_{At-1}}.$$

In the examples that follow, we ignore dividends.) This calculation is easily done in Lotus. Setting up the proper formulas gives:

| month | Asset A price | Asset A return | Asset B price | Asset B return |
|-------|------|---------|------|----------|
| 0  | 25     |          | 45     |          |
| 1  | 24.125 | -0.035   | 44.875 | -0.00277 |
| 2  | 23.375 | -0.03108 | 46.875 | 0.044568 |
| 3  | 24.75  | 0.058823 | 45.25  | -0.03466 |
| 4  | 26.625 | 0.075757 | 50.875 | 0.124309 |
| 5  | 26.5   | -0.00469 | 58.5   | 0.149877 |
| 6  | 28     | 0.056603 | 57.25  | -0.02136 |
| 7  | 28.875 | 0.03125  | 62.75  | 0.096069 |
| 8  | 29.75  | 0.030303 | 65.5   | 0.043824 |
| 9  | 31.375 | 0.054621 | 74.375 | 0.135496 |
| 10 | 36.25  | 0.155378 | 78.5   | 0.055462 |
| 11 | 37.125 | 0.024137 | 78     | -0.00636 |
| 12 | 36.875 | -0.00673 | 78.125 | 0.001602 |

We now make a heroic assumption: We assume that the return data for the 12 months represent the distribution of the returns for the coming month. We thus assume that the past gives us some information about the way returns will behave in the future. This assumption allows us to assume that the average of the historic data represents the *expected monthly return* from each stock. It also allows us to assume that we may learn from the historic data what is the variance of the future returns. Using the @avg and @var functions in Lotus, we calculate as follows:

| | | | |
|---|---|---|---|
| $E(R_A)$ | 0.034113 | $E(R_B)$ | 0.048835 |
| $var(R_A)$ | 0.002525 | $var(R_B)$ | 0.003798 |

Next we want to calculate the *covariance* of the returns. The covariance (and the correlation coefficient, which is derived from it) measures the degree to which the returns on the two assets move together. The definition is

$$\text{Cov}(R_A, R_B) = \frac{1}{M} \sum [R_{At} - E(R_A)][R_{Bt} - E(R_B)],$$

where $M$ is the number of points in the distribution (in our case, $M = 12$). This is easily set up in Lotus:

| month | $R_{At} - E(R_A)$ | $R_{Bt} - E(R_B)$ | product |
|---|---|---|---|
| 1 | -0.06911327 | -0.05161351 | 0.003567 |
| 2 | -0.06520135 | -0.00426749 | 0.000278 |
| 3 | 0.024710258 | -0.08350240 | -0.00206 |
| 4 | 0.041644305 | 0.075473650 | 0.003143 |
| 5 | -0.03880810 | 0.101041408 | -0.00392 |
| 6 | 0.022490502 | -0.07020326 | -0.00157 |
| 7 | -0.00286327 | 0.047234127 | -0.00013 |
| 8 | -0.00381024 | -0.00501104 | 0.000019 |
| 9 | 0.020508577 | 0.086660441 | 0.001777 |
| 10 | 0.121265215 | 0.006626443 | 0.000803 |
| 11 | -0.00997533 | -0.05520516 | 0.000550 |
| 12 | -0.04084727 | -0.04723317 | 0.001929 |

The covariance is @avg(product) = 0.000364. This number is hard to interpret, since its size depends on the units in which we measure the returns. (If we were to write the returns in percentages—i.e., 4 instead of 0.04—then the covariance would be 3.64, which is 10,000 times the number we just calculated.) We can also calculate the *correlation coefficient*, which is defined as

$$\rho_{AB} = \frac{\text{cov}(A, B)}{\sigma_A \sigma_B}.$$

Calculating this gives $\rho_{AB} = 0.117583$.

The correlation coefficient measures the degree of linear relation between the returns of Stock A and Stock B. The following probability theorems relate to the correlation coefficient:

• The correlation coefficient is always between $+1$ and $-1$;

$$-1 \le \rho_{AB} \le 1.$$

• If the correlation coefficient is $+1$, then the returns on the two assets are linearly related with a positive slope; i.e., if $\rho_{AB} = 1$, then

$$R_{At} = c + dR_{Bt}, \quad \text{where } d > 0.$$

• If the correlation coefficient is $-1$, then the returns on the two assets are linearly related with a negative slope. If $\rho_{AB} = -1$, then

$$R_{At} = c + dR_{Bt}, \quad \text{where } d < 0.$$

• If the return distributions are independent, then the correlation coefficient will be zero. (The opposite is not true: If the correlation coefficient is zero, this does not necessarily mean that the returns are independent. See the exercises for an example.)

## 6.2 Calculating Portfolio Means and Variances

Now suppose we form a portfolio composed half of Stock A and half of Stock B. What will be the mean and the variance of this portfolio? It is worth doing the brute calculations at least once in Lotus:

```
proportion     0.5
```

| month | R(A,t) | R(B,t) | R(P,t) |
|-------|--------|--------|--------|
| 1 | -0.035 | -0.00277 | -0.01888 |
| 2 | -0.03108 | 0.044568 | 0.006740 |
| 3 | 0.058823 | -0.03466 | 0.012078 |
| 4 | 0.075757 | 0.124309 | 0.100033 |
| 5 | -0.00469 | 0.149877 | 0.072591 |
| 6 | 0.056603 | -0.02136 | 0.017618 |
| 7 | 0.03125 | 0.096069 | 0.063659 |
| 8 | 0.030303 | 0.043824 | 0.037063 |
| 9 | 0.054621 | 0.135496 | 0.095059 |
| 10 | 0.155378 | 0.055462 | 0.105420 |
| 11 | 0.024137 | -0.00636 | 0.008884 |
| 12 | -0.00673 | 0.001602 | -0.00256 |

```
                  mean     0.041474
                  variance 0.001762
```

It is easy to see that the mean portfolio return is exactly the average of the mean returns of the two assets:

$$E(R_p) = 0.5\,E(R_A) + 0.5\,E(R_B)$$

$$= 0.5(0.034113) + 0.5(0.048835)$$

$$= 0.041474.$$

In general the mean return of the portfolio is the *weighted average return* of the component stocks. If we denote by $\gamma$ the proportion invested in Stock A, then

$$E(R_p) = \gamma\,E(R_A) + (1 - \gamma)E(R_B).$$

On the other hand, the portfolio's variance is hardly the average of the two variances of the stocks! The formula for the variance is

$$\text{Var}(R_p) = \gamma^2\,\text{Var}(R_A) + (1 - \gamma)^2\,\text{Var}(R_B) + 2\gamma(1 - \gamma)\,\text{Cov}(R_A, R_B).$$

Another way of writing this is

$$\sigma_p^2 = \gamma^2\sigma_A^2 + (1 - \gamma)^2\sigma_B^2 + 2\gamma(1 - \gamma)\rho_{AB}\sigma_A\sigma_B.$$

In the case at hand,

$$\text{Var}(R_p) = (0.5)^2(0.002525) + (0.5)^2(0.003798) + 2(0.5)(0.5)(0.000364).$$

A frequently performed exercise is to plot the means and standard deviations for various portfolio proportions $q$. To do this we build a table:

| $\gamma$ | $E(R_p)$ | $\sigma(R_p)$ |
|---|---|---|
| 0 | 0.048835741 | 0.061629034 |
| 0.05 | 0.048099617 | 0.058895888 |
| 0.1 | 0.047363494 | 0.056278665 |
| 0.15 | 0.046627370 | 0.053794288 |
| 0.2 | 0.045891247 | 0.051462000 |
| 0.25 | 0.045155123 | 0.049303390 |
| 0.3 | 0.044419000 | 0.047342221 |
| 0.35 | 0.043682876 | 0.045603971 |
| . | . | . |
| . | . | . |
| . | . | . |
| 0.95 | 0.034849394 | 0.048197403 |
| 1 | 0.034113270 | 0.050250352 |

Such a table is easily set up using Lotus's /Data Table command. The graph

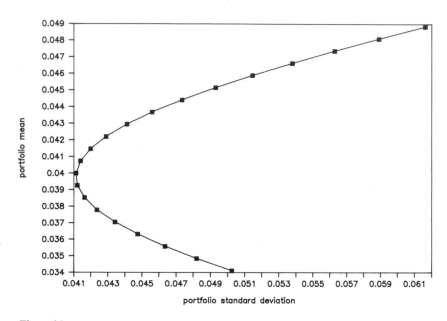

**Figure 6.1**
Portfolio means and variances.

of the means and standard deviations looks like figure 6.1. (Use the /Graph Type XY option.)

## 6.3   Portfolio Mean and Variance—The General Case

In the general case of $N$ assets, suppose that the proportion of asset $i$ in the portfolio is denoted by $\gamma_i$. It is often convenient to write the portfolio proportions as a column vector $\Gamma$:

$$\Gamma = \begin{vmatrix} \gamma_1 \\ \gamma_2 \\ \gamma_3 \\ \vdots \\ \gamma_N \end{vmatrix}.$$

We may then write $\Gamma^{\mathrm{T}}$ as the transpose of $\Gamma$:

$$\Gamma^{\mathrm{T}} = [\gamma_1, \gamma_2, \ldots, \gamma_N].$$

The expected return of the portfolio whose proportions are given by $\Gamma$ is the weighted average of the expected returns of the individual assets:

$$E(R_p) = \sum_{i=1}^{N} \gamma_i E(R_i).$$

Now write $E(R)$ as the column vector of asset returns, and $E(R)^T$ as the row vector of the asset returns:

$$E(R) = \begin{vmatrix} E(R_1) \\ E(R_2) \\ E(R_3) \\ \vdots \\ E(R_N) \end{vmatrix},$$

$$E(R)^T = [E(R_1), \ldots, E(R_N)].$$

Then we may write the expected portfolio return in matrix notation as

$$E(R_p) = \Gamma^T E(R) = E(R)^T \Gamma.$$

The portfolio's variance is given by

$$Var(R_p) = \sum_{i=1}^{N} (\gamma_i)^2 Var(R_i) + \sum_{\substack{i,j=1 \\ i \neq j}}^{N} 2\gamma_i \gamma_j Cov(R_i, R_j).$$

This looks bad, but it is really a straightforward extension of the expression for the variance of a portfolio of two assets which we had before: Each asset's variance appears once, multiplied by the square of the asset's proportion in the portfolio; the covariance of each pair of assets appears once, multiplied by twice the product of the individual assets' proportions.

Another way of writing the variance is to use the notation

$$Var(R_i) = \sigma_{ii}, \quad Cov(R_i, R_j) = \sigma_{ij}.$$

We may then write

$$Var(R_p) = \sum_i \sum_j \gamma_i \gamma_j \sigma_{ij}.$$

The most economical representation of the portfolio variance uses matrix notation. It is also the easiest representation to implement for large portfolios in Lotus. In this representation we call the matrix that has $\sigma_{ij}$ in the $i$th row and the $j$th column the *variance-covariance matrix*:

$$S = \begin{vmatrix} \sigma_{11} & \sigma_{12} & \sigma_{13} \cdots \sigma_{1N} \\ \sigma_{21} & \sigma_{22} & \sigma_{23} \cdots \sigma_{2N} \\ \sigma_{31} & \sigma_{32} & \sigma_{33} \cdots \sigma_{3N} \\ \vdots & & \\ \sigma_{N1} & \sigma_{N2} & \sigma_{N3} \cdots \sigma_{NN} \end{vmatrix}.$$

Then the portfolio variance is given by

$$\text{Var}(R_p) = \Gamma^T S \Gamma.$$

Finally, if we denote by $\Gamma_1 = [\gamma_{11}, \gamma_{12}, \ldots, \gamma_{1N}]$ the proportions of portfolio 1 and by $\Gamma_2 = [\gamma_{21}, \gamma_{22}, \ldots, \gamma_{2N}]$ the proportions of portfolio 2, we can show that the covariance of the two portfolios is given by

$$\text{Cov}(1, 2) = \Gamma_1 S \Gamma_2^T.$$

## 6.4 Efficient Portfolios

An *efficient portfolio* is the portfolio of risky assets that gives the lowest variance of return of all portfolios having the same expected return. Alternatively, we may say that an efficient portfolio has the highest expected return of all portfolios having the same variance. Mathematically, we may define an efficient portfolio as follows: For a given return $m$, an efficient portfolio $p$ is one that solves

$$\min \sum_i \sum_j x_i x_j \sigma_{ij} = \text{Var}(R_p)$$

subject to

$$\sum_i x_i R_i = m = E(R_p),$$

$$\sum_i x(i) = 1.$$

The *efficient frontier* is the set of all efficient portfolios. As was shown by Black (1972),* the efficient frontier is the locus of all convex combinations of any two efficient portfolios. This means that if $X(1) = [x_{11}, \ldots, x_{1N}]$ and $X(2) = [x_{21}, \ldots, x_{2N}]$ are efficient portfolios, then so is any combination

$$\gamma X(1) + (1 - \gamma)X(2) = [\gamma x_{11} + (1 - \gamma)x_{21}, \ldots, \gamma x_{1N} + (1 - \gamma)x_{2N}].$$

* References cited in chapters 6–10 are listed in chapter 11.

Thus, we can find the whole efficient frontier if we can find any two efficient portfolios.

Suppose we are given the expected returns $E(R_i)$ $(i = 1, \ldots, N)$ and the covariances of asset returns $\sigma_{ij}$ $(i, j = 1, \ldots, N)$. A technique for finding a particular efficient portfolio is to solve the following set of $N$ simultaneous linear equations:

$$E(R_i) - C = \sum_j \sigma_{ij} z_j, \quad i = 1, \ldots, N \tag{1}$$

where $C$ is any positive number. (This method was first set out in Sharpe 1970, which is now out of print. For a full discussion of the method, see chapter 4 of Elton and Gruber 1984.) The portfolio proportions of the efficient portfolio are found by normalizing the $z$'s so that they sum to 1:

$$x_i = z_i \Big/ \sum_j z_j.$$

Writing equation 1 in matrix notation gives

$$R - C = SZ. \tag{2}$$

To solve this, we calculate the inverse of $S$ and multiply both sides of equation 2 by this inverse. This gives

$$Z = S^{-1}[R - C].$$

Substituting in two different values of $C$ gives two different vectors $X$ of proportions for two efficient portfolios. Call the vectors $X(1)$ and $X(2)$. In order to calculate the rest of the efficient frontier, we need to find the covariance between the two portfolios. Assume that both vectors are column vectors. Then the covariance is found by solving (again, we use matrix notation)

$$\text{cov}(1, 2) = X(1)^{\mathrm{T}} S X(2),$$

where $X(1)^{\mathrm{T}}$ is a transpose of $X(1)$.

Having found the covariance, we know that all efficient portfolios are given by

$$\gamma X(1) + (1 - \gamma) X(2)$$

for some proportion $\gamma$. Denote by $R(1)$ and $R(2)$ the vectors of the expected returns of portfolios 1 and 2, respectively. Now,

$R(i) = X(i)^\mathrm{T} E(R), \quad i = 1, 2.$

We know that the expected return and variance for any efficient portfolio whose proportions are given by $\gamma$ are

$E(R_p) = \gamma R(1) + (1 - \gamma) R(2),$

$\mathrm{Var}(R_p) = \gamma^2 \mathrm{Var}(1) + (1 - \gamma)^2 \mathrm{Var}(2) + 2\gamma(1 - \gamma) \mathrm{Cov}(1, 2).$

Since Lotus can handle matrix operations, the calculation of the efficient portfolios is within its capabilities. The following chapters discuss the two major problems that arise in the actual implementation of a solution: translating return data to a variance-covariance matrix, and performing the actual calculation of the efficient portfolios.

## Exercises

1. Suppose that $X$ and $Y$ are two random variables, and that $Y = X^2$. Let $X$ have values $-5, -4, -2, 2, 4,$ and 5 with equal probabilities. Show that the correlation coefficient between $X$ and $Y$ is zero. Does this mean that $X$ and $Y$ are independent random variables?

2. Consider two assets, A and B, which have the same expected returns and variances as the assets in the chapter—$E(R_A) = 0.034113$, $E(R_B) = 0.048835$, $\mathrm{Var}(R_A) = 0.002525$, and $\mathrm{var}(R_B) = 0.003798$. Now consider three cases:

$\rho_{AB} = +1,$

$\rho_{AB} = -1,$

$\rho_{AB} = +0.5.$

Graph the combinations of portfolio means and variances for each case. (Graphs like these appear in virtually all elementary finance books. The standard deviation usually appears on the $x$ axis and the portfolio mean return on the $y$ axis. In this case, if you want to put all three graphs on the same set of axes, you will have to reverse this arrangement. Why?)

# 7 Calculating the Variance-Covariance Matrix

The starting point for this calculation is assumed to be a file with data on periodic returns for a group of assets. The spreadsheet looks like this:

```
        num_sec        starttime
            i          stoptime
            j          elapsed
        mean(i)
        mean(j)


        ASSET RETURNS
|   ||       |...|       |       |       ||      ||      |       |--------------------|
|   ||       |...|       |       |       ||      ||      |       |                    |
|date||      |...|       |       |       ||      ||      |       |                    |
|   ||       |...|       |       |       ||      ||      |       |      variance-     |
|   ||secur-|...|secur-|        |PRODUCT||COPY(i)||COPY(j)|      |      covariance    |
|   ||ity 1 |...|ity N |        |       ||      ||      |       |      matrix        |
|   ||       |...|       |       |       ||      ||      |       |      (MATRIX)      |
|   ||       |...|       |       |       ||      ||      |       |                    |
|   ||       |...|       |       |       ||      ||      |       |                    |
|   ||       |...|       |       |       ||      ||      |       |--------------------|

                  cov
```

The column of asset returns gives the percentage return from holding a specific asset from one date to another. Table 7.1 gives an example of some data for the Dow-Jones 30 Industrials; the data are arranged as they would be in the spreadsheet. The dates are given in the form yymmdd, so that 750531 means May 31, 1975. The percentage return for AMR (American Airlines) over that month is defined as

$$\frac{(\text{Price AMR}, 5/31/75) - (\text{Price AMR}, 4/30/75)}{\text{Price AMR}, 4/30/75}.$$

For May 1975, this return was $-15.584$ percent.

The spreadsheet works by copying successive columns from the Asset Returns section into the temporary columns labeled COPY(I) and COPY(J). Once these columns are in place, the spreadsheet calculates the mean return for each asset (MEAN(I) and MEAN(J)). The column PRODUCT then calculates

$$(\text{return}(i, t) - \text{MEAN(I)}) * (\text{return}(j, t) - \text{MEAN(J)}),$$

and the macro calculates @avg(PRODUCT), which is the covariance of assets $i$ and $j$. This covariance is put into the proper place in the variance-covariance MATRIX.

## Chapter 7

**Table 7.1**

Returns on Dow-Jones 30 Industrials.

| date | AMR | ALD | AA | AC | T | BS | .... | UTX | WX | Z |
|---|---|---|---|---|---|---|---|---|---|---|
| 740131 | 11.594 | -7.908 | -0.515 | 7.810 | 0.499 | 1.515 | .... | -1.579 | -9.360 | -0.408 |
| 740228 | 22.078 | 2.116 | 0.176 | 3.604 | 5.499 | 5.299 | .... | 9.947 | 7.578 | 0.000 |
| 740331 | -8.511 | -7.104 | -2.083 | -3.478 | -4.773 | -8.000 | .... | 5.446 | -16.327 | 0.694 |
| 740430 | -3.488 | 3.529 | 5.585 | 3.333 | -5.263 | 0.395 | .... | 5.164 | -8.571 | -3.862 |
| 740531 | -9.639 | -7.670 | -17.713 | -0.889 | -1.016 | -9.764 | .... | -3.571 | -18.243 | -10.949 |
| 740630 | -12.000 | -7.453 | 4.321 | -3.139 | 1.359 | 6.195 | .... | -0.943 | -11.570 | -8.197 |
| 740731 | -10.606 | 0.000 | 10.651 | -3.981 | -9.651 | -0.417 | .... | -7.619 | -8.411 | -6.786 |
| 740831 | -1.695 | -10.508 | -9.979 | -2.463 | 2.908 | -6.276 | .... | 11.856 | -8.220 | -13.725 |
| 740930 | -12.069 | -18.182 | -8.982 | -7.576 | -3.529 | -9.091 | .... | -3.286 | -10.227 | -2.273 |
| 741031 | 27.451 | 16.667 | -13.158 | 12.787 | 12.805 | 13.000 | .... | 11.165 | -3.797 | 2.791 |
| 741130 | -21.538 | 5.397 | -4.667 | 2.475 | -4.649 | -4.425 | .... | 6.550 | -4.021 | -8.140 |
| 741231 | -19.608 | -13.359 | -4.016 | 12.077 | 3.179 | -6.132 | .... | 8.750 | 12.676 | -5.063 |
| 750131 | 48.780 | 13.656 | 12.971 | 10.345 | 8.683 | 27.136 | .... | 4.215 | 12.500 | 35.200 |
| 750228 | 19.672 | 10.698 | 3.956 | 8.800 | 5.619 | -2.372 | .... | 7.353 | 13.271 | 12.121 |
| 750331 | 1.370 | 3.901 | 7.194 | -2.206 | -1.985 | 15.190 | .... | 13.889 | 18.000 | -0.901 |
| 750430 | 4.054 | 1.706 | 23.490 | -11.880 | -1.013 | 15.751 | .... | 17.073 | -0.847 | 18.545 |
| 750531 | -15.584 | 0.537 | 0.728 | 8.261 | 2.506 | -9.810 | .... | 1.042 | 23.884 | -10.938 |
| 750630 | 3.077 | 5.068 | 6.522 | 0.803 | 3.299 | 4.270 | .... | 20.833 | 4.196 | 14.912 |
| 750731 | -4.478 | -2.894 | -9.439 | -4.622 | -3.686 | -6.485 | .... | -7.543 | -4.027 | -5.038 |
| 750831 | 4.688 | -6.755 | 3.572 | 2.979 | -3.878 | 11.679 | .... | 3.263 | -6.333 | 4.918 |
| 750930 | -11.940 | -10.432 | -13.973 | -2.066 | -0.811 | -7.285 | .... | 3.189 | -18.939 | -3.125 |
| 751031 | -1.695 | 6.024 | -8.917 | -0.675 | 7.629 | -3.214 | .... | -7.506 | -2.856 | 27.742 |
| 751130 | 15.517 | 4.015 | 0.238 | 9.957 | 4.253 | 0.369 | .... | -3.580 | 5.882 | 16.026 |
| 751231 | 5.970 | -1.845 | 8.803 | -1.181 | 0.494 | -1.866 | .... | -7.250 | -0.926 | -2.762 |
| 760131 | 11.268 | 24.060 | 18.447 | 6.135 | 8.108 | 26.616 | .... | 15.903 | 16.822 | 13.295 |

....

list of symbols and names....

| | | | |
|---|---|---|---|
| AMR | AMERICAN AIRLINES | HR | INTERNATIONAL HARVESTER |
| ALD | ALLIED CHEMICAL AND DYE | MCD | McDONALDS CORP |
| AA | ALUMINUM CO AMER | MRK | MERCK & CO. |
| AC | AMERICAN CAN CO | MMM | MINNESOTA MINING AND MANUFACTURING |
| T | AMERICAN TEL & TEL | OI | OWENS ILLINOIS |
| BS | BETHLEHEM STEEL | MO | PHILIP MORRIS |
| C | CHRYSLER | PG | PROCTER AND GAMBLE |
| DD | DUPONT E I DE NEMOURS | S | SEARS ROEBUCK |
| EK | EASTMAN KODAK | SD | STANDARD OIL OF CALIFORNIA |
| XON | EXXON | TX | TEXACO |
| GE | GENERAL ELECTRIC | UK | UNION CARBIDE |
| GF | GENERAL FOODS | X | UNITED STATES STEELPORTATION CO |
| GM | GENERAL MOTORS | UTX | UNITED AIRCRAFT & TRANS |
| GT | GOODYEAR TIRE AND RUBBER | WX | WESTINGHOUSE |
| IBM | INTERNATIONAL BUSINESS MACHINES | Z | WOOLWORTH |

The procedure of the previous paragraph is repeated once for each pair of I and J. If the number of securities (here denoted by the range name NUM_SEC) is 30, then the procedure is repeated 487 times.

The specific macro entries are the following:

\A gets the initial data and sets the timer.

```
\A          initialization
{let STARTTIME,@now}{blank STOPTIME}{blank ELAPSED}
{getnumber How many securities are there?    ,NUM_SEC}
{let I,1}{let J,1}~
{windowsoff}{paneloff}{branch \B}~
```

\B and the macro listed under the range name UPDATE are the heart of the program. \B calculates the covariance between two asset returns and puts this covariance in the proper place of the variance-covariance matrix.

```
\B
{if I=J}{goto}DATA~{right i-1}/c{end}{down}~COPY(I)~{let MEAN(I),@avg(COPY(I))}~
'/c{end}{down}~COPY(J)~{right}
{let MEAN(J),@avg(COPY(J))}~{calc}
{let COV,@avg(PRODUCT)}
{put MATRIX,I-1,J-1,COV}
{if J=NUM_SEC#and#I=NUM_SEC}{branch \C}
{branch UPDATE}
```

UPDATE sees to it that we don't repeat calculations, by first doing (for example) the calculation for $I = 2$ and $J = 5$ and then later doing the calculation for $I = 5$ and $J = 2$.

```
UPDATE
{if J<=NUM_SEC}{let J,J+1}~
{if J=NUM_SEC+1}{let I,I+1}{let J,I}~
{branch \B}
```

The macro repeatedly returns to UPDATE until all the data have been entered into the variance-covariance matrix.

DATA is the label for the upper left corner of the columns of asset returns (i.e., asset 1's return for the first period). The second line of the macro copies the return vector for asset I into the column labeled COPY(I). The third line of the macro repeats this procedure for asset J. There is no need to recopy every time the asset I returns, since we are calculating cov(1, 1), cov(1, 2), cov(1, 3), .... Only when we get to cov(2, 2) do we need to copy a new column to COPY(I). This is accomplished by {if I = J} in the second line.

The fifth line of \B puts the covariance term in the correct cell of the variance-covariance MATRIX; because Lotus numbers ranges starting with row 0 and column 0, it is necessary to subtract 1 from I and from J. The sixth line of \B checks to see if we are finished. If so, we set the timer and {quit}. If not, we go back to UPDATE for another round.

When we reach the last macro, \C, we have half a variance-covariance matrix in place, the diagonal and the cells below it. \C uses /range transpose to copy the cells below the diagonal to those above it. It then sets the timer, and quits.

```
\C   the end
'/rtMATRIX~MATRIX~
{let STOPTIME,@now}{let ELAPSED,STOPTIME-STARTTIME}{calc}{quit}~
```

The macro requires that you have predefined the following ranges:

| | |
|---|---|
| COPY(I) | MEAN(I) |
| COPY(J) | MEAN(J) |
| COV | NUMBER |
| DATA | NUM_SEC |
| ELAPSED | PRODUCT |
| I | STARTTIME |
| J | STOPTIME |
| MATRIX | UPDATE |

To speed calculations, we have set the spreadsheet to manual recalculation. This means that we have to recalculate the spreadsheet before entering results in the variance-covariance matrix. Hence the {calc} in \B. If we didn't put in the last {calc} in \C, the screen would show CALC on the bottom when the macro stopped, which would be disturbing to fastidious souls.

Using an IBM PC with an 8087 chip, the time required to calculate the variance covariance matrix for the Dow-Jones Industrials (monthly data for 10 years for 30 shares) was 54 minutes.

## Exercise

Below you will find the annual returns for 1974 through 1983 for six stocks from among the Dow-Jones 30 Industrials (AMR is American Airlines, BS is Bethlehem Steel, GE is General Electric, HR is International Harvester, and UK is Union Carbide). Calculate the variance-covariance matrix of the six stocks. (The answer is given in the exercises the end of the next chapter.)

It is helpful to write a little macro to put the data into a spreadsheet. If you are recording across rows, this one will do:

```
\F    {?}{right}{?}{right}{?}{right}{?}{right}{?}{right}{?}{right}{?}
      {down}{left 6}{branch \F}
```

You can now push NUM LOCK and use the number pad to enter the data.

| year | AMR | BS | GE | HR | MO | UK |
|------|-----|-----|-----|-----|-----|-----|
| 1974 | -0.35052 | -0.11543 | -0.42462 | -0.21065 | -0.07585 | 0.23308 |
| 1975 | 0.70831 | 0.24715 | 0.37193 | 0.22267 | 0.02135 | 0.35688 |
| 1976 | 0.73293 | 0.36651 | 0.25497 | 0.58149 | 0.12759 | 0.07814 |
| 1977 | -0.20337 | -0.42709 | -0.04901 | -0.09376 | 0.07120 | -0.27210 |
| 1978 | 0.16631 | -0.04523 | -0.05734 | 0.27508 | 0.13722 | -0.13455 |
| 1979 | -0.26585 | 0.01577 | 0.08984 | 0.07927 | 0.02150 | 0.22536 |
| 1980 | 0.01241 | 0.47512 | 0.33497 | -0.18943 | 0.20022 | 0.36567 |
| 1981 | -0.02636 | -0.20423 | -0.02755 | -0.74268 | 0.09133 | 0.04791 |
| 1982 | 1.06420 | -0.14927 | 0.69682 | -0.26149 | 0.22429 | 0.04560 |
| 1983 | 0.19422 | 0.36804 | 0.31105 | 1.86823 | 0.20661 | 0.26397 |

# 8 Calculating Efficient Portfolios

The spreadsheet for calculating efficient portfolios looks like this:

```
constant      starttime      MEAN(1)      VAR(1)
counter       stoptime       MEAN(2)      VAR(2)
num_sec       elapsed                     COV(1,2)

|---------------------|      |    ||    |      |    ||    |      |    ||    |
|                     |      |    ||    |      |    ||    |      |    ||    |
|                     |      |vector||vector|   |vector||vector|   |vector||vector|
|    variance-        |      |of    ||of    |   |      ||      |   |      ||      |
|    covariance       |      |means ||means |   | Z(1) || Z(2) |   | X(2) || X(2) |
|    matrix           |      |      ||minus |   |      ||      |   |      ||      |
|    (MATRIX)         |      |(MEANS)||con-  |   |      ||      |   |      ||      |
|                     |      |      ||stant |   |      ||      |   |      ||      |
|                     |      |    ||    |      |    ||    |      |    ||    |
|---------------------|      |    ||    |      |    ||    |      |    ||    |


---------------------|
                     |                       ---------------------------------
                     |                       row vector X(1)T
    inverse of       |                       ---------------------------------
    variance-        |
    covariance       |                       ---------------------------------
    matrix           |                       row vector X(2)T
    (INVERSE)        |                       ---------------------------------
                     |
---------------------|                       ---------------------------------
                                             INTERIM calculations
                                             ---------------------------------
```

The capitalized items in the layout of this spreadsheet correspond to range names used in the macros that calculate the efficient frontier.

Before you start the macro, you have to input the following items:

• The variance-covariance matrix. This has to be copied from the spreadsheet discussed in the chapter 7. One good way to do this is to use the /File Combine command.

• The vector of means. This column vector contains the mean return of each of the assets.

• In the column vector of "means minus constant" you have to insert a formula that puts in each cell the mean of the asset return minus the current value of CONSTANT. For example, if the first five items of MEANS are 2.147, 0.028, 1.195, 1.348, and 0.932 and the current value of CONSTANT is 5, the vector of MEANS and that of means minus constant will look as follows:

```
means   means-con
2.147  -2.85344
0.028  -4.97161
1.195   -3.8048
1.348  -3.65165
0.932  -4.06774
```

• the number of securities in the range labeled NUM_SEC.

The first macro, \A, initiates the spreadsheet program by setting the timer and turning off the windows and panel, so that the macro as a whole will run faster.

```
\A        finding an efficient portfolio
{let STARTTIME,@now}{blank ELAPSED}{blank STOPTIME}~{paneloff}{windowsoff}~
/dmiMATRIX~INVERSE~
{let CONSTANT,0}~/dmmINVERSE~MEANS-CON~Z(1)~
{let CONSTANT,5}~/dmmINVERSE~MEANS-CON~Z(2)~
{branch \B}~
```

The second line of \A inverts the variance-covariance matrix. For a $30 \times 30$ matrix, this inversion can take about 2 minutes on an IBM PC with a numerical coprocessor. The next line takes an arbitrary value for the CONSTANT, substracts this CONSTANT from the vector of MEANS, and multiplies the inverse of the covariance matrix by the resulting vector. The product, a column vector, is stored in the range $Z(1)$. The fourth line of \A repeats the process for a different value of CONSTANT. (The values are arbitrary and do not affect the shape of the efficient frontier; they must, however, be different.)

Macros \B and \C calculate the values of the column vectors $X(1)$ and $X(2)$; each of these column vectors contains the proportions of an optimal portfolio.

```
\B        loop for X(1) and X(2)
{for COUNTER,1,NUM_SEC,1,\c}~
{branch \D}~

\C        calculating X(1) and X(2)
{put X(1),0,COUNTER-1,@index(Z(1),0,COUNTER-1)/@sum(Z(1))}
{put X(2),0,COUNTER-1,@index(Z(2),0,COUNTER-1)/@sum(Z(2))}~
```

Macro \D uses the /Range Transpose function of Lotus to turn the column vectors $X(1)$ and $X(2)$ into row vectors $X(1)T$ and $X(2)T$ respectively.

```
\D        transposes
/rtX(1)~X(1)T~
/rtX(2)~X(2)T~
{branch \E}~
```

Macro \E calculates the mean of portfolios 1 by multiplying the row vector of portfolio proportions, X(1)T, into the column vector of asset mean returns, MEANS. The result (a scalar) is placed in the cell labeled MEAN(1). The process is then repeated for portfolio 2.

```
\E        calculating the means
/dmmX(1)T~MEANS~MEAN(1)~
/dmmX(2)T~MEANS~MEAN(2)~
{branch \F}~
```

The label of \F is self-explanatory.

```
\F        calculating VAR(1), VAR(2), COV(1,2)
/dmmX(1)T~MATRIX~INTERIM~/dmmINTERIM~X(1)~VAR(1)~
/dmmX(2)T~MATRIX~INTERIM~/dmmINTERIM~X(2)~VAR(2)~
/dmmX(1)T~MATRIX~INTERIM~/dmmINTERIM~X(2)~COV(1,2)~
{let STOPTIME,@now}{let ELAPSED,STOPTIME-STARTTIME}~{quit}~
```

This macro first calculates the variance of portfolio 1 by calculating the product

$$X(1)T*MATRIX*X(1),$$

and placing the result in the cell labeled VAR(1). Because Lotus handles only stepwise matrix multiplications, we place the result of the multiplication of X(1)T*MATRIX in the range INTERIM. INTERIM is then multiplied by X(1) to give VAR(1). The same process is repeated for VAR(2). In order to calculate COV(1, 2), we multiply

$$X(1)T*MATRIX*X(2).$$

The spreadsheet used here constructs a table of various combinations of the two efficient portfolios.

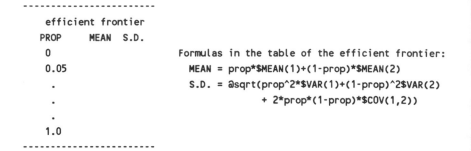

```
--------------------------
     efficient frontier
     PROP      MEAN   S.D.
     0                          Formulas in the table of the efficient frontier:
     0.05                        MEAN = prop*$MEAN(1)+(1-prop)*$MEAN(2)
       .                         S.D. = @sqrt(prop^2*$VAR(1)+(1-prop)^2$VAR(2)
       .                                     + 2*prop*(1-prop)*$COV(1,2))
       .
     1.0
--------------------------
```

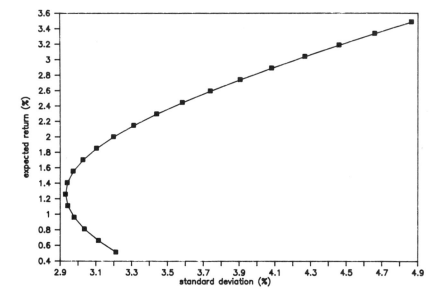

**Figure 8.1**
The efficient frontier.

This table has its formulas built in, which adds to the time it takes to do the spreadsheet calculations.

When you graph the means and returns of the portfolios in the table, you should see the familiar curve of the efficient frontier (figure 8.1).

The last line of the macro calculates the time needed for the macro. For a 30 × 30 covariance matrix and an IBM PC with an 8087 numeric coprocessor, the time needed is about 2 minutes, 53 seconds. If you don't put in the table to graph the efficient frontier (an aesthetic folly, though perhaps a more sensible approach), the time drops to 2:36.

An efficient portfolio usually contains negative proportions of some assets. This means that the asset is sold short in that particular efficient portfolio.

The efficient portfolios found by the technique illustrated in this chapter may be either close together or far apart on the efficient frontier. If the portfolios are far apart, you can assign values between 0 and 1 to the proportion PROP in the able, which calculates the efficient frontier (as illustrated above). If the portfolios are close together, however, you may have to let PROP be greater than 1, or less than 0 (depending on the two particular efficient portfolios you found).

## Exercises

1. In a well-known article, Roll (1978) discusses the ability of the Capital Asset Pricing Model to classify portfolio performance. Roll uses an example in which there are four assets, which have the following variance-covariance matrix:

$$S = \begin{vmatrix} 10 & 2 & 4 & 5 \\ 2 & 20 & 4 & 1 \\ 4 & 4 & 40 & 10 \\ 5 & 1 & 10 & 60 \end{vmatrix}.$$

The vector of expected asset returns is given by

$$R(1) = 6, \quad R(2) = 7, \quad R(3) = 8, \quad R(4) = 9.$$

Roll asserts that the following five portfolios are efficient (the numbers in parentheses are the percentage weights of the four assets):

portfolio 1: $(59.6, 27.6, 7.69, 5.08)$
portfolio 2: $(40.7, 31.9, 14.0, 13.4)$
portfolio 3: $(-4.4, 42.2, 29.0, 33.3)$
portfolio 4: $(-49.6, 52.4, 44.1, 53.1)$
portfolio 5: $(18.2, 37, 21.5, 23.3)$

Is Roll correct? (The numbers may contain some rounding errors; this is not to be held against Roll.)

2. If you did the exercise at the end of chapter 7 correctly, you calculated the following variance-covariance matrix for the six stocks:

```
0.205951 0.037520 0.107749 0.0492612 0.020834 0.005857
0.037520 0.079038 0.035480 0.1028379 0.008906 0.040579
0.107749 0.035480 0.086735 0.0442907 0.019443 0.014840
0.049261 0.102837 0.044290 0.4435255 0.019252 0.027357
0.020834 0.008906 0.019443 0.0192526 0.008311 -0.00148
0.005857 0.040579 0.014840 0.0273574 -0.00148 0.039209
```

Assuming that these are the only stocks in your investment universe, find the efficient frontier.

# 9 Estimating Betas and the Security-Market Line

## 9.1 Introduction

The Capital Asset Pricing Model (CAPM) is an equilibrium model of capital markets. The model's main conclusion is that the equilibrium relation between risk and return is given by the Security-Market Line (SML):

$$E(R_i) = R_f + \beta_i[E(R_M) - R_f],$$

where $E(R_i)$ is the expected return on a particular risky security $i$, $E(R_M)$ is the expected return on the market portfolio M, $R_f$ is the return on a risk-free asset, and $\beta_i$ is a measure of the riskiness of asset $i$:

$$\beta_i = \frac{\text{Cov}(R_i, R_M)}{\text{Var}(R_M)}.$$

An alternative version of the model (Black 1972) does not require the assumption that there is a risk-free asset. In this case the equilibrium relation between expected return and $\beta$ is shown to be

$$E(R_i) = E(R_Z) + \beta_i[E(R_M) - E(R_Z)],$$

where $E(R_Z)$ is the expected return of an asset whose $\beta$ is zero.

In this chapter we will look at some typical capital-market data and replicate a simple test of the CAPM. This means that we have to calculate the betas for a set of assets, and we then have to determine the equation of the SML.

Warning: The test in this chapter is the simplest possible test of the CAPM. There is an enormous literature in which the possible statistical and methodological pitfalls of this test are discussed. A classic reference is Miller and Scholes 1972. Surveys can be found in Elton and Gruber 1984 and Levy and Sarnat 1984.

Another caveat relates to the role of the market portfolio M. Roll (1977, 1978) shows that the linear relationship

$$E(R_i) = R_f + \beta_i[E(R_M) - R_f]$$

should hold when M is replaced by *any* efficient portfolio. Following Roll, we can distinguish between two kinds of tests: a statistical test that determines whether we have been able to find an efficient portfolio on which to run our regressions, and an economic test to see whether the portfolio we picked is really the market portfolio. See section 9.6 for an illustration of this problem.

Section 9.2 discusses the general form of our test, and section 9.3 shows how to set up the test using Lotus.

## 9.2 Testing the CAPM

Tests of the CAPM start with return data on a set of assets. For our test we shall discuss the data used in the chapter on efficient portfolios, which include monthly returns for the thirty Dow-Jones industrial stocks.

The steps in the test are as follows:

• Determine a candidate for the market portfolio M. We shall use the Standard & Poor's 500 Index (S&P500) as a candidate for M.

• For each of the assets in question, determine the asset $\beta$.

• Regress the mean returns of the assets on their respective betas; this should give the Securities-Market Line.

## 9.3 Setting Up the Spreadsheet

Our spreadsheet looks very much like those in chapter 8:

```
            counter      starttime
            num_sec      stoptime
                         elapsed

            ASSET RETURNS
|    ||     ||DATA |...|    ||      ||      |
|    ||     ||     |...|    ||      ||      |  the column PRODUCT
|date||     ||     |...|    ||      ||      |  contains the formula:
|    ||     ||     |...|    ||      ||      |  (R_it - MEAN(I))*(S&P_t-MEAN(S&P)),
|    ||S&P  ||secur-|...|secur-||COPY(I)||PRODUCT|  where R_it is the entry on row i of
|    || 500 ||ity 1 |...|ity N ||      ||      |  the column COPY(I), and MEAN(I) is the
|    ||     ||     |...|    ||      ||      |  average of the entries of COPY(I), recorded
|    ||     ||     |...|    ||      ||      |  two lines below COPY(I).
|    ||     ||     |...|    ||      ||      |
|    ||     ||     |...|    ||      ||      |

means                               BETA(I)    This cell contains the formula:
standard deviations                            @AVG(PRODUCT)/VAR(S&P)
betas
```

The range name DATA is attached to the first cell of the return vector of security 1. Below the vectors of returns are two rows in which we have calculated the mean return of each security and the variance of that security's return. We have attached a third row in which we shall record the beta of each security. As in chapter 8, we let the macro record the time it takes to calculate the betas. The spreadsheet is set to recalculate manually.

The first macro starts the clock, freezes the screen, and sends the cursor to the cell DATA. It then initiates a loop (the {for ...} command), which transfers the execution to \B. Each iteration of the loop calculates the beta for one asset. The third line of \A is invoked only after the loop is finished. It merely sets the clocks and {quits} the macro.

```
\A
{let STARTTIME,@now}~{paneloff}{windowsoff}{goto}DATA~
{for COUNTER,1,NUM_SEC,1,\B}
{let STOPTIME,@now}~{let ELAPSED,STOPTIME-STARTTIME}~{quit}~
```

```
\B
/c{end}{down}{end}{down}~COPY(I)~{calc}
{end}{down}{down 4}~+BETA(I)~/RV~~
{right}{up 4}{end}{up}~
```

During its first iteration, the first line of the macro \B copies a column of return data for security 1 *and* the mean return of security 1 to the column labeled COPY(I). The command {calc} on the first line of \B recalculates the formulas in the column PRODUCT. This is crucial, since we have set the spreadsheet for manual recalculation.

When we finish the first line of \B, the cell at the bottom of PRODUCT contains the $\beta$ of security 1. The cursor is still at DATA. The second line of \B puts the cursor at the bottom of the vector of security 1's returns, in the proper place to record $\beta_1$. It does this by putting +BETA(I) in the cell and then using the /Range Value command to turn the formula into a number.

The last line of \B sends the cursor to the top of the next column, to the first item in the security 2 return vector.

When we complete the {for ...} loop, we will have calculated all the betas.

## 9.4    An Alternative Method for Calculating Beta

An alternative way to calculate the beta for each asset is to regress the returns of asset $i$ on the returns of the market (in this case, the S&P500). It is easy to do this in Lotus: Use /Data Regression, defining the X range as the column of S&P 500 returns and the Y range as the column of security $i$ returns (of course, the procedure has to be repeated NUM_SEC times). Choose a place in the spreadsheet to record the output (at least nine rows deep and four columns wide). The beta of the asset is the slope of the regression line (labeled X Coefficient). Make sure that the beta is recorded in the proper place on the spreadsheet before you go on to the next column.

For the first asset in the data used here, the output looks as follows:

```
        Regression Output:
Constant                       0.495318
Std Err of Y Est              11.83299
R Squared                      0.253993
No. of Observations                 120
Degrees of Freedom                  118

X Coefficient(s)  1.456161
Std Err of Coef.  0.229735
```

The X coefficient is the beta of the asset. You can verify numerically that these two methods give the same answer.

## 9.5    Estimating the Securities-Market Line

Once we have calculated all the betas, we have to run a second regression. This time we define the independent variable (the $X$ range called for in /Data Regression) as the betas of the assets, and we define the $Y$ range (the dependent variable) as the mean returns of the assets. (There is a technical problem here which is easily solved: Lotus demands that ranges for regressions be *columns*. In our original calculations we put both the means and the betas in row vectors. So we have to find an empty spot on the spreadsheet and use /Range transpose to transform the rows into columns before we can run the regression.)

```
ESTIMATING THE SECURITIES MARKET LINE
          Regression Output:
Constant                    0.656346
Std Err of Y Est            0.453320
R Squared                   0.050024
No. of Observations               30
Degrees of Freedom                28


X Coefficient(s)   0.486706
Std Err of Coef.   0.400823
```

How well does this SML predict returns? The $R^2$ of the regression is piteously low, indicating that only about 5 percent of the variance is explained by the regression. We can compare the constant to the average Treasury-bill return for the period, 0.693933, and come to the conclusion that it is not far off. The $X$ coefficient, however, does not compare well with the difference between the mean of the S&P500 return and the mean of the Treasury bills (this difference is 0.258725). Furthermore, comparing the constant and the $X$ coefficient against their respective standard errors does not indicate that they are significantly different from zero.

Finally, we can use Lotus to plot the predicted means (from the regression line) versus the actual means. Given the regression results, and given a $\beta$ for a particular asset, we calculate the predicted mean return for the asset as follows:

Predicted mean return $= 0.656346 + 0.486706\beta$.

The table of betas, actual means, and predicted means is given on page 98. (For ease in graphing with Lotus, we have used /Data sort to rearrange the data so that the betas are in ascending order.) The graph is given as figure 9.1.

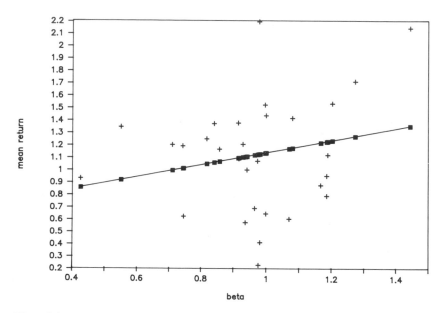

**Figure 9.1**
Security-market line versus actual means. (■): Predicted means; (+): actual means.

| actual | | predicted | | actual | | predicted |
|---|---|---|---|---|---|---|
| mean | beta | mean | | mean | beta | mean |
| 0.932 | 0.424257 | 0.862836 | | 0.232 | 0.975470 | 1.131114 |
| 1.348 | 0.548939 | 0.923519 | | 2.197 | 0.976797 | 1.131760 |
| 1.206 | 0.709444 | 1.001638 | | 0.416 | 0.979877 | 1.133260 |
| 1.195 | 0.741219 | 1.017103 | | 1.527 | 0.995064 | 1.140651 |
| 0.627 | 0.743797 | 1.018358 | | 0.649 | 0.997889 | 1.142026 |
| 1.252 | 0.816773 | 1.053876 | | 1.440 | 0.998660 | 1.142401 |
| 1.375 | 0.839393 | 1.064885 | | 0.608 | 1.068491 | 1.176389 |
| 1.169 | 0.856075 | 1.073004 | | 1.420 | 1.078794 | 1.181403 |
| 1.381 | 0.913598 | 1.101001 | | 0.880 | 1.166103 | 1.223897 |
| 1.093 | 0.915315 | 1.101837 | | 0.957 | 1.184401 | 1.232803 |
| 1.210 | 0.927572 | 1.107802 | | 0.795 | 1.184571 | 1.232885 |
| 0.578 | 0.935292 | 1.111560 | | 1.124 | 1.187424 | 1.234274 |
| 1.004 | 0.939672 | 1.113691 | | 1.538 | 1.201133 | 1.240946 |
| 0.693 | 0.963709 | 1.125391 | | 1.716 | 1.271498 | 1.275193 |
| 1.075 | 0.972614 | 1.129724 | | 2.147 | 1.442863 | 1.358598 |

## 9.6   Is Our "Market Portfolio" Merely Efficient?

In addition to the five efficient portfolios listed in exercise 2 of chapter 8, Roll (1978) gives eleven other portfolios:

| | ASSET PROPORTIONS | | | |
|---|---|---|---|---|
| portfolio | 1 | 2 | 3 | 4 |
| 6 | 1 | 0 | 0 | 0 |
| 7 | 0 | 1 | 0 | 0 |
| 8 | 0 | 0 | 1 | 0 |
| 9 | 0 | 0 | 0 | 1 |
| 10 | 0.5 | 0.5 | 0 | 0 |
| 11 | 0.333333 | 0.333333 | 0.333333 | 0 |
| 12 | 0.4 | 0.3 | 0.2 | 0.1 |
| 13 | 0.25 | 0.25 | 0.25 | 0.25 |
| 14 | 0.1 | 0.2 | 0.3 | 0.4 |
| 15 | 0 | 0.333333 | 0.333333 | 0.333333 |
| 16 | 0 | 0 | 0.5 | 0.5 |

Suppose we take portfolio 5 of chapter 8 to be the "market" portfolio. This produces the following betas (this table also shows each portfolio's expected return):

| portfolio | mean | beta |
|---|---|---|
| 6 | 6 | 0.417092 |
| 7 | 7 | 0.805712 |
| 8 | 8 | 1.195150 |
| 9 | 9 | 1.583769 |
| 10 | 6.5 | 0.611402 |
| 11 | 6.999993 | 0.805984 |
| 12 | 7 | 0.805957 |
| 13 | 7.5 | 1.000431 |
| 14 | 8 | 1.194904 |
| 15 | 7.999992 | 1.194876 |
| 16 | 8.5 | 1.389459 |

Regressing the expected returns on the betas produces the following output:

```
        Regression Output:
Constant                    4.927958
Std Err of Y Est            0.000328
R Squared                   0.999999
No. of Observations               11
Degrees of Freedom                 9


X Coefficient(s)  2.570931
Std Err of Coef.  0.000298
```

Does this mean that portfolio 5 is the true market portfolio? Has Roll discovered the Holy Grail? Surprisingly, Roll's answer is No. Portfolio 5 is merely an efficient portfolio. Were we to repeat the experiment using portfolio 1, 2, 3, or 4 (or any other efficient portfolio, for that matter), the results would be the same (see the exercises).

### Exercises

1. This continues our series of exercises involving six stocks. The table below gives return data for the Standard & Poor's 500 stock index. Assuming that the S&P500 is the market portfolio, calculate the $\beta$ of each of the six stocks and find the SML.

| year | S&P500 |
|------|---------|
| 1974 | -0.26458 |
| 1975 | 0.37212 |
| 1976 | 0.23849 |
| 1977 | -0.07179 |
| 1978 | 0.06574 |
| 1979 | 0.18424 |
| 1980 | 0.32408 |
| 1981 | -0.04909 |
| 1982 | 0.21409 |
| 1983 | 0.22514 |

2. Repeat the experiment of section 9.6 for the other four efficient portfolios given in Roll's article (see exercise 1 of chapter 8). Show that in each case you will get an "SML" with an $R^2$ of 1.

# 10 Entering Portfolio Information—A Macro

## 10.1 Introduction

One of the problems when doing portfolio calculations is entering masses of data into the spreadsheet. This chapter illustrates a macro that allows you to enter the portfolio information into a spreadsheet. The object is to create a spreadsheet that looks like the following:

| SECURITY | EXPECTED RETURN | VARIANCE-COVARIANCE MATRIX | | | |
|----------|-----------------|--------|----|----|----|
| 1 | 6 | 10 | 2 | 4 | 4 |
| 2 | 7 | 2 | 20 | 4 | 1 |
| 3 | 8 | 4 | 4 | 40 | 10 |
| 4 | 9 | 5 | 1 | 10 | 60 |

It is not difficult to insert the relevant numbers by putting the cursor on a particular cell, putting in the number, then going on to the next cell. However, what we want to do in this chapter is create a macro that will prompt us to put in the right numbers. This is easier (once the macro is written) than doing it manually. It is also more fun, and a useful learning exercise.

## 10.2 The Structure of the Spreadsheet

The spreadsheet has three sections. The top one is illustrated above. The macro (really six macros joined by BRANCH statements) is another part of the spreadsheet. A third part contains "working variables"—elements you need to make the right questions appear on the panel of the screen and the right numbers appear in the spreadsheet.

Before starting, you must designate the cell that will always be the top left corner of the covariance matrix as the range STARTMAT. Similarly, the cell designated STARTRET is the first cell in the vector of returns. STARTSEC is the first cell in the vector that labels the securities (the first vector above). You also must designate three ranges as MATRIX, RETURNS, and SECURITIES. (There are quite a few other ranges in this macro, but they will be obvious as we go on. The above ranges have to exist *before* you start the macro the first time, since the macro erases them.)

## 10.3   The Macro

Your macros and working variables should be placed well away from the data area of the spreadsheet. Otherwise, the data you enter may erase the macros or the working variables. Since Lotus cannot invert a matrix bigger than 90 × 90, you are safe if you leave at least 90 rows between the data area and the macros. (You should also use /Range Protect to make sure no data can be put on the macros. You can't use this on all the working variables, because you need some of them for the temporary storage of data.)

   There are six macros, labeled from \B through \G. The first macro sets up the two vectors (one counts the securities; the other lists the security returns) and the covariance matrix:

```
\B                       setting up the return vector and the covariance matrix
{goto}PORTFOLIO~
{GETNUMBER How many securities are there?    ,number}~
{PANELOFF}~{WINDOWSOFF}~
{GOTO}STARTMAT~
/REMATRIX~/RNDMATRIX~
/RNCMATRIX~{DOWN NUMBER-1}{RIGHT NUMBER-1}~
/RERETURNS~/RNDRETURNS~
{GOTO}STARTRET~/RNCRETURNS~{DOWN NUMBER-1}~
/RESECURITIES~/RNDSECURITIES~
{GOTO}STARTSEC~/RNCSECURITIES~{DOWN NUMBER-1}~
{LET COUNTERi,0}{let counterj,0}~
{GOTO}STARTSEC~/DFSECURITIES~1~~~
{GOTO}PORTFOLIO~{WINDOWSON}{PANELON}~
{branch \c}~
```

   Macro \B first sends the cursor to the top of the spreadsheet, to a cell named PORTFOLIO, just to keep you from looking at the macro while it is working. The macro then asks you how many securities you have, and places that number in a cell named NUMBER in the working-variables area.

   Next the macro goes to the top left corner of the covariance matrix, erases the range MATRIX, and deletes the name. This takes care of any previous data in the matrix. It then creates the range MATRIX, and makes it the proper size. (Why do you have to delete the range name MATRIX? Lotus can make problems if you don't. Try it and see.) Macro \B then does the same thing for the vectors RETURNS and SECURITIES. The vector SECURITIES is then filled with numbers starting with 1 and going up to the number of securities.

```
\C                    entering expected returns
{PANELOFF}{WINDOWSOFF}~
{LET COUNTERi,COUNTERi+1}~
{IF COUNTERi>NUMBER}{goto}PORTFOLIO~{WINDOWSON}{PANELON}~{let counteri,0}{BRANCH \D}~
{GOTO}DUMMYNUM~{LET DUMMYNUM,COUNTERi}~{EDIT}{HOME}'{END}~
{GOTO}superdummy~@S(MESSAGE)~
{GETNUMBER What is the expected return of asset  4?  ,BUFFER}
{PUT RETURNS,0,COUNTERi-1,BUFFER}~
{BRANCH \C}~
```

Macro \C calls up a series of messages on the panel. The first message says "What is the expected return of asset 1?" and puts the answer in the first cell of the vector RETURNS. The massages repeat themselves until all the expected return data are filled in.

The way \C works is the following: In the working-variable area there are three cells labeled DUMMYNUM, ENDMESSAGE, and DUMMYMESS. \C first puts the current counter_i number in DUMMYNUM and transforms it from a number to a label. The cell MESSAGE combines the contents of the three cells DUMMYNUM, ENDMESSAGE, and DUMMYNESS (the formula in MESSAGE is +DUMMYMESS&DUMMYNUM&ENDMESSAGE) to form the string:

{GETNUMBER What is the expected return of asset 1?   ,BUFFER}

The third line from the bottom of \C is given a range name SUPERDUMMY. The *fourth* line from the bottom of \C says: Go to SUPERDUMMY (i.e., the next line) and put in it the contents of MESSAGE. The macro then goes on to the next line and flashes the message on the panel.

In the macro \F a similar trick is used to create a series of commands that say

{GETNUMBER What is the covariance of asset i and asset j?   ,BUFFER}

for combinations of $j \leq i$.

When you have finished \F, you have the bottom half of the covariance matrix. Since the matrix is symmetrix, \G uses /Range Transpose to copy the bottom half of the matrix onto the top half.

```
\D                      resetting the counters
{let counteri,0}{let counterj,0}~
{BRANCH \E}~

\E                      entering the covariance matrix
{windowsoff}{paneloff}~
{let counteri,counteri+1}~
{for counterj,counteri,number,1,\f}~
{if counteri>number}{CALC}{BRANCH \G}~
{branch \e}~


\F
{goto}dummyi~{let dummyi,counteri}{edit}{home}' {end} and ~
{goto}dummyj~{let dummyj,counterj}{edit}{home}' ~
{goto}SUPERDUMMY2~@s(MESS2)~
{GETNUMBER What is the covariance of  4 and  4?  ,BUFFER}
{put MATRIX,COUNTERi-1,counterj-1,buffer}~


\G                      filling up the covariance matrix
{goto}matrix~/rtmatrix~~
{GOTO}PORTFOLIO~{WINDOWSON}{PANELOFF}{QUIT}~
```

## 10.4   The Working-Variable Area

The working-variable area will look like this:

```
              WORKING VARIABLES

NUMBER          4
BUFFER                  30
DUMMYNUM        4
DUMMYMESS       {GETNUMBER What is the expected return of asset
ENDMESSAGE      ?  ,BUFFER}
MESSAGE         {GETNUMBER What is the expected return of asset  4?  ,BUFFER}



dummyi          4 and
dummyj          4
covmessage      {GETNUMBER What is the covariance of
mess2           {GETNUMBER What is the covariance of  4 and  4?  ,BUFFER}



counteri            5
counterj            5
```

## Exercise

Write a macro that inverts the covariance matrix, placing it next to the variance matrix (spaced one column over).

# 11 References for Portfolio Theory

The literature on the capital asset pricing model and its tests is vast. A selective set of references is given below. For a full set of references, see any of the texts on portfolio theory cited below.

Black, F. 1972. "Capital Market Equilibrium with Restricted Borrowing." *Journal of Business* 45 (July): 444–455.

Elton, E. J., and M. J. Gruber. 1984. *Modern Portfolio Theory and Investment Analysis.* Second edition. New York: Wiley.

Haugen, R. A. 1986. *Modern Investment Theory.* Englewood Cliffs, N.J.: Prentice-Hall.

Jensen, M. C., ed. 1972. *Studies in the Theory of Capital Markets.* New York: Praeger.

Levy, H., and M. Sarnat. 1984. *Portfolio and Investment Selection: Theory and Practice.* Englewood Cliffs, N.J.: Prentice-Hall.

Lintner, J. 1965. "The Valuation of Risk Assets and the Selection of Risky Investments in Stock Portfolios and Capital Budgets." *Review of Economics and Statistics* 47 (February): 13–37.

Markowitz, H. M. 1952. "Portfolio Selection." *Journal of Finance* 7 (March): 77–91.

Merton, R. C. 1972. "An Analytic Derivation of the Efficient Portfolio Frontier." *Journal of Financial and Quantitative Analysis* 7 (September): 1851–1872.

Miller, M. H., and M. Scholes. 1972. "Rates of Return in Relation to Risk: A Re-Examination of Some Recent Findings." In M. C. Jensen (ed.), *Studies in the Theory of Capital Markets* (New York: Praeger).

Modigliani, F., and G. A. Pogue. 1974. "An Introduction to Risk and Return." *Financial Analysts Journal* 30 (March–April): 68–80; May–June: 69–88.

Roll, R. 1977. "A Critique of the Asset Pricing Theory's Tests; Part I: On Past and Potential Testability of the Theory." *Journal of Financial Economics* 4 (March): 129–176.

Roll, R. 1978. "Ambiguity When Performance Is Measured by the Securities Market Line." *Journal of Finance* 33 (September): 1051–1069.

Sharpe, W. F. 1964. "Capital Asset Prices: A Theory of Market Equilibrium under Conditions of Risk." *Journal of Finance* 19 (September): 425–442.

Sharpe, W. F. 1970. Portfolio Theory and Capital Markets. New York: McGraw-Hill.

# III OPTIONS

# Overview

The Black-Scholes options pricing model is one of the main advances in modern finance theory. The model appears to be well-substantiated empirically and is easily implemented on a spreadsheet program. Unfortunately, the Black-Scholes model involves considerable mathematical overhead. In order to implement the model, we need to calculate the normal distribution. It is also helpful to realize what underlying assumptions about stock-price distributions the model makes. Chapters 12–16 introduce the mathematical overhead, then to proceed to the options-pricing model and its applications. These chapters progress as follows.

*Chapter 12: The normal distribution.* This chapter discusses the normal distribution and shows how to calculate its values in a spreadsheet.

*Chapter 13: The lognormal distribution.* A basic assumption of the Black-Scholes model is that stock prices are lognormally distributed. This chapter discusses the meaning of this assumption.

*Chapter 14: Simulating the normal and the lognormal distribution.* One way to get a feeling for the meaning of the statistical assumptions is to simulate them.

*Chapter 15: Option pricing.* This chapter covers the basics of options, implements the Black-Scholes model, discusses the put-call parity theorem, and explains how to find the implied standard deviation. (It *does not* give a derivation of the Black-Scholes model; such a derivation requires extensive motivation and would take us too far off our path. The interested reader should see one of the several good textbooks on this topic. Extensive treatments can be found in Cox and Rubinstein 1985, Jarrow and Rudd 1983, and Ritchken 1987. For shorter expositions, see Elton and Gruber 1984, Haugen 1986, and Levy and Sarnat 1984.

*Chapter 16: Portfolio insurance.* This chapter discusses and simulates the important elements of portfolio insurance.

# 12 The Normal Distribution

## 12.1 Background

The normal distribution is the most frequently used probability distribution. There are several reasons for this: normally distributed variables crop up in a large number of empirical applications, the normal distribution provides a good approximation to many other probability distributions, and the normal distribution is easy to work with.

In succeeding chapters we will use the normal distribution to describe the uncertainty relating to the movement of stock prices movements. We shall also use the normal distribution to price options. In this chapter we shall be concerned only with a technical issue: how to generate the normal distribution in a spreadsheet.

A random variable $X$ is said to be normally distributed with mean $\mu$ and variance $\sigma$ if the distribution is given by

$$F(x) = \int_{-\infty}^{x} f(y)\,dy,$$

where

$$f(x) = \frac{e^{-(x-\mu)^2/2\sigma^2}}{\sigma\sqrt{2\pi}}.$$

When $\mu = 0$ and $\sigma = 1$, the resulting distribution is called the standard normal distribution and is denoted by $N(x)$:

$$F(x) = \int_{-\infty}^{x} f(y)\,dy,$$

where

$$f(x) = \frac{e^{-x^2/2\sigma^2}}{\sigma\sqrt{2\pi}}.$$

The integral $N(x)$ cannot be evaluated directly. An approximation to $N(x)$ is given by

$$N(x) = 1 - h(x)t(b_0 + b_1 t + b_2 t^2 + b_3 t^3 + b_4 t^4) + \text{error}, \quad x > 0$$

where

$$h(x) = (1/\sqrt{2\pi})e^{-x^2/2},$$

$$t = 1/(1 + px),$$

$$p = +0.2316419,$$

$$b_0 = +0.319381530,$$

$$b_1 = -0.356563782,$$

$$b_2 = +1.781477937,$$

$$b_3 = -1.821255978,$$

$$b_4 = +1.330274429.$$

The error for this approximation is less than $7.5 \times 10^{-8}$. To find $N(x)$ for $x < 0$, set $N(x) = 1 - N(-x)$.

## 12.2    A Long Exercise

A spreadsheet can be used to create a table of the normal distribution. The first step is to make a column:

```
x
N(x)
h(x)
t
p
b(0)
b(1)
b(2)
b(3)
b(4)
```

Next, use /Range Names Labels Right to name the cells in the second column by the names of the cells to their left. (We cannot write subscripts or superscripts in the spreadsheet. Instead, we write b1 as b(1), and so on. Why the parentheses? If we didn't use them, Lotus wouldn't be able to differentiate between cell b(1) and cell B1. That could be disastrous!) In the next column, enter either the appropriate values or the formulas. To make the formulas work for negative values of $x$, you have to use some 1-2-3 logic. For instance, $t$ is given by

```
@IF(x>0,1/(1+$p*x),1/(1-$p*x)).
```

(An alternative is to use absolute values and write the formula for $t$ as $1/(1 + @abs(x)*$p)$.) Why the $ signs? Soon we are going to copy the first two rows of the table (it is a waste of valuable memory to copy all the rows), and we want to make sure Lotus knows that $p$ and all the $b$'s are absolute and not relative values.)

How do we write $N(x)$? Given the above definition for $t$, we have that $N(x)$ is given by

```
@IF(x>0,1-h(x)*t*(b(0)+b(1)*t+b(2)*t^2+b(3)*t^3+b(4)*t^4),
       h(x)*t*(b(0)+b(1)*t+b(2)*t^2+b(3)*t^3+b(4)*t^4))
```

After doing this, check your work: Get a table for the standard normal distribution, plug different values of $x$ into your worksheet, and see that you get the same answer as the table. Some values for the normal distribution are $N(0) = 0.5$, $N(0.5) = 0.6915$, and $N(-0.5) = 0.3085$.

Next, create your own table: Copy the contents of the first two rows of the second column to (say) the next 60 columns. Let the initial $x$ be $-3$, and go up to $+3$ in steps of 0.1. It might be worthwhile to check your values of $N(x)$ against the table one more time, just to make sure you didn't make some stupid mistakes when you copied. A fairly common error is to forget the $ signs when copying.

At some point you should have an $x$ whose value is 0. Lotus may surprise you by printing out something strange, such as $1.45678932 \times 10 - 15$. The reason for this is that the internal representation of the numbers in the computer differs from the decimal representation. Of course, there is no big difference between 0 and what Lotus writes. However, this should make you exercise care when writing IF statements that start out @IF $(x = 0, \ldots)$. A better way to do this is to define an $e$ (a very small number) and write @IF(@abs(x)<e,...).

You can have some fun drawing pretty graphs. The probability that $x$ lies between 1.2 and 1.3 is given by $N(1.3) - N(1.2)$. Make a table of such differences. You should get something like:

| x | 1.25 |
|---|---|
| N(x) | 0.018269 |

If you graph these two rows, putting the $x$ values on the $x$ axis (naturally), you should get a pretty bell curve, as in figure 12.1.

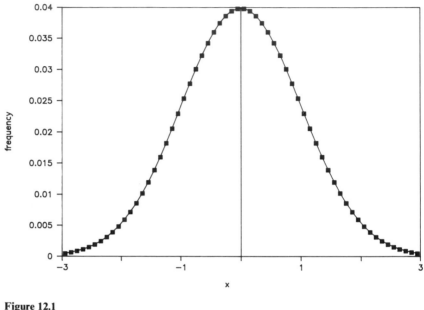

**Figure 12.1**
Normal curve.

## 12.3   How to Prevent Your Spreadsheet from Thinking

Unless you tell it to do otherwise, Lotus will recalculate the spreadsheet
every time you make an entry. Large spreadsheets can take a lot of time to
recalculate, and this otherwise laudable property of Lotus can occasionally
become very irritating. One way to stop this from happening is to use
/Worksheet Global Recalculation Manual. This option allows you to
make as many entries to the spreadsheet as you wish, and prevents the
spreadsheet from recalculating. After you have made your first entry, Lotus
notifies you that the values you see are not the recalculated values by
writing CALC at the bottom of the screen. Pressing [F9] recalculates
the spreadsheet.

A more drastic solution is to use /Range Value (/RV). This command
tells Lotus to stop relating to the entries in cells as formulas to be recalculated
and to start relating to them as numbers only. Suppose you want to
create a table of the standard normal distribution. You use the above
approximation and create a table that looks like

| x | −3.0 | −2.9 | ... | +2.9 | +3.0 |
|---|---|---|---|---|---|
| N(x) | | | | | |
| h(x) | | | | | |
| t | | | | | |
| p | | | | | |
| b(0) | | | | | |
| b(1) | | | | | |
| b(2) | | | | | |
| b(3) | | | | | |
| b(4) | | | | | |

(Only the first line is shown here; the rest is left to your imagination.) Once you are satisfied that the calculations are correct, you want to throw away everything from this table except for the first two lines. If you use /Range Erase to erase the rows from h(x) to b(4), Lotus will show ERR, because it no longer knows how to calculate N(x). What to do? Use /Range Value and put the cursor over the first two lines of the table. When Lotus asks where to put the values, indicate the top left cell in the range. Lotus will then no longer look to calculate these two lines, but will understand them as simply numerical entries into the spreadsheet. Now you can erase rows h(x) through b(4).

Using /RV is a bit like erasing; you can easily destroy a lot of valuable work. Before you do this, save the file under another name so you will have a copy of the file with the formulas and one without them.

## Exercises

1. Set up a spreadsheet program to calculate the normal distribution using the first approximation. Let the values of $x$ range from $-3$ to $+3$ with intervals of 0.1.

2. Redo the previous exercise, but this time use the /Data Table 1 command. If you don't know how to use this command, see chapter 25. Notice how the /Data Table command eliminates the difficulties with spreadsheet recalculation discussed above.

3. If $X$ is normally distributed with mean $\mu$ and standard deviation $\sigma$, then

$$F(x) = N((x - \mu)/\sigma).$$

Revise your spreadsheet so that you can insert the mean and the variance as parameters. Play around with the graphs.

## References

Abramowitz, M., and I. A. Stegun, eds. 1964. *Handbook of Mathematical Functions*. New York: Dover.

Knuth, D. 1969. *The Art of Computer Programming, Volume 2*. Reading, Mass.: Addison-Wesley.

Larson, H. J. 1969. *Introduction to Probability Theory and Statistical Inference*. New York: Wiley.

Latour, A. 1986. "Polar Normal Distribution." *Byte* (August): 131–132.

Miller, A. R. 1981. *Pascal Programs for Scientists and Engineers*. Berkeley: Sybex.

# 13 The Lognormal Distribution

## 13.1 A Crude Introduction

What are reasonable assumptions to be made about the way stock prices behave over time? Clearly the price of a stock (or any other risky financial asset) is uncertain. What is its distribution? This is a perplexing question. One way to answer this question is to ask what are reasonable properties of a stock price.

Five reasonable properties follow:

1. The stock price is uncertain.

2. The stock price is never zero. (We exclude stocks of "dead" companies.)

3. The return from holding a stock tends to increase over time.

4. Changes in stock prices are continuous. Over short periods of time, changes in a stock's price are very small, and the change goes to zero as the time span goes to zero.*

5. The *uncertainty* associated with the return from holding a stock also tends to increase the longer you hold the stock. Thus, given the stock's price today, the variance of the stock price tomorrow is small; however, the price variance in one month is larger, and the variance in one year is larger still.

Suppose we denote by $S_t$ the price at time $t$ of a share of stock. One way to describe the uncertainties about $S_t$ is to assume that the change in the price between time $t$ and time $t + \Delta t$ can be divided into two components, one certain and the other uncertain. We can do this by dividing the return to $S_t$ into two components, one certain and the other uncertain:

$$S_{t+\Delta t} = S_t \exp(\mu \Delta t + \sigma \sqrt{\Delta t} Z), \tag{1}$$

where $Z$ is a standard normal variable (mean 0, standard deviation 1).

To see what this means, suppose first that $\sigma = 0$. In this case we have

$$S_{t+\Delta t} = S_t \exp(\mu \Delta t),$$

---

* If you have watched stock prices, you know that continuity is usually not a bad assumption. Sometimes, however, it can be disastrous (look at the way prices behaved on October 19, 1987, for a dramatic example). It is possible to build a stock-price model that assumes that stock prices are usually continuous but have occassional (and random) jumps. See Cox and Ross 1976, Merton 1976, and Jarrow and Rudd 1983.

which simply says that the stock price grows at an exponential rate with certainty. In this case the stock is like a riskless bond that bears interest rate $m$, continuously compounded.

Suppose, however, that $\sigma > 0$. In this case, equation 1 says that, although the tendency is for the stock price to increase, there is an uncertain element (normally distributed) that must be taken into account. Note that equation 1 fulfills our conditions for the behavior of the stock price. In particular, the stock price will never be negative. If you had followed your first inclination and made the distribution of the stock price normal, you would have allowed for the possibility that it could also be negative. Intuitively, we are saying that to determine the rate of growth of the stock price between $t$ and $t + \Delta t$ we should do this:

1. Multiply $\Delta t$ (the elapsed time interval) by $\mu$ (the average rate of growth).

2. Take a draw from a random variable which is standard normal, multiply this by $\sqrt{\Delta t}$, and multiply by the standard deviation $\sigma$. This is the uncertain portion of the return. (The square root implies that the variance of the stock's log return is linear in time. See below.)

3. Add the two results and exponentiate.

## 13.2   Some Properties of Equation 1

First, divide through by $S_t$ and take the logarithm of both sides. This gives

$$\ln(S_{t+\Delta t}/S_t) = \mu \Delta t + \sigma \sqrt{\Delta t} Z.$$

Taking the expectation of this expression, we get

$$E[\ln(S_{t+\Delta t}/S_t)] = \mu \Delta t.$$

This follows, since $E[Z] = 0$. Taking the variance gives

$$\text{Var}[\ln(S_{t+\Delta t}/S_t)] = \sigma^2 \Delta t.$$

We have done what we set out to do: The stock price fulfills properties 1–5.

The name "lognormal distribution" derives from the fact that the logarithm of the returns is normally distributed, with mean $\mu$ and variance $\sigma^2$.

## 13.3    Calculating a Lognormal Distribution

We can use Lotus to calculate the density function of a lognormally distributed random variable. To do this, we first calculate the densities for a standard normal distribution. For this we need the approximation to the normal from chapter 12. We will get a table that looks like the following:

| NORMAL Z | -2.975 | -2.925 | -2.875 | -2.825 | -2.775 | -2.725 ... |
|----------|--------|--------|--------|--------|--------|------------|
| PROB | 0.000239 | 0.000277 | 0.00032 | 0.00037 | 0.000424 | 0.000487 ... |

The probabilities are the differences between the cumulative probabilities. For example,

$$\text{Prob}\{Z = 0.025\} = N(0.05) - N(0).$$

Thus, we are attaching the probability of an interval to its midpoint; as an approximation this is fine.

The lognormal calculates

$$@\exp(\text{mean} * \text{del}(t) + \text{sig} * @\text{sqrt}(\text{del}(t)) * Z).$$

The probabilities of the standard normal are then assigned to the lognormal. Implementing this gives the following:

LOGNORMAL DISTRIBUTION

| MEAN | 0.2 |
|------|-----|
| SIG | 0.5 |
| DEL(T) | 1 |

| VALUE | 0.275959 | 0.282945 | 0.290108 | 0.297452 | 0.304982 | 0.312703 ... |
|-------|----------|----------|----------|----------|----------|--------------|
| PROB | 0.000239 | 0.000277 | 0.00032 | 0.00037 | 0.000424 | 0.000487 ... |

The graph of this function is shown as figure 13.1.

## 13.4    From Price Data to Distributional Parameters

Suppose we are given monthly price data for a stock, and that we wish to estimate the parameters $\mu$ and $\sigma$ of the stock's *annual* logarithmic rate of return from these data. The table on page 122 shows how to do this.

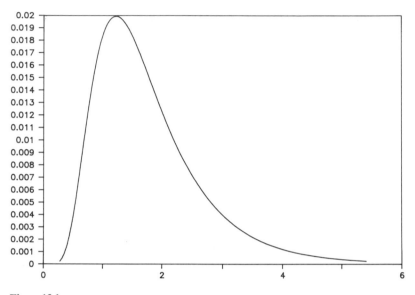

**Figure 13.1**
Lognormal density.

| month | closing price | 1+ return | ln(1+ return) |
|---|---|---|---|
| 0 | 25 | | |
| 1 | 24.69219 | 0.987687 | -0.01238 |
| 2 | 23.68760 | 0.959315 | -0.04153 |
| 3 | 22.88975 | 0.966317 | -0.03426 |
| 4 | 22.80182 | 0.996158 | -0.00384 |
| 5 | 22.88009 | 1.003432 | 0.003426 |
| 6 | 22.56180 | 0.986088 | -0.01400 |
| 7 | 23.93675 | 1.060941 | 0.059156 |
| 8 | 24.36041 | 1.017699 | 0.017544 |
| 9 | 24.97833 | 1.025365 | 0.025049 |
| 10 | 26.08291 | 1.044221 | 0.043271 |
| 11 | 26.12551 | 1.001633 | 0.001632 |
| 12 | 26.88987 | 1.029257 | 0.028837 |

$\mu$ =     @AVG(ln 1+return)*12              0.072874
$\sigma$ =     @STD(ln 1+return)*@SQRT(12)        0.099871

We multiply the average log return by 12 to get $\mu$, and we multiply the standard deviation of the log returns by $\sqrt{12}$ because of the relation

$$S_{t+\Delta t} = S_t \exp(\mu \Delta t + Z\sigma\sqrt{\Delta t}).$$

We write this relation as

$$S_{t+\Delta t} = S_t \exp(R),$$

where $\ln(R)$ has mean $\mu$ and standard deviation $\sigma$. This means that the end-of-the-year price, $S_{12}$, can be expressed as

$$S_{12} = S_0 \exp(R_1 + R_2 + \cdots + R_{12}).$$

If we assume that the log rates of return $R_1, \ldots, R_{12}$ are independent, then the annual log return, $\ln(S_{12}/S_0)$, has an expectation of $12\mu$ and a variance of $12\sigma^2$. Suppose we calculate $\mu$ and $\sigma$ from monthly data. Then if we want annual parameters from these data (and no matter what units the data are expressed in, it is standard to express the parameters in annual terms), we have to use $12\mu$ for the annual mean and $\sigma\sqrt{12}$ for the annual standard deviation.

## Exercises

1. Graph the lognormal density. What happens to the graph when the standard deviation $\sigma$ gets larger? (Warning: Lotus plots most graphs symmetrically on the $x$ axis. If you want your graph to appear to scale, use the /Graph Type XY option.)

2. Calculate the *annual* log mean and standard deviation of returns from the following *daily* data:

| day | price | day | price |
|-----|-------|-----|-------|
| 0 | 25.00 | 13 | 28.53 |
| 1 | 25.69 | 14 | 27.38 |
| 2 | 24.74 | 15 | 26.95 |
| 3 | 26.07 | 16 | 28.08 |
| 4 | 27.02 | 17 | 26.68 |
| 5 | 28.70 | 18 | 27.00 |
| 6 | 28.38 | 19 | 26.61 |
| 7 | 28.23 | 20 | 26.51 |
| 8 | 26.69 | 21 | 25.56 |
| 9 | 26.11 | 22 | 25.96 |
| 10 | 25.21 | 23 | 25.28 |
| 11 | 24.93 | 24 | 26.61 |
| 12 | 26.14 | 25 | 27.55 |

# References

Aitchison, J., and J. Brown. 1957. *The Lognormal Distribution.* Cambridge University Press.

Cox, J., and S. Ross. 1976. "The Valuation of Options for Alternative Stochastic Processes." *Journal of Financial Economics* 3 (January–March): 145–166.

Cox, J., S. Ross, and M. Rubinstein. 1979. "Option Pricing: A Simplified Approach." *Journal of Financial Economics* 8 (September): 229–263.

Jarrow, R. A., and A. Rudd. 1983. *Option Pricing.* Homewood, Ill.: Irwin.

Merton, R. 1976. "Option Pricing When Underlying Stock Returns Are Discontinuous." *Journal of Financial Economics* 3 (May): 125–144.

# 14 Simulating the Normal and Lognormal Distributions

## 14.1 Introduction

It is often useful and instructive to generate numbers that look as if they have been taken from a normal or a lognormal distribution. This chapter tells how to create such numbers. The method we use is proved in Knuth 1981; for further references, see Latour 1986 and Press et al. 1986. We start with the normal distribution (sections 14.2–14.4) and then apply the method to the lognormal distribution (sections 14.5 and 14.6). Section 14.7 discusses the implications of the simulations for the technical analysis of stock prices.

## 14.2 Simulating the Normal Distribution: A General Description

The method consists of several steps:

1. First generate two independent random variables, uniformly distributed between $-1$ and 1. Since the Lotus random-number generator @RAND generates numbers between 0 and 1, take $2@rand - 1$. Designate the two random numbers random1 and random2.

2. Calculate $S(1) = (random1)^2 + (random2)^2$. If $S(1) < 1$, go on to the next step. If $S(1) \geq 1$, go back to the previous step.

3. Calculate $S(2) = [-2\ln(S(1))/S(1)]^{0.5}$.

4. Let $X(1) = S(2)random1$ and $X(2) = S(2)random2$.

$X(1)$ and $X(2)$ are two independent normal variables distributed with mean 0 and standard deviation 1.

## 14.3 The Macro Program

The program below implements the method just described.

• It allows repetition of the algorithm as many times as desired. Each run of the algorithm produces two numbers: $X(1)$ and $X(2)$.

• It makes a table of frequencies.

• It records the amount of time it takes to do the algorithm for the specified number of runs. This has nothing in particular to do with the problem at hand, but it is a nice thing to know.

Schematically, the spreadsheet looks like this:

```
results      --------------------------     runnumber     1000 starttime 21:11:15
-------|        |      FREQUENCY        |     random1  0.015988 stoptime  21:18:54
       |        |       |        |      |     random2  0.137243 elapsed   00:07:39
       |        |       |        |      |     S(1)     0.019091
       |        | actual|  pre-  |      |     S(2)     20.36397
       |        | freq- | dicted |      |     X(1)     0.325590
RESULT-|        | uencies| freq- |      |     X(2)     2.794821
 COL   |        |       | uency  |      |     maxrun       1000
       |        |       |        |      |
       |        |       |        |      |
       |        |       |        |      |     \A
       |        |       |        |      |     .
       |        |       |        |      |     .
                                             \B
                                              .
                                              .
                                              .
```

Macro \A starts off everything. The range RESULTCOL is the column of the worksheet in which we are going to record our results.

```
\A        starting
{let starttime,@now}
{blank stoptime}{blank elapsed}{blank resultcol}~
{branch \B}
```

This macro assumes that a range called FREQUENCY has been set up. FREQUENCY has three columns. The first is called GROUPLINE (more about that when we get to \E). The second column is for recording the frequencies themselves. The third column of FREQUENCY contains the predicted frequency for each interval; these have to be calculated using the formula for the standard normal distribution given in chapter 13 (the area of the spreadsheet where these calculations are done has not been shown).

Macro \A records the time in three ranges, labeled STARTTIME, STOPTIME, and ELAPSED. The first line of \A records the current time in STARTTIME and blanks out the ranges STOPTIME and ELAPSED. Make sure you have formatted these ranges correctly, so that the spreadsheet will show the time. The correct formatting is /Range Format Date Time. At this point you have a choice about the time format. The example uses format 3, Long International.

Before the algorithm starts, the ranges STARTTIME, STOPTIME, ELAPSED, and RESULTCOL are BLANKed—that is, any results recorded in them from previous runs are wiped out.

Macro \B runs the algorithm in \C MAXRUN times, thus creating 2*MAXRUN numbers (which are, we hope, normally distributed).

```
\B        running the loop
{for runnumber,1,maxrun,1,\C}
{branch \E}
```

Each run of macro \C creates the two normal deviates. Note that \C does not go on to the next stage until it has created two random numbers whose squares sum to less than unity. Each run of \C goes on to \D, where the results are recorded. When \B has looped the requisite number of times, it will go on to \E.

```
\C        creating two normal deviates
{let random1,2*@rand-1}{let random2,2*@rand-1}
{let S(1),random1^2+random2^2}
{if S(1)>=1}{branch \C}
{let S(2),@sqrt(-2*@ln(S(1))/S(1))}
{let X(1),random1*S(2)}{let X(2),random2*S(2)}
{branch \D}
```

Macro \D records the results. Because RESULTCOL starts with row 0, the results of run 1 are recorded in rows 0 and 1 of RESULTCOL, the results of run 2 in rows 2 and 3, and so on.

```
\D        recording the results
{put resultcol,0,2*runnumber-2,X(1)}
{put resultcol,0,2*runnumber-1,X(2)}
```

The last macro, \E, calculates the frequencies. The operative part of this macro is the second line, which uses /Data Distribution to calculate the frequencies. /Data Distribution requires two pieces of input: First, you have to tell Lotus where to get the data. In this case the answer is RESULTCOL, the column where we have recorded all the normal deviates. Second, you have to tell Lotus the column in which the groups for the frequency distribution are listed. In our case this is the first column of FREQUENCY (called GROUPLINE). GROUPLINE looks like this:

```
-3.0
-2.8
-2.6
...
2.8
3.0
```

Lotus will record the entries in RESULTCOL that are less than or equal to $-3.0$ in the cell to the right of $-3.0$. It will record all the entries that are less than or equal to $-2.8$ but greater than $-3.0$ in the cell next to $-2.8$. The spillover (i.e., all entries in RESULTCOL that are greater than 3.0) will be recorded in the cell to the right of the blank cell below 3.0.

Because \E is the only part of this program that requires any screen action from Lotus, we can set {windowsoff} and {paneloff} to save time. The last two lines of \E record the time we finished (in STOPTIME), calculate the elapsed time (in ELAPSED), and execute a QUIT. If we need to do more runs, the macro returns to \B.

```
\E        calculating the frequencies
{windowsoff}{paneloff}
/ddresultcol~groupline~
{let stoptime,@now}{let elapsed,stoptime-starttime}
{calc}{quit}
```

## 14.4   Some Output

A run of 1,000 iterations generates 2,000 normal deviates. Part of the output looks like this:

```
results
-0.57528
-1.25115
1.300617
-0.44717
-0.57371
0.168718
-0.85655
-0.60777
-0.47538
-0.09695
0.344853
-0.50183
-1.10901
-0.14462
-0.16140
1.649269
-0.85010
-1.69770
-1.16999
-1.30419
```

The elapsed time is around 7 minutes (using an IBM PC compatible with an 8087 numerical co-processor).

The frequency-distribution table is as follows:

| group | frequency actual | predicted | group | frequency actual | predicted |
|---|---|---|---|---|---|
| -3.0 | 4 | 1.325530 | 0.2 | 165 | 158.5193 |
| -2.8 | 3 | 2.410446 | 0.4 | 158 | 152.3240 |
| -2.6 | 6 | 4.212062 | 0.6 | 168 | 140.6504 |
| -2.4 | 5 | 7.072614 | 0.8 | 129 | 124.7954 |
| -2.2 | 10 | 11.41174 | 1.0 | 105 | 106.4001 |
| -2.0 | 14 | 17.69332 | 1.2 | 86 | 87.17105 |
| -1.8 | 32 | 26.36040 | 1.4 | 67 | 68.62604 |
| -1.6 | 39 | 37.73804 | 1.6 | 50 | 51.91484 |
| -1.4 | 45 | 51.91484 | 1.8 | 38 | 37.73804 |
| -1.2 | 71 | 68.62604 | 2.0 | 28 | 26.36040 |
| -1.0 | 99 | 87.17105 | 2.2 | 16 | 17.69332 |
| -0.8 | 98 | 106.4001 | 2.4 | 16 | 11.41174 |
| -0.6 | 121 | 124.7954 | 2.6 | 4 | 7.072614 |
| -0.4 | 140 | 140.6504 | 2.8 | 6 | 4.212062 |
| -0.2 | 130 | 152.3240 | 3.0 | 1 | 2.410446 |
| 0 | 141 | 158.5193 | | 5 | 1.325530 |

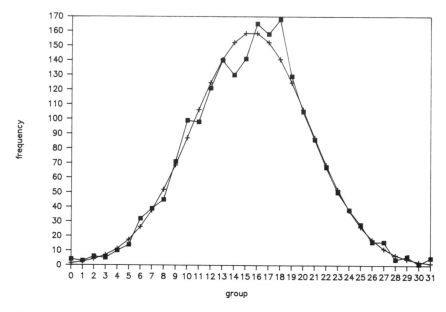

**Figure 14.1**
Actual frequency (■) versus preducted frequency (+).

The predicted frequency is calculated by using differences of the cumulative standard normal distribution. The probability that a standard normal random variable $X$ is less than or equal to $-0.6$—$\Pr\{X \le -0.6\}$—is 0.274253. $\Pr\{X \le -0.8\}$ is 0.211855. Thus, the probability that $X$ will lie in the interval between $-0.8$ and $-0.6$ is

$$0.274253 - 0.211855 = 0.062398.$$

Since we have 2,000 points, we predict that

$$0.062398 \times 2,000 = 124.7954$$

lie in the interval. In the event, 129 points lie in the interval. The actual and the predicted frequencies are plotted in figure 14.1.

## 14.5 Simulating the Lognormal Distribution

Once we know how to simulate the normal distribution, we can simulate the lognormal distribution. In many finance applications this is important, since a reasonable assumption for the movement of a stock price over time is that it is distributed lognormally.

Suppose the price of a stock is distributed lognormally, with an annual log mean return of $\mu$ and an annual log standard deviation of $\sigma$. If we denote by $S_0$ the price of a share of the stock today, then after an interval $\Delta t$ the price of the stock will be

$$S_{\Delta t} = S_0 \exp(\mu \Delta t + \sigma Z \sqrt{\Delta t}),$$

where $Z$ is a standard normal variable. In general we will have

$$S_{t+\Delta t} = S_t \exp(\mu \Delta t + \sigma Z \sqrt{\Delta t}). \tag{1}$$

This means that

$$S_{n\Delta t} = S_t \exp(n\mu \Delta t + \sigma Z \sqrt{n\Delta t}).$$

We want to simulate a lognormal price process. As a learning exercise this is certainly interesting, but there are other reasons to do it. Not least, the simulation will give us some insight into the meaning of price uncertainty and will help us understand the irrelevance of "technical analysis."

## 14.6   The Simulation

We will try to understand, through simulation, the meaning of the following sentences: "The price of a stock today is $25. The price of the stock is distributed lognormally, with an annual log mean return of 4 percent and an annual log standard deviation of 10 percent." We want to know how the price of the stock will behave on a daily basis throughout the next year. There are an infinite number of *price paths* for the stock. What we will do is simulate (randomly) one of these paths. If we want another price path, we can merely rerun the simulation. Every time we run the simulation we will get a different price path. (Actually, not every time: Since all computer random-number generators have cycles, eventually a price path will return. However, the Lotus random-number generator has a cycle of about 1,000,000, so you will have to run quite a few simulations before seeing the same data.)

There are about 250 business days in a year. This means that the daily price movement of the stock between day $t$ and day $t + 1$ can be simulated by setting $\Delta_t = 1/250$, $\mu = 0.04$, $\sigma = 0.1$ in equation 1:

$$S_{t+1} = S_t \exp(0.04/250 + 0.1Z\sqrt{1/250}).$$

Minor changes in our normal simulation program will do the trick.

The layout of the spreadsheet is even simpler this time than in the previous simulation. There is a two-column range for recording the data, called PRICE. The first column records the price of the asset at each period (starting with the asset's initial price), and the second column lists the periods of the simulation. (Since each run of the simulation produces two random numbers, there will be twice as many periods as there are MAXRUNs.) Here is how the spreadsheet looks:

```
price   period                              runnumber        125
-------|------|    starttime    10:30:59     random1     0.080152
       |      |    stoptime     10:32:16     random2     -0.48723
       |      |    elapsed      00:01:17     S(1)        0.243824
       |      |                              S(2)        3.402408
       |      |                              X(1)        0.272713
    PRICE     |                              X(2)        -1.65778
       |      |                              maxrun          125
       |      |
       |      |                              mean           0.04
       |      |                              standdiv        0.1
       |      |                              deltat        0.004
       |      |                              initial price    25
       |      |
```

The new variables here are the MEAN, the standard deviation STANDDIV ($\sigma$), DELTAT ($\Delta t$), and the INITIAL PRICE of the stock.

Most of what \A does has been covered in the discussion of the normal simulation. The third line of \A inputs the first line of the two-column range PRICE: the initial price of the stock and the initial period (which is always zero).

```
\A              starting
{let starttime,@now}{blank stoptime}{blank elapsed}
{blank price}{let deltat,1/(2*maxrun)}
{put price,0,0,initial price}{put price,1,0,0}~
{branch \B}
```

The next macro, \B, runs the critical loop (the {for} statement is the essential line) and does the cleanup (lines 2 and 3 of \B).

```
\B              running the loop
{for runnumber,1,maxrun,1,\C}
{let stoptime,anow}{let elapsed,stoptime-starttime}
{calc}{quit}
```

The macro \C creates the two normal deviates; it is the same as the macro we used in the simulation of the normal distribution.

```
\C        creating two normal deviates
{let random1,2*arand-1}{let random2,2*arand-1}
{let S(1),random1^2+random2^2}
{if S(1)>=1}{branch \C}
{if S(1)<1}{let S(2),asqrt(-2*aln(S(1))/S(1))}
{let X(1),random1*S(2)}{let X(2),random2*S(2)}
{branch \D}
```

The next macro, \D, records the price of the stock at the end of the time period Wt and records the period in which the price occurred:

```
\D          recording the results
{put price,0,2*runnumber-1,aexp(mean*deltat+standdiv*|sqrt(deltat)*x(1))*aindex(price,0,2*runnumber-2)}
{put price,0,2*runnumber,aexp(mean*deltat+standdiv*|sqrt(deltat)*x(2))*aindex(price,0,2*runnumber-1)}
{put price 1,2*runnumber-1,2*runnumber-1}
{put price 1,2*runnumber,2*runnumber}
```

The output looks like this:

| price    | period |
|----------|--------|
| 25       | 0      |
| 24.78760 | 1      |
| 25.01177 | 2      |
| 25.08762 | 3      |
| 25.07903 | 4      |
| 25.13519 | 5      |
| 25.34761 | 6      |
| 25.55202 | 7      |
| 25.23397 | 8      |
| 25.33506 | 9      |
| 25.21644 | 10     |
| 24.76368 | 11     |
| 24.75911 | 12     |
| 24.88392 | 13     |
| 25.04754 | 14     |
| 25.43039 | 15     |
| 25.24913 | 16     |
| 25.12834 | 17     |
| 25.13259 | 18     |
| 25.22704 | 19     |

... and so on for a few hundred more rows.

A more instructive way of looking at the data is through a graph, as in figure 14.2. If you're lucky, maybe you can simulate a stock-market crash, as in figure 14.3.

## 14.7   Technical Analysis

Security analysts are divided into "fundamentalists" and "technicians." This division has nothing to do with their outlook on the Creator of the Universe, but rather with the way they regard stock prices. Fundamentalists believe that the value of a stock is ultimately determined by underlying economic variables. Thus, when a fundamentalist analyzes a company, he will look at its earnings, its debt/equity ratio, its markets, and so forth.

Technicians, on the other hand, think that stock prices are determined by patterns. They believe that, by examining the pattern of past prices of

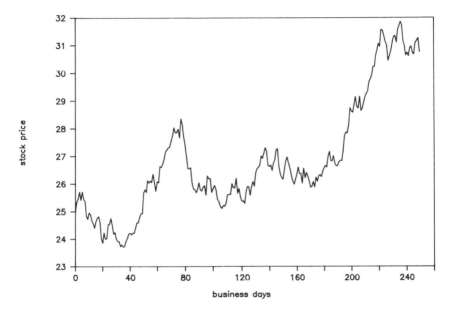

**Figure 14.2**
Lognormal simulation (mean $= 0.04$, $\sigma = 0.10$).

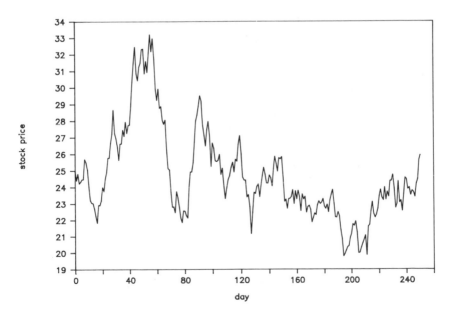

**Figure 14.3**
Simulated stock-market crash.

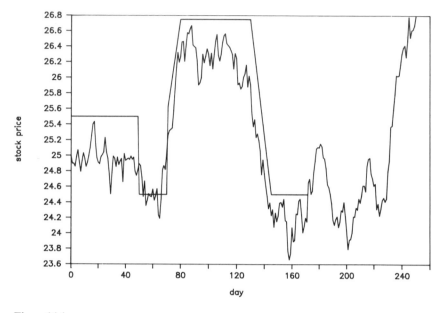

**Figure 14.4**
Head and shoulders.

a stock, they can predict its future prices. A technician may tell you "we're currently in a head-and-shoulders pattern," by which he means that a graph of the stock price looks like figure 14.4. Other terms used by technicians include "floors," "rebound levels," and "pennants." A good reference for this terminology is Chicago Board of Trade 1985.

The orthodox (some would say ivory-tower) view of technical analysis is that it is worthless. A basic theorem of financial theory says that markets efficiently incorporate the information known about the securities traded on them. There are several versions of this theory; one of them, the *weak efficient markets hypothesis*, says that at the very least all information about past prices is incorporated into the current price. This already means that technical analysis cannot make predictions of future prices, since it is based solely on past price information. (For a discussion of this point, see chapter 13 of Brealey and Myers 1984; for a more advanced treatment, see chapter 9 of Copeland and Weston 1983.)

Nevertheless, a lot of people believe in technical analysis. The simulations we are running in this chapter will allow us to generate a myriad of patterns which, when analyzed, will yield "good" predictions of future prices. For example, in figure 14.2 it appears that $23.50 is a floor for the stock price, since it never goes any lower. A perspicacious analyst can detect a clear head-and-shoulders pattern between days 0 and 120. From day 220 on, it appears that a new floor of $30.25 is developing. Thus, a technician might predict that the stock price will stay above $30.25 unless it drops below that level. (If you are going to be a technician, you have to learn to say these things with a straight face.)

## Exercises

1. Run a few of the lognormal simulations. Examine the price pattern for trends. Find at least one of the following:

support area

resistance area

uptrend/downtrend

head and shoulders

inverted head and shoulders

double top/bottom

rounded top/bottom

triangle (ascending, symmetrical, descending)

flag

(These terms are from Chicago Board of Trade 1985.)

2. Use /Data Table 1 to create the predicted frequency distribution of the standard normal needed for the normal simulation program.

3. A reasonable assumption about exchange rates is the following: Let $e_t$ be the natural logarithm of the exchange rate between two currencies at time $t$. Then $e_t$ is normally distributed, with

Expectation $= (e_0 - E)e^{\gamma t} + E$

and

Variance    $= (e^{2\gamma t} - 1)\delta^2/2\gamma$,

where $\gamma < 0$ and $E$ is the log of the purchasing-power-parity rate (the exchange rate that equilibrates the cost of baskets of goods in the two countries). Simulate this process. Note that over time the expected exchange rate approaches $E$ asymptotically. See Franke 1986 and Lessard 1979.

## References

Brealey, R., and S. Myers. 1984. *The Principles of Corporate Finance*. New York: McGraw-Hill.

Chicago Board of Trade. 1985. *Commodity Trading Manual*.

Copeland, T. E., and J. F. Weston. 1983. *Financial Theory and Corporate Policy*. Reading, Mass.: Addison-Wesley.

Franke, G. 1986. "Exchange Rate Volatility and International Trade: The Option Approach." Manuscript, University of Konstanz.

Knuth, D. E. 1981. *The Art of Computer Programming, Vol. 2: Seminumerical Algorithms*. Second edition. Reading, Mass.: Addison-Wesley.

Latour, A. 1986. "Polar Normal Distribution." *Byte* (August): 131–132.

Lessard, D. R., ed. 1979. *International Financial Management*. Boston: Warren, Gorham, Lamont.

Press, W. H., B. P. Flannery, S. A. Teukolsky, and W. T. Vetterling. 1986. *Numerical Recipes: The Art of Scientific Computing*. Cambridge University Press.

# 15 Option Pricing

## 15.1 Introduction

This section and the next can, at best, serve as an introduction to the already informed. If you know nothing whatsoever about options, read an introduction to the topic in a basic finance text. Some texts that give more advanced treatments of the topic are listed at the end of chapter 14.

An *option on a stock* is a security that gives the holder the right to buy or to sell one share of the stock on or before a particular date for a predetermined price. The following is a brief glossary of terms and notation used in the field of options.

*Call*: An option that gives the holder the right to buy a share of stock.
*Put*: An option that gives the holder the right to sell a share of stock.
*Exercise price, $K$*: The price at which the holder can buy or sell the underlying stock.
*Expiration date, $T$*: The date on or before which the holder can buy or sell the underlying stock.
*Stock price*: The price at which the underlying stock is selling at date $t$, denoted by $S_t$.
*Option price*: The price at which the option is sold or bought.

We shall use $C_t$ to denote the price of a call on date $t$, and $P_t$ to denote a put price. When we need fuller notation, we shall write $C_t(S_t, K, T)$ for the price of a call on date $t$ when the price of the underlying stock is $S_t$, the exercise price is $K$, and the expiration date is $T$.

### American Options vs. European Options

In the jargon of options markets, an American option can be exercised on or before the terminal date, whereas European options can be exercised only on their terminal date. Just to confuse matters further, the options sold on both American and European options markets are usually American options!

### Writing Options vs. Purchasing Options

The purchaser of a call option acquires the right to buy a share of stock for a given price and pays for this right at the time of purchase. The *writer* of a call option is the seller of his right: The writer collects the option price today in return for obligating herself to deliver one share of stock in the future for the exercise price, if the purchaser of the call demands. In terms of cash flows, the purchaser of an option always has an initial negative cash flow (the price of the option) and a future cash flow which is at worst zero (if it is not worthwhile exercising the option) and otherwise positive (if the option is exercised). The cash-flow position of the writer of the option is reversed: An initial positive cash flow is followed by a terminal cash flow which is at best zero.

### Example

A "General Pills, September 50 call option" is a security that gives the holder the right to buy one share of General Pills on or before a specified day in September (in most American markets, the day is the third Friday in the month) for the price of $50. If the price of the GP September 50 call today is $4, then you pay this price for the privilege of being able, between now and September, to purchase one share of GP stock for $50, irrespective of its market price at the time you exercise the option. (It will usually not be optimal to exercise a call before its expiration date. One of the remarkable theorems in option-pricing theory states that early exercise is optimal only if the underlying stock pays dividends before the expiration date. Even then, one should consider early exercise only at the moment before the dividend payment; see Jarrow and Rudd 1983 or Cox and Rubinstein 1985. The upshot of this theorem is that in many cases an American call option can be analyzed as if it were a European call option.)

A "General Pills September 50 put option" is the right to *sell* one share of GP in September (on or before the same day in the month as the call) for $50. Paying $2 for this put option today gives you the right to sell a share of GP stock for $50 between now and September, irrespective of the market price of the stock. Of course, you will exercise this option only if the market price at the time of exercise is less than $50. (As opposed to a call option, early exercise of an American put may be optimal even in the absence of dividend payments.)

### Payoff Patterns at Expiration

One of the attractions of options is that they allow their owners to change the payoff patterns of the underlying assets.

Suppose you buy a share of General Pills stock in July at its current market price of $50. If in September the price of the stock is $70, you will have made $20 profit; if its price is $40, you will have lost $20. Denoting the price of the stock in September by $S_T$ and its price in July by $S_0$, we may write your profit function from the stock as following:

Profit from stock $= S_T - S_0 = S_T - 50$.

On the other hand, suppose that in July you bought one GP September 50 call for $4. In September you will exercise the call only if the market price of GP is then higher than $50. If we write the call price as $C_0$, we can write your profit function from the call in September as follows:

$$\text{Call profit in Sept.} = \max(0, S_T - K) - C_0$$
$$= \max(0, S_T - 50) - 4$$
$$= \begin{cases} -4 & \text{if } S_T \le 50 \\ S_T - 54 & \text{if } S_T > 50. \end{cases}$$

(Our use of the word *profit* in this section constitutes an abuse of the English language and the standard finance concept, since we are ignoring the interest costs associated with buying the asset. In the case at hand, this is both traditional and harmless.)

If in July you bought a September 50 put for $2, your terminal payoff would be $\max(50 - S_T, 0)$ giving

$$\text{Put profit in Sept.} = \max(0, K - S_T) - P_0$$
$$= \max(0, 50 - S_T) - 2$$
$$= \begin{cases} 48 - S_T & \text{if } S_T \le 50 \\ -2 & \text{if } S_T > 50. \end{cases}$$

The graphs of these three basic profit patterns are shown in figure 15.1.

Suppose you bought one share of stock in GP for $50 and simultaneously purchased a put on the stock with an exercise price of $50. (For reasons that will become clear shortly, this combination is often called a *protective put* or *portfolio insurance*.) If the put price is $2, your profit pattern at the expiration date of the option will be the sum of the profits from the stock and those from the put:

$$S_T - 50 + \max(50 - S_T, 0) - 2$$
$$= \begin{cases} S_T - 50 + 50 - S_T - 2 = -2 & \text{if } S_T \le 50 \\ S_T - 50 - 2 & \text{if } S_T > 50. \end{cases}$$

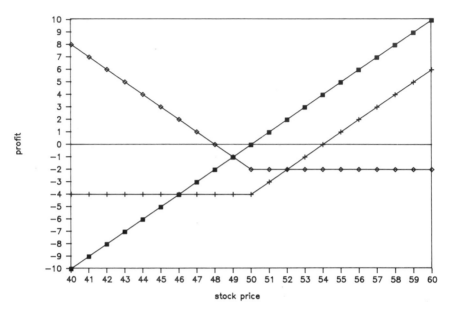

**Figure 15.1**
Basic profit patterns. (■): Stock; (+): call; (◇): put.

Thus, the combination of the stock and the put offers an insurance policy, limiting your maximum loss to the put price (more will be said about this in the next chapter). The payoff pattern is shown in figure 15.2.

Another combination involves buying and writing calls with different exercise prices. When the bought call has a low exercise price and the written call has a higher exercise price, the combination is called a *bullish spread*. As an example, suppose you bought a call (for $4) with an exercise price of $50 and wrote a call (for $2) with an exercise price of $55. This bullish spread gives a profit of

$$\max(S_T - 50, 0) - 4 + 2 - \max(S_T - 55, 0).$$

This gives

$$\text{Bullish spread profit} = \begin{cases} -2 & \text{if } S_T \le 50 \\ S_T - 50 - 2 & \text{if } 50 < S_T < 55 \\ 3 & \text{if } S_T \ge 55. \end{cases}$$

See figure 15.3.

Many more interesting combinations are possible. For further examples, see the exercises at the end of this chapter.

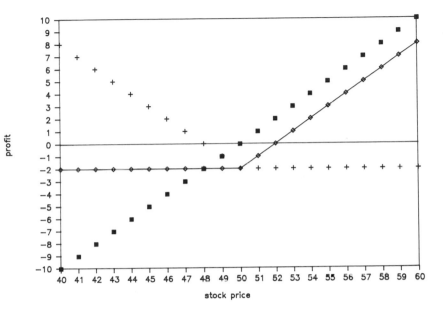

**Figure 15.2**
Protective put payoff. (■): Stock; (+): put; (◇): put + stock.

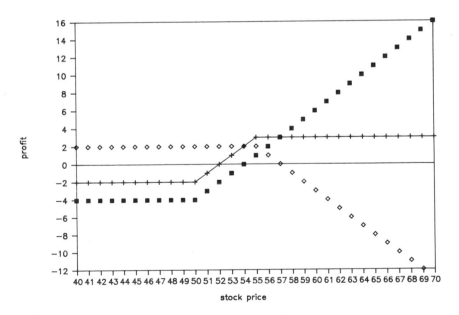

**Figure 15.3**
Bullish spread. (■): Low call; (+) spread; (◇): high call.

**Factors Influencing the Option Price**

What determines the price of a call option? How much should I be willing to pay today for the right to be able to buy one share of stock in the future for a predetermined price? There is a numerical answer to this question, which we shall get to in the next section. For the moment, let us look at some general factors that influence the price of a call option with exercise price $K$ and expiration data $T$, written on a stock whose price today is $S_t$:

• *the exercise price of the option, K*. Obviously, the higher the exercise price, the less worthwhile (everything else being equal) it is to exercise the option. Thus, a higher exercise price makes for a lower call-option value.

• *the current market price of the stock, $S_t$*. The higher the current price, the more the option is worth. The intuitive reason for this is that the higher the current price of the stock, the greater the probability that the option will be worth exercising.

• *the time remaining until exercise, $T - t$*. The more time you have to exercise the option, the greater the probability that it will be worth exercising.

• *the variability of the stock price*. Like the two previous factors, this increases the probability that you will be able to exercise the option profitably. (We usually think of variability as implying lower value, since we identify variability with risk. For options, the case is reversed. Why? A call option protects its holder against downward movements of the stock price. The holder of the call option is therefore interested in upward movements only.)

## 15.2   The Black-Scholes Equation for Option Pricing

Black and Scholes (1973) have derived a formula that can be used to price European call options. The Black-Scholes formula assumes that the call option is a European option, written on a stock that pays on dividends. The stock's price return is assumed to be lognormally distributed with a standard deviation of log return $\sigma$. (The Black-Scholes formula depends only on the $\sigma$ of the log returns, and not on the expected value of these returns, $\mu$.)

As before, we denote the current price of the stock by $S_t$, the exercise price of the option by $K$, and the expiration date of the option by $T$. The time to expiration, denoted by $\tau$, is equal to $T - t$, and $r$ denotes the risk-free interest rate (assumed to be continuously compounded). For future reference, note that if $r$ is in annual terms then so is $\tau$. Black and Scholes show that the value of a call option is given by

$$C_t = S_t N(d_1) - Ke^{-r\tau}N(d_2),$$

where

$$d_1 = \frac{\ln(S_t/K) + (r + \sigma^2/2)\tau}{\sigma\sqrt{\tau}},$$

$$d_2 = \frac{\ln(S_t/K) + (r - \sigma^2/2)\tau}{\sigma\sqrt{\tau}} = d_1 - \sigma\sqrt{\tau}$$

and where $N(\ )$ is the cumulative normal distribution.

**A Numerical Example**

Consider a call option with exercise price $K = 50$ written on a stock whose $S_t$ is 50. Suppose that the stock price is lognormally distributed with $\sigma = 0.35$. If $r = 0.08$ and if $\tau = 0.25$ (approximately 3 months), then

$$d_1 = 0.20178,$$

$$d_2 = 0.02678,$$

$$N(d_1) = 0.5800,$$

$$N(d_2) = 0.5107,$$

$$e^{-r\tau} = 0.9802,$$

giving a Black-Scholes price of

$$S_t N(d_1) - Ke^{-r\tau}N(d_2) = 3.9693.$$

## 15.3  Pricing Puts

The Black-Scholes formula can be used to price European puts as well as calls. One way to do this is to use the *put-call parity theorem*, which states that a European put on a stock with exercise price $K$ and expiration date $T$ is equivalent to a portfolio in which four asset positions are combined:

• the purchase of a call on the stock, with the call exercise price $K$ and expiration date $T$. This has initial cash flow $-C_t$ and terminal payoff $\max(S_T - K, 0)$.

• the purchase of $Ke^{-rt}$ of the riskless asset. This has payoff $K$ at time $T$.

• selling short one share of the stock. This has cash flow $S_t$ at time $t$ and cash flow $-S_T$ on the expiration date of the option.

• writing a European put. This has positive cash flow $P_t$ at time $t$. At time $T$ the cash flow is $-\max(K - S_T, 0)$.

The total terminal cash flow of this portfolio is zero, as can be seen from the following.

If $S_T \leq K$,

| | |
|---|---|
| call: | 0 |
| riskless asset: | $K$ |
| stock: | $-S_T$ |
| put: | $-(K - S_T)$. |

If $S_T \geq K$,

| | |
|---|---|
| call: | $S_T - K$ |
| riskless asset: | $K$ |
| stock: | $-S_T$ |
| put: | 0. |

It follows from arbitrage considerations that the total initial cash flow of the portfolio must likewise be zero. This implies that

$$-C_t - Ke^{-rt} + S_t + P_t = 0,$$

or (rearranging)

$$P_t = C_t - S_t + Ke^{-rt}.$$

This is the put-call parity theorem.

We can use this theorem directly with the Black-Scholes pricing equation for calls to give an equivalent formula for pricing puts:

$$P_t = -S_t N(-d_1) + Ke^{-rt} N(-d_2),$$

where $d_1$ and $d_2$ are as defined for calls and where $N(\ )$ is the cumulative normal distribution.

## 15.4   Calculating the Implied Variance

Of all the variables in the Black-Scholes option-pricing equation, the most difficult to estimate is $\sigma$, the standard deviation of the stock's logarithmic return. A common exercise is the following: Given the call price, the current stock price, the time to expiration, and the interest rate, calculate the *implied* $\sigma$.

There is no closed-form solution for the $\sigma$. The general way to calculate the implied $\sigma$ is to use the Black-Scholes formula to iterate to a solution. Suppose we are given a call option whose price is $C$. We do not know the share price $\sigma$, but we know the other parameters that go into the Black-Scholes pricing formula $S_t$, $K$, $\tau$, and $r$. Our problem is thus to find $\sigma$ such that

$$C = S_t N(d_1) - Ke^{-r\tau}N(d_2).$$

For notational simplicity, we write

$$f(\sigma) = S_t N(d_1) - Ke^{-r\tau}N(d_2).$$

Our problem may be restated as follows: Given $C$, $S_t$, $r$, $\tau$, and $K$, find $\sigma$ such that $f(\sigma) = C$.

There are several ways to solve this problem. We shall consider two of them.

### Method 1

By this method we find two values of $\sigma$ that bracket the given value of $C$. This is made simpler by the fact that $f(\sigma)$ is monotonic in $\sigma$, achieving its lowest value when $\sigma = 0$ and rising from there. For example, when $\sigma = 0$, it may be shown that

$$\lim_{\sigma \to 0} f(\sigma) = \max(0, S_t - Ke^{-r\tau}).$$

Suppose $f(\sigma_{\text{LOW}}) < C < f(\sigma_{\text{HIGH}})$, where $\sigma_{\text{LOW}}$ and $\sigma_{\text{HIGH}}$ are two specific values of $\sigma$. We can then use the following algorithm to find the implicit $\sigma$:

1. Let $\sigma_{\text{AVG}} = (\sigma_{\text{LOW}} + \sigma_{\text{HIGH}})/2$. If $f(\sigma_{\text{AVG}}) < C$, replace $\sigma_{\text{LOW}}$ with $\sigma_{\text{AVG}}$. If $f(\sigma_{\text{AVG}}) > C$, replace $\sigma_{\text{HIGH}}$ with $\sigma_{\text{AVG}}$.
2. Repeat step 1 until $|f(\sigma) - C|$ is sufficiently small.

The following spreadsheet illustrates this technique. Though not shown here, it is assumed that you have incorporated the Black-Scholes model in your spreadsheet, and that the worksheet is set for automatic recalculation.

|        |           | runnumber    | 15          |
|--------|-----------|--------------|-------------|
| S      | 100       | LOWSTD       | 0.403442382 |
| K      | 125       | HIGHSTD      | 0.403503418 |
| r      | 0.12      |              |             |
| tau    | 0.25      |              |             |
| sigma  | 0.403472  |              |             |
| d(1)   | -0.85653  | Target_call  | 2           |
| d(2)   | -1.05827  |              |             |
|        |           |              |             |
| call price | 1.999904 |           |             |

Macro \A is self-explanatory.

```
\A                starting off, entering highstd
{windowsoff}{paneloff}~
{GETNUMBER Enter a "high guess" for the standard deviation.    ,highstd}~
{let lowstd,0}{let runnumber,0}~
{let sigma,highstd}~
{if call price>=target_call}{branch \c}~
{branch \b}~
```

The {GETNUMBER} command prompts the user to enter a guess for the standard deviation. This guess must be too high; otherwise, macro \B prompts the user to enter another guess, until finally he makes a guess that is high enough. The initial low guess for $\sigma$ is set at 0.

```
\B                making sure highstd is high enough
{getnumber Your first guess is too low.  Enter a new guess.  ,highstd}~
{let sigma,highstd}~
{if call price>target_call}{branch \c}~
{branch \b}~
```

Macro \C does the actual calculation. At each iteration, \C takes the average of the current high and low s. If this average gives too low a price for the call, then its value is put into the low standard deviation; otherwise, it replaces the current high s.

```
\c
{let runnumber,runnumber+1}~
{let sigma,(highstd+lowstd)/2}~
{if @abs(call price-target_call)<0.0001}{quit}~
{if call price<target_call}{let lowstd,sigma}~
{if call price>target_call}{let highstd,sigma}~
{if runnumber>20}{quit}~
{branch \c}~
```

## Method 2

This method employs the Newton-Raphson technique to find a root of the equation $C - f(\sigma)$.

The monotonicity of $f$ guarantees that only one such root exists. The Newton-Raphson technique employs successive substitutions for $\sigma$, where

$$\sigma(i+1) = \sigma(i) - \frac{f(\sigma(i)) - C}{f'(\sigma)}.$$

The trick here is to start from a $\sigma$ that will always lead to convergence. Manaster and Koehler (1982) show that one such $\sigma$ is given by

$$\sigma^2 = |\ln(S_t/K) + r\tau|\frac{2}{\tau}.$$

The one other additional piece of information required for this method is

$$f'(\sigma) = \frac{\partial f(\sigma)}{\partial \sigma}.$$

This is not a trivial calculation. However, it can be shown (see Jarrow and Rudd 1983) that

$$f'(\sigma) = S_t\sqrt{\tau}N'(d_1),$$

where

$$N'(x) = \frac{1}{\sqrt{2\pi}}e^{-x^2/2}.$$

The Manaster-Koehler approach is more efficient (i.e., converges faster) than the first method. It is also simple to implement in a spreadsheet. Here is the way the spreadsheet looks initially (we have not put in that part of the spreadsheet that calculates the normal distribution):

```
s                  100
K                  125 marker              9
r                 0.12 initial      1.243039
tau               0.25
sigma      1.243039987 derivative    9.973557
d(1)        -2.7322E-17 N'(d(1))      0.199471
d(2)        -0.62151999 target              2

call price   -7.40423315
```

MARKER is a variable that starts the process. If MARKER $\neq$ 0, then $\sigma$ is set to its initial value (as in the example above). Setting MARKER = 0 starts the iterations.

Here are the formulas:

```
initial      @SQRT(@ABS(@LN(S/K)+R*TAU)*2/TAU)
sigma        @IF(MARKER<>0,INITIAL,SIGMA-(CALL PRICE-TARGET)/DERIVATIVE)
derivative   +S*@SQRT(TAU)*N'(D(1))
N'(d(1))     (1/@SQRT(2*@PI))*@EXP(-D(1)^2/2)
d(1)         (@LN(S/K)+(R+SIGMA^2/2)*TAU)/(SIGMA*@SQRT(TAU))
d(2)         +D(1)-SIGMA*@SQRT(TAU)
call price   +S*N(D(1))-K*@EXP(-R*TAU)*N(D(2))
```

Here is the way the spreadsheet looks six iterations later:

```
s                  100
K                  125 marker              0
r                 0.12 initial      1.243039
tau               0.25
sigma      0.403479783 derivative   13.82214
d(1)        -0.85651904 N'(d(1))      0.276442
d(2)        -1.05825893 target              2

call price           2
```

## Exercises

1. Consider the General Pills, September 30, 60 call options. Suppose that one share of General Pills is currently selling for $55, and that the calls are selling for $8.

a. Graph the net payoff from buying a call, given various terminal prices $S(T)$. Include the cost of purchasing the call; that is, graph the following:

Net payoff $= \max(0, S(T) - 60) - 8$.

b. Graph the net payoff from buying one share of stock now and selling it on September 30: $S(T) - 55$.

c. What is the payoff from buying one share of stock now and selling a call option? Note that the seller of a call (the technical jargon is *writing a call*) collects the call price today, but has to supply the stock to the purchaser of the call by or on the terminal date if the purchaser of the call wants to exercise it.

d. On a single graph, show the net payoffs from buying one share of General Pills stock, buying a share of GP stock and writing a call on the stock, buying a share of GP stock and writing two calls, and buying a share of GP stock and writing three calls.

In answering the following three questions, make use of the data in the following table:

| Type of option | Exercise price | Price |
|---|---|---|
| call | 40 | 13 |
| call | 50 | 6 |
| call | 60 | 3 |
| put | 40 | 1 |
| put | 50 | 4 |
| put | 60 | 10 |

2. A *bearish spread* involves buying a call with a high exercise price and writing a call with a low exercise spread. Give a numerical example of such a spread and graph the net terminal profits.

3. An investor purchases two calls, each with an exercise price of 50, and sells one with an exercise price of 40 and one with an exercise price of 60. Graph the net terminal profits. (Such a position is called a *butterfly spread*).

4. In a *straddle*, an investor purchases both a put and a call on the same stock with the same expiration date and the same exercise price. Graph the payoffs for the three possible straddles for the options listed above.

5. Build a spreadsheet that will calculate the Black-Scholes value of a call option. Assume that there are 365 days in a year, and use Lotus to calculate the number of days between the current date and the expiration date of the option.

6. Calculate the value of a call written on one share of a stock currently selling for $50. Assume that the exercise price is $40, the riskless rate of interest is 6 percent, and the standard deviation of the stock's return is 20 percent. The expiration date of the option is March 23, 1987, and today is October 18, 1986. The expiration date of the option is March 23, 1987, and today is October 18, 1986.

7. A share of stock in the XYZ Corporation is currently selling for $38. The risk-free interest rate is 6 percent. Both puts and calls on the stock are sold with expiration dates 3 and 6 months hence and with exercise prices of $35, $40, and $45. Use the spreadsheet implementation of the Black-Scholes formula to answer the following questions:
a. What is the effect of changing $\sigma$ on the valuation of the options? Let your answer be in the form of graphs. Show that

$$\lim_{\sigma \to 0} f(\sigma) = \max(0, S_t - Ke^{-r\tau}).$$

b. Suppose that the $\sigma$ of XYZ is 38 percent. What is the effect of changing the risk-free rate on the option prices?
c. Repeat the previous question, but this time allow the maturity of the option to get very small.

8. Suppose $S_t = \$122$, $E = \$125$, $r = 0.10$, and $\tau = 0.25$ (approximately 3 months to maturity). If $C = \$3$, what is the implied $\sigma$? Build the two spreadsheet programs that iterate to the solution. First use Method 1 of the chapter, then use the Manaster-Koehler technique (Method 2).

9. Adapt the macro of Method 1 for finding the implied variance so that the macro sets the initial value of the high standard deviation.

## References

Black, F. 1975. "Fact and Fantasy in the Use of Options." *Financial Analysts Journal* 31 (July–August): 36–41, 61–72.

Black, F., and M. Scholes. 1972. "The Valuation of Option Contracts and a Test of Market Efficiency." *Journal of Finance* 27 (May): 399–417.

Black, F., and M. Scholes. 1973. "The Pricing of Options and Corporate Liabilities." *Journal of Political Economy* 81 (May): 673–659.

Boyle, P., and A. Ananthanarayanan. 1977. "The Impact of Variance Estimation in Option Valuation Models." *Journal of Financial Economics* 5 (December): 375–387.

Cox, J. C., and S. A. Ross. 1976. "The Valuation of Options for Alternative Stochastic Processes." *Journal of Financial Economics* 3 (January–March): 145–166.

Cox, J. C., and M. Rubinstein. 1985. *Options Markets.* Englewood Cliffs, N.J.: Prentice-Hall.

Elton, E. J., and M. J. Gruber. 1984. *Modern Portfolio Theory and Investment Analysis.* Second edition. New York: Wiley.

Garman, M., and M. Klass. 1980. "On the Estimation of Security Price Volatilities from Historical Data." *Journal of Business* 53 (January): 67–79.

Geske, R. 1979. "A Note on an Analytic Valuation Formula for Unprotected American Call Options on Stocks with Known Dividends." *Journal of Financial Economics* 7 (December): 375–380.

Geske, R. 1979. "The Valuation of Compound Options." *Journal of Financial Economics* 7 (March): 63–81.

Geske, R., and R. Roll. 1984. "On Valuing American Call Options with the Black-Scholes European Formula." *Journal of Finance* 39 (June).

Geske, R., R. Roll, and K. Shastri. 1982. "Over-the-Counter Option Market Dividend Protection and Biases in the Black-Scholes Model." *Journal of Finance* 37 (September): 1271–1277.

Haugen, R. A. 1986. *Modern Investment Theory.* Englewood Cliffs, N.J.: Prentice-Hall.

Jarrow, R. A., and A. Rudd. 1983. *Option Pricing.* Homewood, Ill.: Irwin.

Latane, H., and R. Rendleman. 1976. "Standard Deviations of Stock Price Ratios Implied in Option Prices." *Journal of Finance* 31 (May): 369–382.

Levy, H., and M. Sarnat. 1984. *Portfolio and Investment Selection: Theory and Practice.* Englewood Cliffs, N.J.: Prentice-Hall.

MacBeth, J., and L. Merville. 1979. "An Empirical Examination of the Black-Scholes Call Option Pricing Model." *Journal of Finance* 34 (December): 1173–1186.

Manaster, S., and G. Koehler. 1982. "A Note on the Calculation of Implied Variances from the Black-Scholes Model." *Journal of Finance* 37 (March): 227–230.

Merton, R. 1973. "Theory of Rational Option Pricing." *Bell Journal of Economics and Management Science* 4 (spring): 141–183.

Merton, R. 1976. "Option Pricing When the Underlying Stock Returns Are Discontinuous." *Journal of Financial Economics* 3 (January–March): 125–144.

Merton, R. 1976. "The Impact on Option Pricing of Specification Error in the Underlying Stock Price Returns." *Journal of Finance* 31 (May): 333–350.

Parkinson, M. 1977. "Option Pricing: The American Put." *Journal of Business* 50 (January): 21–36.

Parkinson, M. 1980. "The Extreme Value Method for Estimating the Variance of the Rate of Return." *Journal of Business* 53 (January): 61–67.

Ritchken, P. 1987. *Options: Theory, Strategy, and Applications.* Glenview, Ill.: Scott, Foresman.

Ritchken, P. 1987. *Options—Theory, Strategy, and Applications.* Glenview, Ill.: Scott, Foresman.

Roll, R. 1977. "An Analytical Valuation Formula for Unprotected American Call Options on Stocks with Known Dividends." *Journal of Financial Economics* 5 (November): 251–258.

Sterk, W. 1982. "Tests of Two Models for Valuing Call Options on Stocks with Dividends." *Journal of Finance* 37 (December): 1229–1238.

Sterk, W. 1983. "Comparative Performance of the Black-Scholes and Roll-Geske-Whaley Option Pricing Models." *Journal of Financial and Quantitative Analysis* 18 (September): 345–354.

Whaley, R. 1981. "On the Valuation of American Call Options on Stocks with Known Dividends." *Journal of Financial Economics* 9 (June): 207–211.

Whaley, R. (1982). "Valuation of American Call Options on Dividend-Paying Stocks: Empirical Tests." *Journal of Financial Economics* 10 (March): 29–58.

# 16 Portfolio Insurance

## 16.1 Insuring Stock Returns

Options can be used to guarantee minimum returns from stock investments. When you purchase a stock and simultaneously purchase a put on the stock, you can be sure that the dollar return from the purchase will never be lower than the exercise price on the put.

To see this, consider the following example: You decide to invest in one share of General Pills stock, which currently costs $56. The stock pays no dividends. You hope for a large capital gain at the end of the year, but you worry that the stock's price may decline. To guard against a decline in the stock's price, you decide to purchase a put on it. The put you purchase allows you to sell the stock at the end of one year for $50. The cost of the put, $2.38, is derived from the Black-Scholes option model (see chapter 15 above) using the following data: $S_0 = \$56$, $K = \$50$, $\sigma = 0.30$, and $r = 0.08$.

This *protective put* or *portfolio insurance* strategy guarantees that you will lose no more than $6 on your share of General Pills stock. If the stock's price at the end of the year is more than $50, you will simply let the put expire without exercising it. On the other hand, if the stock's price at the end of the year is less than $50, you will exercise the put and collect $50. It is as if you had purchased an insurance policy on share with a $6 deductible.

Of course this protection doesn't come for free: Instead of investing $56 in your single share of stock, you have invested $58.38. You could have deposited the additional $2.38 in the bank and earned interest of $0.08 \times 2.38 = \$0.19$ in the course of the year.

## 16.2 Portfolio Insurance on More Complicated Assets

What if you want to purchase portfolio insurance on a more complicated basket of assets? If your basket matches one on which options are sold, you simply buy the basket and buy the put on the basket in the options market. But in many cases you will be unable to find a put option on a portfolio of assets that exactly matches the portfolio in which you want to invest. (You might consider buying an option for each asset in the portfolio you want to purchase, but this won't work: A portfolio of options does not constitute an option on a portfolio.)

It is here that the Black-Scholes option-pricing model comes to our aid. An option on a stock (from here on, "stock" will be used to refer to a portfolio of stocks as well as a single stock) is simply a portfolio consisting of a short position in the stock and a long position in the risk-free asset, with both positions being adjusted continuously.

For example, a put in the Black-Scholes model has value at time $0 \le t \le 1$ of

$$P_t = -S_t \mathrm{N}(-h) + Ke^{-r\tau}\mathrm{N}(\sigma\sqrt{\tau} - h),$$

where $h = \ln(S_t e^{rt}/K)/\sigma\sqrt{\tau} + 0.5\sigma\sqrt{\tau})$, $\tau = 1 - t$, $r$ is the risk-free rate of interest, $\sigma$ is the standard deviation of the log return of the stock, and $K$ is the exercise price of the put. Thus, buying a put is equivalent to investing $Ke^{-rt}\mathrm{N}(\sigma\sqrt{\tau} - h)$ in a risk-free bond that matures at $t = 1$ and investing $-S_t \mathrm{N}(-h)$ in the stock (i.e., selling short this amount of stock).

This means that buying one share of stock and buying a put on the share with exercise price $K$ is equivalent to buying $S_t[1 - \mathrm{N}(-h)]$ of the stock and $Ke^{-rt}\mathrm{N}(\sigma\sqrt{\tau} - h)$ of the risk-free bond.

The total investment required to buy one share of the stock plus the put is $S_t + P_t$. In terms of portfolio proportions, we will be investing

$$\omega_t = \frac{S_t[1 - \mathrm{N}(-h)]}{S_t + P_t}$$

$$= \frac{S_t[1 - \mathrm{N}(-h)]}{S_t[1 - \mathrm{N}(-h)] + Ke^{-rt}\mathrm{N}(\sigma\sqrt{\tau} - h)}$$

of our wealth in the risky asset (the right-hand side follows from the Black-Scholes formula).

To sum up: If you want to buy a specific portfolio of assets *and* an insurance policy guaranteeing that at $t = 1$ your total investment will not be worth less than $K$, then at each point in time, $t$, you should invest a proportion $\omega_t$ of your wealth in the specific portfolio you have chosen and a proportion $1 - \omega_t$ in riskless, pure discount bonds that mature at $t = 1$.

### Example

Suppose you decide to invest all your wealth in General Pills stock (currently selling at $56) and in protective puts on the shares with an exercise price of $50. This insures that your dollar return per share at the end of one year will be no less than $50. Suppose there is no traded put on General Pills, so that you will have to create your own put by investing in the share and in riskless discount bonds. The riskless rate is 8 percent, and the standard deviation of General Pills' log return is 30 percent. Then your investment strategy should be to invest

$$\omega_0 = \frac{S_0[1 - N(-h)]}{S_0 + P_0} = \frac{56(1 - 0.2135)}{58.38} = 75.44\%$$

in shares of General Pills and to invest

$$1 - \omega_0 = 24.56\%$$

in riskless discount bonds maturing in one year. (If traded puts on GP existed, these would be trading at $2.38 for an exercise price one year from now of $50. Your strategy would then consist of buying 17.13 shares of GP (cost = $959.23) and 17.13 puts (cost = $40.76). Buying $754.40 of shares and $245.60 of bonds exactly duplicates the initial investment in 17.13 shares and 17.13 puts. This equivalence is guaranteed by Black and Scholes.)

One week later, $\tau$ (the time remaining until the end of the year) is $51/52 = 0.9808$. The stock has risen to $60. The riskless rate is still 8 percent. You should now be investing

$$\omega_{0.0192} = \frac{S_0[1 - N(-h)]}{S_0 + P_0} = \frac{60(1 - 0.1524)}{60 + 1.63} = 82.52\%$$

in shares of General Pills. If you had started off at $\tau = 1$ with $1,000, your investment strategy would look like

| beginning of week | | | end of week | | |
|---|---|---|---|---|---|
| shares | bonds | portfolio value | shares | bonds | portfolio value |
| $754.40 | $245.60 | $1000 | $808.28 | $245.98 | $1054.26 |

for week 1 and like

| beginning of week | | | end of week | | |
|---|---|---|---|---|---|
| shares | bonds | portfolio value | shares | bonds | portfolio value |
| $869.98 | $184.28 | $1054.26 | ??? | $184.56 | ??? |

for week 2.

The value of your bonds grows by a factor of $1.00154 = e^{(1/52)0.08}$ per week. On the other hand, the value of your shares depends on the weekly rate of growth in the price of General Pills stock. During week 0, this rate of growth was $60/56 = 1.0714$.

Now suppose that at the end of week 2, the price of a share of General Pills tumbled to 52. Your position now looks like this:

| beginning of week | | | end of week | | |
|---|---|---|---|---|---|
| shares | bonds | portfolio value | shares | bonds | portfolio value |
| $869.98 | $184.28 | $1054.26 | $753.98 | $184.56 | $938.54 |

Since another week has passed, your investment in General Pills should now be

$$\omega_{0.0385} = \frac{S_0[1 - N(-h)]}{S_0 + P_0} = \frac{52(1 - 0.2939)}{52 + 3.33} = 66.36\%.$$

This gives

| beginning of week | | | end of week | | |
|---|---|---|---|---|---|
| shares | bonds | portfolio value | shares | bonds | portfolio value |
| $622.82 | $315.72 | $938.54 | ??? | $316.21 | ??? |

Of course, the above example is somewhat misleading, since the Black-Scholes model assumes that portfolio proportions are continuously adjusted, whereas we have waited a whole week to readjust our proportions. In the background lurks a pious hope that finite (but short) adjustment intervals will approximate the Black-Scholes continuous-readjustment scheme. (Since we are only human, we can't in fact make continuous adjustments to our portfolio. Moreover, since readjustment of the portfolio involves transaction costs to the investor, only finite adjustment is possible. In a later section of this chapter, we will consider a portfolio-insurance strategy that includes transaction costs.)

## 16.3   Some Properties of Portfolio Insurance

The above example illustrates some of the typical properties of portfolio insurance. Three important properties are the following.

### Property 1

When the stock price is above the exercise price $K$, then $\omega_t > 0.5$.

The proof of this property requires a little manipulation of our formula for $\omega_t$. Rewrite $\omega_t$ (dropping the index $t$ on $S_t$) as

$$1 \Big/ \left(1 + \frac{Ke^{-r\tau}N(\sigma\sqrt{\tau} - h)}{S[1 - N(-h)]}\right).$$

When $S \geq K$, the denominator of $\omega_t$ is $<2$. This will prove the proposition. First note that when $S \geq K$, $K/S \leq 1$. Next, note that $e^{-rt} < 1$ for all $t$. Finally, examine the expression

$$\frac{N(\sigma\sqrt{\tau} - h)}{1 - N(-h)} = \frac{N(\sigma\sqrt{\tau} - h)}{N(h)}$$

$$= \frac{N(0.5\sigma\sqrt{\tau} - [\ln(S/K) + r\tau]/\sigma\tau)}{N(0.5\sigma\sqrt{\tau} + [\ln(S/K) + r\tau]/\sigma\tau)} < 1.$$

This proves the property.

**Property 2**

When the stock's price increases, $\omega_t$ increases, and vice versa. To see this, it is enough to see that when $S$ increases, the value of the put decreases and $N(-h)$ decreases. Rewrite the original definition of $\omega_t$ as

$$\omega_t = \frac{S_t[1 - N(-h)]}{S_t + P_t} = \frac{1 - N(-h)}{1 + P_t/S_t}.$$

Thus, when $S_t$ increases, the denominator of $\omega_t$ decreases and the numerator increases. This proves that $\omega_t$ increases.

**Property 3**

When $t \to 1$, one of two things happens: If $S_t > K$, then $\omega_t \to 1$. If $S_t < K$, then $\omega_t \to 0$. To see this, note that when $S_t > K$ and $t \to 1$, $N(h) \to 1$ and $N(-h) \to 0$; thus, for this case, $\omega_t \to 1$. Conversely, when $S_t < K$ and $t \to 1$, $N(h) \to 0$ and $N(-h) \to 1$ and thus $\omega_t \to 0$. (Strictly speaking, these statements are true only as "probability limits"—see Billingsley 1968. What about the case when, as $t \to 1$, $S_t/K \to 1$? In this case, $\omega_t \to \frac{1}{2}$. However, the probability of this occurring is zero.)

## 16.4   A Simulation Macro

What do portfolio-insurance strategies look like? In this section we consider this question by simulating such a strategy by means of a macro. The macro, which is based on the simulation macros of chapter 14, initially generates two normal deviates. These are then turned into lognormal deviates. Returns on the stock are calculated, and the required portfolio proportions (stock versus risk-free asset) are calculated.

The variables used are the following:

| | | | | | |
|---|---|---|---|---|---|
| | | runnumber | | 26 NORMAL DISTRIBUTION | |
| starttime | 15:06:22 | random1 | 0.386591 | h(1) | h(2) |
| stoptime | 15:07:44 | random2 | 0.571726 | -6.84986 | 6.891464 |
| elapsed | 00:01:22 | S(1) | 0.476323 | N( )  3.7E-12 | 1 |
| | | S(2) | 1.764678 | | |
| | | X(1) | 0.682209 | q  0.386590 | 0.385155 |
| | | X(2) | 1.008913 | h(x)  2.6E-11 | 1.9E-11 |
| | | maxrun | 26 | | |
| | | | | p | 0.231641 |
| | | mean | 0.2 | b(0) | 0.319381 |
| | | sigma | 0.3 | b(1) | -0.35656 |
| | | deltat | 0.019230 | b(2) | 1.781477 |
| | | initial price | 56 | b(3) | -1.82125 |
| | | riskfree | 0.08 | b(4) | 1.330274 |
| | | tau | 0 | | |
| | | K | 50 | | |
| | | initial wealth | 1000 | | |

Data are recorded in a range called DATA, which has five columns:

| period | stock | value of previous risky | portfolio value | risky propor. |
|---|---|---|---|---|

The first column records the dates. The second column gives the simulated stock price at each date. The third column gives the value, at the start of the current period, of the amount of money invested in the stock in the previous period. The fourth column records the total value of the portfolio (risk-free assets and stock) at the start of the current period. The last column records the proportion of the portfolio invested in the risky asset at the end of the current period.

The first macro, \A, sets up the variables.

```
\A              starting
{let starttime,@now}{blank stoptime}{blank elapsed}
{blank data}{let deltat,1/(2*maxrun)}{let tau,1}{windowsoff}{paneloff}
{put data,0,0,0}{put data,1,0,initial price}
{let h(1),(@ln(@index(data,1,0)*@exp(riskfree*tau)/K)/(sigma*@sqrt(tau))+sigma*@sqrt(tau)/2)}
{let h(2),sigma*@sqrt(tau)-h(1)}
{calc}
{put data,4,0,@index(data,1,0)*N(h(1))/
       (@index(data,1,0)*N(h(1))+K*@exp(-riskfree*tau)*N(h(2)))}
{put data,3,0,initial wealth}
{branch \B}
```

The variable $h(1)$ is what we have been calling $-h$, and the variable $h(2)$ is equal to $\sigma\sqrt{\tau} - h$. At the {calc} command, the spreadsheet calculates the values of the normal distribution needed to calculate the portfolio proportions. The {put} commands insert the appropriate numbers into the table. After \A, the table looks like this:

| period | stock | value of previous risky | portfolio value | risky propor. |
|--------|-------|-------------------------|-----------------|---------------|
| 0      | 56    |                         | 1000            | 0.754401      |

The third column is empty, because there is no previous period yet. Note that this is the same result we got in section 16.2.

Macro \B runs the loop, and macro \C is the same macro we used in chapter 14 to simulate the normal distribution:

```
\B              loop
{for runnumber,1,maxrun,1,\C}

\C              creating two normal deviates
{let random1,2*@rand-1}{let random2,2*@rand-1}
{let S(1),random1^2+random2^2}
{if S(1)>=1}{branch \C}
{if S(1)<1}{let S(2),@sqrt(-2*@ln(S(1))/S(1))}
{let X(1),random1*S(2)}{let X(2),random2*S(2)}
{branch \D}
```

Macro \D records most of the results. It is essentially the same as lines 3–8 of \A. Because each run gives two normal deviates, we have to repeat all the lines twice. And because we do not want to calculate the proportion of assets invested in the risky asset at the end of time 1 (i.e., when $\tau = 0$), \D ends with a branch which depends on whether we are at $t < 1$ (in which case we go to \E) or we have finished (in which case we go to \F).

```
\D              recording the results
{put data,0,2*runnumber-1,2*runnumber-1}
{put data,1,2*runnumber-1,
        @index(data,1,2*runnumber-2)*@exp(mean*deltat+sigma*X(1)*@sqrt(deltat))}
{put data,2,2*runnumber-1,@index(data,4,2*runnumber-2)*
        @index(data,3,2*runnumber-2)*@exp(mean*deltat+sigma*X(1)*@sqrt(deltat))}
{put data,3,2*runnumber-1,@index(data,2,2*runnumber-1)+
        (1-@index(data,4,2*runnumber-2))*@index(data,3,2*runnumber-2)*@exp(riskfree*deltat)}
{let tau,1-(2*runnumber-1)/(2*maxrun)}
{let h(1),(@ln(@index(data,1,
        2*runnumber-1)*@exp(riskfree*tau)/K)/(sigma*@sqrt(tau))+sigma*@sqrt(tau)/2)}
{let h(2),sigma*@sqrt(tau)-h(1)}
{calc}
{put data,4,2*runnumber-1,@index(data,1,2*runnumber-1)*N(h(1))/
        (@index(data,1,2*runnumber-1)*N(h(1))+K*@exp(-riskfree*tau)*N(h(2)))}
{put data,0,2*runnumber,2*runnumber}
{put data,1,
        2*runnumber,@index(data,1,2*runnumber-1)*@exp(mean*deltat+sigma*X(2)*@sqrt(deltat))}
{put data,2,2*runnumber,@index(data,4,2*runnumber-1)*
        @index(data,3,2*runnumber-1)*@exp(mean*deltat+sigma*X(2)*@sqrt(deltat))}
{put data,3,2*runnumber,@index(data,2,2*runnumber)+
        (1-@index(data,4,2*runnumber-1))*@index(data,3,2*runnumber-1)*@exp(riskfree*deltat)}
{let tau,1-runnumber/maxrun}
{if tau>0}{branch \E}
{branch \F}




\E              recording proportion for tau>0 (i.e. t<1)
{let h(1),(@ln(@index(data,1,2*runnumber)*@exp(riskfree*tau)/K)
        /(sigma*@sqrt(tau))+sigma*@sqrt(tau)/2)}
{let h(2),sigma*@sqrt(tau)-h(1)}
{calc}
{put data,4,2*runnumber,@index(data,1,2*runnumber)*N(h(1))
        /(@index(data,1,2*runnumber)*N(h(1))+K*@exp(-riskfree*tau)*N(h(2)))}




\F              ending
{let stoptime,@now}{let elapsed,stoptime-starttime}
{calc}{quit}
```

One year's simulation, with weekly revisions, generates data that look like the following:

| period | stock | value of previous risky | portfolio value | risky propor. |
|--------|-------|-------------------------|-----------------|---------------|
| 0 | 56 | | 1000 | 0.754401 |
| 1 | 58.60046 | 789.5383 | 1035.414 | 0.802773 |
| 2 | 58.97971 | 836.5823 | 1041.108 | 0.809784 |
| 3 | 58.86261 | 841.3997 | 1039.739 | 0.808551 |
| 4 | 56.64903 | 809.0685 | 1008.431 | 0.768702 |
| 5 | 58.84598 | 805.2467 | 1038.853 | 0.809813 |
| 6 | 58.46183 | 835.7857 | 1033.665 | 0.803939 |
| 7 | 59.78782 | 849.8532 | 1052.826 | 0.827287 |
| 8 | 59.04736 | 860.2029 | 1042.318 | 0.815942 |
| etc. | | | | |

For this particular run, investing in portfolio insurance paid off, as figure 16.1 shows.

## 16.5  Insuring Total Portfolio Returns

So far we have considered only the problem of constructing artificial puts, one per share. A slightly different version of this problem involves constructing a portfolio of puts and shares that guarantees the *total* dollar returns on the *total* initial investment. A typical story goes like this:

You have $100, and you want to guarantee than a year from now you will have at least $100 \times Z$. You want to invest in a risky asset (a stock, whose current price is $S_0$) and in a put on the stock with exercise price $K$. You want the number of puts be equal to the number of shares. Every $K$ gives a put price $P_0(S_0, K)$ and therefore means that you buy $\alpha$ shares, where

$$\alpha = \$100/[S_0 + P_0(S_0, K)].$$

Since you have bought $\alpha$ shares, the minimum dollar return from your portfolio is $\alpha K$. You want this to be equal to $100Z$, and therefore you solve to get $\alpha = 100Z/K$. Thus, you can guarantee your minimum return if

$$S_0 + P_0(S_0, K) = K/Z.$$

This equality corresponds to

$$S_0 N(h) + K e^{-r} N(\sigma - h) = K/Z,$$

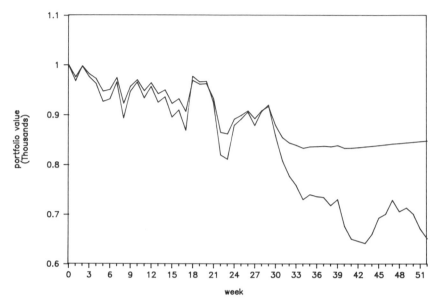

**Figure 16.1**
Insured (upper line) versus uninsured portfolio.

where

$$h = \ln(S_0 e^r/K)/\sigma + 0.5\sigma).$$

Dividing through by $K$ gives

$$S_0/K \, N(h) + e^{-r}N(\sigma - h) = 1/Z.$$

The first thing we can establish about the preceding equation is that its graph looks like figure 16.2.

Next, it is easily seen that there is no solution to the equation unless $Z < e^r$. The economic meaning of this is that you cannot use a strategy of buying both shares and puts and still guarantee yourself the riskless rate of return. If you want the riskless rate of return, you should invest all your wealth in a riskless asset, and forego the upside return you hope for in an insured-portfolio strategy. (There is no free lunch!)

To see that a feasible $Z$ must be $< e^r$, note that as $K \to \infty$

$$S_0/K \, N(h) + e^{-r}N(\sigma - h) \to e^{-r}.$$

To complete the proof, note that, for every $K < \infty$,

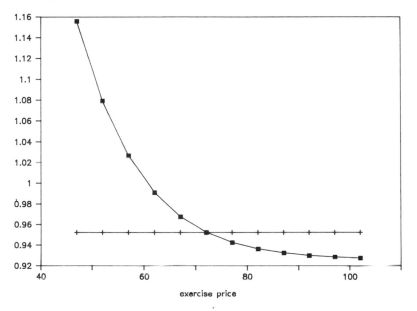

**Figure 16.2**
Insuring total portfolio returns. (■): $(1/E)[S(O) + \text{Put}]$; (+): $1/Z$. Here, $Z = 1.05$.

$$S_0/K \, N(h) + e^{-r}N(\sigma - h) > e^{-r}.$$

To actually calculate $K$ we need to solve

$$S_0/K \, N(h) + e^{-r}N(\sigma - h) = 1/Z$$

for $K$. This equation is not readily solvable analytically, but it can easily be solved by a simple macro, which will be given below.

The idea behind the macro is explained by the following steps:

1. $S(0)$, $r$, $\sigma$, and $Z$ are given.

2. Find a $K$ (called LOW K) for which

$$S_0/K \, N(h) + e^{-r}N(\sigma - h) > 1/Z.$$

3. Find another $K$ (HIGH K) for which

$$S_0/K \, N(h) + e^{-r}N(\sigma - h) < 1/Z.$$

4. Let $K$ equal the average of LOW K and HIGH K, and calculate

$$S_0/K \, N(h) + e^{-r}N(\sigma - h).$$

If this expression (called PORT in the macro) is $< 1/Z$, replace the current value of HIGH K with $K$. If this expression is $> 1/Z$, replace the current value of LOW K with $K$.

5. Repeat step 4 until some desired degree of accuracy is reached.

The shape of the curve (see figure 16.2) guarantees that the procedure will converge.

Here is the macro, with some additional notes where necessary:

CALCULATING THE OPTIMAL K FOR TOTAL PORTFOLIO INSURANCE

|  |  |  |  |  |  |  |
|---|---|---|---|---|---|---|
|  |  |  | NORMAL DISTRIBUTION |  |  |  |
| S(0) | 56 |  | h(1) | h(2) | starttime | 18:15:41 |
| K | 58.5481872 |  | 0.268338539 | 0.031661460 | stoptime | 18:16:32 |
| r | 0.08 |  | N(h(1)) | N(h(2)) | elapsed | 00:00:51 |
| sigma | 0.3 |  | 0.605780570 | 0.512629040 |  |  |
| port | 1.05263148 |  |  |  |  |  |
| low K | 58.5476074 | q | 0.941479118 | 0.992719276 |  |  |
| high K | 58.5481872 | h(x) | 0.384834726 | 0.398742371 |  |  |
| low port | 7 |  |  |  |  |  |
| high port | 0.92996417 | p | 0.2316419 |  |  |  |
| epsilon | 0.0000001 | b(0) | 0.31938153 |  |  |  |
|  |  | b(1) | -0.35656378 |  |  |  |
| z | 0.95 | b(2) | 1.781477937 |  |  |  |
| 1/z | 1.05263157 | b(3) | -1.82125597 |  |  |  |
|  |  | b(4) | 1.330274429 |  |  |  |

\A puts in two arbitrary values for LOW K and HIGH K. If LOW K isn't low enough, \B halves it repeatedly until

$$S_0/K \, N(h) + e^{-r} N(\sigma - h) > 1/Z.$$

If HIGH K isn't low enough, \C doubles it repeatedly until a satisfactory value is reached.

```
\A
{windowsoff}{paneloff}{let low K,8}~
{let high K,20}~
{let starttime,@now}{branch \B}~
```

```
\B          checking to make sure that low K is low enough
{let h(1),aln(S(0)*aexp(r)/LOW K)/sigma+0.5*sigma}~
{let h(2),sigma-h(1)}~
{let LOW PORT,S(0)/LOW K*N(h(1))+aexp(-r)*N(h(2))}~
{IF LOW PORT<1/Z}{LET LOW K,LOW K/2}{BRANCH \B}~
{BRANCH \C}~
```

```
\C          checking to make sure that high K is high enough
{LET h(1),aln(S(0)*aexp(r)/high K)/sigma+0.5*sigma}~
{LET H(2),sigma-h(1)}~
{LET HIGH PORT,S(0)/low K*N(h(1))+aexp(-r)*N(h(2))}~
{IF HIGH PORT>1/Z}{LET HIGH K,2*HIGH K}~{BRANCH \C}~
{BRANCH \D}~
```

\D takes the average value of LOW K and HIGH K and does step 5 above. The macro stops (recording the stopping time and calculating elapsed time for the calculation) when

$$|S_0/K\,\mathrm{N}(h) + e^{-r}\mathrm{N}(\sigma - h) - 1/Z| < \varepsilon,$$

where $\varepsilon$ is the desired degree of accuracy.

```
\D          the algorithm
{LET K,(HIGH K+LOW K)/2}~
{LET h(1),aln(S(0)*aexp(r)/K)/sigma+0.5*sigma}~
{LET H(2),sigma-h(1)}~
{LET PORT,S(0)/K*N(h(1))+aexp(-r)*N(h(2))}~
{IF PORT>1/Z}{LET LOW K,K}~
{IF PORT<1/Z}{LET HIGH K,K}~
{IF aABS(PORT-1/Z)<EPSILON}~{let stoptime,anow}{let elapsed,stoptime-starttime}{QUIT}~
{BRANCH \D}~
```

## 16.6   Transaction Costs

Thus far we have ignored transaction costs. To model these costs well, you have to know their exact structure, and this can vary from investor to investor. In this section we shall model the simplest kind of transaction costs, leaving a slightly more complicated case for the exercises.

Consider only a percentage transactions cost on purchases of stock. (Buying and selling riskless assets involve no costs.) Suppose your desired percentage invested by the risky asset is $y$. Obviously, transaction costs mean that you have to purchase a different percentage, $x$. What is the relation between $x$ and $y$?

Denote the transaction costs by $\gamma$. Then if your initial wealth is $W_0 = 1$ and you order $x_0$ percent stock and $(1 - x_0)$ percent risk-free asset, your wealth *immediately after your order* will be

$$x_0(1 - \gamma) + (1 - x_0) = 1 - \gamma x_0.$$

Thus, your transaction cost is $\gamma x_0$. If your intention is that the percentage of your wealth invested in the risky asset should be $y_0$, you want

$$y_0 = \frac{x_0(1 - \gamma)}{1 - \gamma x_0},$$

which solves to give

$$x_0 = y_0/(1 - \gamma + \gamma y_0).$$

Now suppose that the risky asset grows by a factor of $\beta_0$ over the next time period, and that the riskless asset grows by a factor of $e^{r\Delta t}$. Then your initial wealth at the start of the next period will be

$$(1 - \gamma x_0)[y_0\beta_0 + (1 - y_0)e^{r\Delta t}] = W_1.$$

Given this initial wealth and the stock price, you decide you want to have proportion $y_1$ invested in the risky asset. Considering that you have to pay transaction costs on sales or purchases of the stock, how much should you say you want to have invested? Denote this proportion by $x_1$. Having ordered this new proportion, you have to pay the transaction cost on the difference between $x_1$ and the current proportion of the risky asset in your portfolio:

$$\left| \frac{y_0\beta_0}{W_1} - x_1 \right| \equiv \delta_1.$$

Having paid the transaction cost $\delta_1\gamma$, you will be left with wealth $W_1(1 - \delta_1\gamma)$. Thus, the problem is to find a value of $x_1$ that solves

$$\frac{(x_1 - \delta_1\gamma)W_1}{W_1(1 - \gamma\delta_1)} = y_1.$$

This has two solutions. If $y_0\beta_0/W_1 > x_1$, then

$$x_1 = \frac{y_1}{1 + \gamma(1 - y_1)}\left(1 - \frac{y_0\beta_0}{W_1}\right);$$

if $y_0\beta_0/W_1 < x_1$, then

$$x_1 = \frac{y_1}{1 + \gamma(1 - y_1)}\left(1 + \frac{y_0\beta_0}{W_1}\right).$$

## 16.7 Implicit Puts and Asset Values

Up to this point in the chapter, we have been discussing the construction of puts in order to construct portfolio insurance. We will now reverse the logic and consider situations in which one is offered a package that includes an implicit put. The problem is how to deduce the true value of the underlying asset that is part of the package.

Many commonly encountered situations include implicit puts. Consider the situation in which you are offered an asset plus an option to have the seller repurchase the asset. Some examples that come to mind are irrevocable tender offers, "satisfaction guaranteed or your money back" offers, and computer sales where you get to return the item but have to pay a 15 percent "restocking charge." (See Bhagat, Brickley, and Loewenstein 1987 for an application of these ideas to cash tender offers.)

Were you in possession of the asset's variance, you could deduce from the offer the true value of the asset. Without this information, you can deduce the locus of the asset's standard deviation and its true value. To do this, let $V_a$ denote the true value of the asset (stripped of any puts or repurchase offers). Let $V_p$ denote the value of the put. Let $Y$ denote the purchase price (which, of course, includes the put), and let $K$ denote the price at which you can get your money back. Then it follows that

$$Y = V_a + V_p.$$

If we assume that the put option can be priced by the Black-Scholes formula, we will have

$$V_p = -V_a N(-h) + Ke^{-r\tau}N(\sigma\sqrt{\tau} - h),$$

where

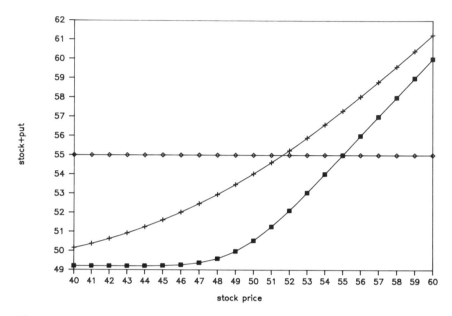

**Figure 16.3**
Implicit puts and asset prices. (■): Low $\sigma$; (+): high $\sigma$; ($\Diamond$): Y.

$$h = \frac{\ln(V_a/Ke^{-rt})}{\sigma\sqrt{\tau}} + 0.5\sigma\sqrt{\tau}.$$

Thus, to solve this problem we must find a $\sigma$ and $V_a$ that simultaneously solve

$$Y = V_a(1 - N(-h)) + Ke^{-rt}N(\sigma\sqrt{\tau} - h)$$
$$= V_aN(h) + Ke^{-rt}N(\sigma\sqrt{\tau} - h).$$

The right-hand side of the preceding equation is increasing in $\sigma$. A graphical representation of the solution is given in figure 16.3. Finding a numerical solution is left to you as an exercise.

## Exercises

1. One of the problems with portfolio insurance is the risk of missing your target because of finite revision intervals. To get a feeling for this problem, set up the macro of section 16.4 and run it repeatedly using

RUNNUMBER = 12 (this corresponds to 24 portfolio revisions a year). Note how many times you miss your target (i.e., for how many runs the final portfolio value is less than your desired wealth).

It follows from the discussion of section 16.2 that the portfolio-insurance strategy for the stock with an initial price of $56 and with $K = $50$ where $\sigma = 0.3$ is like buying 17.13 shares. Thus, the reasonable way to define your target is to say that it is $17.13 \times \$50 = \$856.50$.

2. Set up a macro to do exercise 1 for you, using the Lotus FOR statement.

3. Implement section 16.6 in your portfolio-insurance spreadsheet.

4. Consider a transaction-cost structure in which each purchase or sale of stock involves a fixed cost $C$ and a percentage cost $\gamma$. Redo section 16.6 and implement it in a spreadsheet.

5. You have been offered the chance to purchase stock in a firm. The seller wants $55 per share but offers to repurchase the stock at the end of 60 days for $52 per share. If the $\sigma$ of the share's log returns is 30 percent, what is the true value per share? Assume that the interest rate is 12 percent.

## References

Benninga, S., and M. Blume. 1985. "On the Optimality of Portfolio Insurance." *Journal of Finance* 40 (December): 1341–1352.

Bhagat, S., J. A. Brickley, and U. Loewenstein. 1987. "The Pricing Effects of Interfirm Cash Tender Offers." *Journal of Finance* 42 (September): 965–986.

Billingsley, P. 1968. *Convergence of Probability Measures.* New York: Wiley.

Brennan, M. J., and E. S. Schwartz. 1976. "The Pricing of Equity-Linked Life Insurance Policies with an Asset Value Guarantee." *Journal of Financial Economics* 3 (June): 195–213.

Brennan, M. J., and E. S. Schwartz. 1979. "Alternative Investment Strategies for the Issuers of Equity-Linked Life Insurance Policies with an Asset Value Guarantee." *Journal of Business* 52 (January): 63–93.

Brennan, M. J., and R. Solanki. 1981. "Optimal Portfolio Insurance." *Journal of Financial and Quantitative Analysis* 16 (September): 279–300.

Gatto, M. A., R. Geske, R. Litzenberger, and H. Sosin. 1980. "Mutual Fund Insurance." *Journal of Financial Economics* 8 (September): 283–317.

Jacobs, B. 1983. "The Portfolio Insurance Puzzle." *Pensions and Investment Age* (August 22): 26.

Jacques, W. E. 1987. "Portfolio Insurance or Job Insurance?" *Financial Analysts Journal* (January–February): 7.

Jarrow, R. A., and A. Rudd. 1983. *Option Pricing.* Homewood, Ill.: Irwin.

Leland, H. E. 1985. "Option Pricing and Replication with Transaction Costs." *Journal of Finance* 40 (December): 1283–1301.

Leland, H. E. 1980. "Who Should Buy Portfolio Insurance?" *Journal of Finance* 35 (May): 581–594.

Pozen, R. C. 1978. "When to Purchase a Protective Put." *Financial Analysts Journal* (July–August): 47–60.

Rubinstein, M. 1985. "Alternative Paths to Portfolio Insurance." *Financial Analysts Journal* (July–August): 42–52.

Rubinstein, M., and H. E. Leland. 1981. "Replicating Options with Positions in Stock and Cash." *Financial Analysts Journal* (July–August): 3–12.

Schwartz, E. S. 1986–87. "Options and Portfolio Insurance." *Finanzmarkt und Portfolio Management* 1: 9–17.

Somes, S. P., and M. A. Zurack. 1987. "Pension Plans, Portfolio Insurance and FASB Statement No. 87: An Old Risk in a New Light." *Financial Analysts Journal* (January–February): 10–13.

# IV DURATION AND IMMUNIZATION

# Overview

These two chapters survey some of the theory and the numerical applications relating to duration and immunization strategies.

Duration, a measure of the sensitivity of a bond's price to changes in interest rates, is widely used in the management of bond portfolios. Chapter 17 covers some of the concepts of the classical duration theory, concentrating on the calculational problems. Not surprisingly, a spreadsheet can simplify duration calculations tremendously.

Chapter 18 discusses immunization strategies. An immunization strategy is "one in which a portfolio of ... bonds is managed so that its value is always as close as possible to the value of another asset" (Nelson and Schaefer 1983; see references at end of chapter 18). This topic is a natural outgrowth of the duration concept.

# 17 Duration

## 17.1 Introduction

Duration is a measure of the sensitivity of the price of a bond to changes in the interest rate at which the bond is discounted.

Consider a bond with payments of $C(t)$, where $t = 1, \ldots, N$. Ordinarily, the first $N - 1$ of the payments will be interest payments, and $C(N)$ will be the sum of the repayment of principal and the last interest payment.

Now consider the net present value of the weighted average of the bond payments:

| Time | Payment | Time × Payment | NPV |
|------|---------|----------------|-----|
| 1 | $C(1)$ | $C(1)$ | $C(1)/(1 + r)$ |
| 2 | $C(2)$ | $2\,C(2)$ | $2\,C(2)/(1 + r)^2$ |
| 3 | $C(3)$ | $3\,C(3)$ | $3\,C(3)/(1 + r)^3$ |
| ⋮ | ⋮ | ⋮ | ⋮ |
| $N$ | $C(N)$ | $N\,C(N)$ | $N\,C(N)/(1 + r)^N$ |

The time-weighted average of the bond payments is

$$\sum_{t=1}^{N} \frac{t\,C(t)}{(1 + r)^t}.$$

The *duration* is defined as the time-weighted average of the bond payments, as a percentage of the bond price:

$$D = \frac{1}{P} \sum_{t=1}^{N} \frac{t\,C(t)}{(1 + r)^t}.$$

## 17.2 Two Examples

Consider two bonds. Bond A has just been issued. Its face value is $1,000, it bears the current market interest rate of 7 percent, and it will mature in 10 years. Bond B was issued 5 years ago, when interest rates were high. This bond has a $1,000 face value and bears a 13 percent coupon rate. When issued, this bond had a 15-year maturity, so its remaining maturity is 10 years. Since the current market rate of interest is 7 percent, Bond B's market price is given by

$$\$1,421.41 = \sum_{t=1}^{10} \frac{\$130}{(1.07)^t} + \frac{\$1,000}{(1.07)^{10}}.$$

To calculate the duration of each bond, we set up a table:

| year | C(t,A) | $\dfrac{tC(t,A)}{1000*(1.07)^t}$ | C(t,B) | $\dfrac{tC(t,B)}{1421*(1.07)^t}$ |
|------|--------|--------------------------------|--------|--------------------------------|
| 1 | 70 | 0.06542 | 130 | 0.08548 |
| 2 | 70 | 0.12228 | 130 | 0.15977 |
| 3 | 70 | 0.17142 | 130 | 0.22397 |
| 4 | 70 | 0.21361 | 130 | 0.27909 |
| 5 | 70 | 0.24955 | 130 | 0.32604 |
| 6 | 70 | 0.27986 | 130 | 0.36566 |
| 7 | 70 | 0.30515 | 130 | 0.39869 |
| 8 | 70 | 0.32593 | 130 | 0.42584 |
| 9 | 70 | 0.34268 | 130 | 0.44773 |
| 10 | 1070 | 5.43934 | 1130 | 4.04130 |
| duration | | 7.51523 | | 6.75356 |

As might be expected, the duration of Bond A is longer than that of Bond B, since the average payoff of Bond A takes longer than that of Bond B. To look at this another way, the net present value of Bond A's first-year payoff ($70) represents 6.54 percent of the bond's price, whereas the net present value of Bond B's first-year payoff ($130) is 8.55 percent of its price. The figures for the second-year payoffs are 12.23 percent and 15.98 percent, respectively. (For the second-year figures you have to divide the appropriate line of the preceding table by 2, since in the duration formula each payoff is weighted by the period in which it is received.)

## 17.3   Using Duration to Measure Price Volatility

To see how duration may be used to measure price volatility, write the *current market price* of the bond as

$$P = \sum_{t=1}^{N} \frac{C(t)}{(1 + r)^t},$$

where $r$ is the current market interest rate. The *change in the price of the bond* due to a change in the interest rate is given by

$$\frac{dP}{dr} = \sum_{t=1}^{N} \frac{-t\,C(t)}{(1 + r)^{t-1}}.$$

This can be written as

$$\frac{dP}{dr} = \frac{-DP}{1 + r},$$

which transforms into two useful interpretations of duration: First, duration can be regarded as the *discount-rate elasticity of the bond price*:

$$\frac{dP/P}{dr/(1 + r)} = -D.$$

Second, duration can be used to measure the *price volatility* of the bond, as can be seen from the following transformation of the previous equation:

$$\frac{dP}{P} = -D\frac{dr}{1 + r}.$$

Let us go back to the examples of the previous section. Suppose that the market interest rate rises by 10 percent, from 7 percent to 7.7 percent. What will happen to the bond prices? The price of Bond A will be

$$\$952.39 = \sum_{t=1}^{10} \frac{\$70}{(1.077)^t} + \frac{\$1,000}{(1.077)^{10}}.$$

A similar calculation shows the price of Bond B to be

$$\$1,360.50 = \sum_{t=1}^{10} \frac{\$130}{(1.077)^t} + \frac{\$1,000}{(1.077)^{10}}.$$

As predicted by the price-volatility formula, the changes in the bond prices are approximated by

$$\Delta P \simeq -DP\Delta r.$$

To see this, work out the numbers for each bond:

| Bond | $\Delta P$ | $D$ | $P$ | $\Delta r$ | $-DP\Delta r$ |
|------|--------|------|-------|--------|----------|
| A    | −47.61 | 7.52 | 1,000 | 0.007  | −52.64   |
| B    | −60.91 | 6.75 | 1,421 | 0.007  | −67.14   |

## 17.4   Closed-Form Formulas for Duration

### Chua's Derivation

The duration formula requires a lot of tedious calculation. For the special case in which we are calculating the duration of a bond with unchanging coupon payments over time, Chua (1984) and Babcock (1985) have derived closed-form formulas. These formulas save a lot of time, and they also provide useful insights into the nature of duration.

Let us first derive Chua's formula. Consider a bond with $N$ periods remaining until maturity. Suppose that at each $n$, where $n = 1, \ldots, N$, the bond pays a coupon payment of $I$, and that at $n = N$ (the final period) the bond pays, in addition to this coupon payment, a payment of $F$ (the return of the face value of the bond). If the current market price of the bond is $P$, then the *yield to maturity* of the bond, $r$, is given by the internal rate of return on the bond at its current price:

$$P = \sum_{t=1}^{N} \frac{C}{(1 + r)^t} + \frac{F}{(1 + r)^N}.$$

The duration formula is given by

$$D = \frac{1}{P} \sum_{t=1}^{N} \frac{tC}{(1 + r)^t} + \frac{NF}{(1 + r)^N}.$$

If we write

$$\sum_{t=1}^{N} \frac{t}{(1 + r)^t} = X,$$

we can rewrite the duration formula as

$$D = \frac{CX + NF/(1 + r)^N}{P}.$$

Now we start to do some computational gymnastics:

$$\frac{X}{1+r} - X = -\frac{1}{1+r} + \frac{1}{(1+r)^2} - \frac{2}{(1+r)^2} + \frac{2}{(1+r)^3} - \frac{3}{(1+r)^3} + \cdots$$

$$+ \frac{N-1}{(1+r)^N} - \frac{N}{(1+r)^N} + \frac{N}{(1+r)^{N+1}}$$

$$= -\frac{1}{1+r} - \frac{1}{(1+r)^2} - \frac{1}{(1+r)^3} + \cdots$$

$$- \frac{1}{(1+r)^N} + \frac{N}{(1+r)^{N+1}}.$$

Next we write

$$\sum_{t=1}^{N} \frac{1}{(1+r)^t} = \text{PVIF}(r, N),$$

where $\text{PVIF}(r, N)$ is the present-value interest factor of an $N$-period annuity of \$1 per period, discounted at interest rate $r$. (It can be calculated with the Lotus formula @PV(1, $r$, $N$).) Thus, it follows that

$$\text{PVIF}(r, N) + \frac{X}{1+r} - X = \frac{N}{(1+r)^{N+1}}.$$

Now, it is well known (see, for example, Brealey and Myers 1984, p. 31) that

$$\text{PVIF}(r, N) = \frac{(1+r)^N - 1}{r(1+r)^N}.$$

Thus, we can write

$$X = \left( \text{PVIF}(r, N) - \frac{N}{(1+r)^{N+1}} \right) \frac{1+r}{r}.$$

Substituting in the value for $\text{PVIF}(r, N)$ and doing a bit of manipulation gives

$$X = \frac{(1+r)^{N+1} - (1+r) - rN}{r^2(1+r)^N}.$$

This gives Chua's *closed-form solution for the duration calculation*:

$$D = \frac{1}{P} \left( \frac{C[(1+r)^{N+1} - (1+r) - rN]}{r^2(1+r)^N} + \frac{NF}{(1+r)^N} \right).$$

**Babcock's Formula**

Rewrite Chua's formula as

$$D = \frac{1}{P}\left(\frac{C[(1+r)^{N+1} - (1+r)]}{r^2(1+r)^N}\right) + \frac{N}{P}\left(\frac{F}{(1+r)^N} - \frac{C}{r(1+r)^N}\right).$$

The first term of this expression can be rewritten as

$$\frac{1}{P}\left(\frac{C[(1+r)^{N+1} - (1+r)]}{r^2(1+r)^N}\right) = \frac{\text{PVIF}(r, N)(1+r)C/P}{r}$$

$$= \frac{\text{PVIF}(r, N)(1+r)y}{r},$$

where $y \equiv C/P$ (this is usually called the "current yield" of the bond).
The second term can be simplified as follows:

$$\frac{N}{P}\left(\frac{F}{(1+r)^N} - \frac{1}{r(1+r)^N}\right) = \frac{N}{P}\left(P - \sum_{1}^{N}\frac{C}{(1+r)^t} - \frac{C}{r(1+r)^N}\right)$$

$$= \frac{N}{P}\left(P - \frac{C[(1+r)^N - 1]}{r(1+r)^N} - \frac{C}{r(1+r)^N}\right),$$

$$= N\{1 - y/r\}.$$

Thus we arrive at Babcock's expression for duration:

$$D = N(1 - y/r) + (y/r)\text{PVIF}(r, N)(1+r).$$

Babcock's expression gives us two useful insights into the standard duration measure:

• Duration is a weighted average of the maturity of the bond and of $(1 + r)$ times the PVIF associated with the bond.

• In many cases the current yield of the bond, $y$, is not greatly different from its yield to maturity, $r$. In these cases, duration is not very different from $(1 + r)$PVIF.

## 17.5  Duration and the Yield to Maturity

We an use Chua's formula to calculate the effect of changes in the yield to maturity (YTM) on duration. Consider the following example: A bond

with a maturity of 10 years and an annual coupon payment of 155 currently
has a YTM of 7 percent. This gives a bond price of $1,597 and a duration of
6.55. What is the effect of a change in the YTM on the bond's duration?

To calculate this, we set up a spreadsheet that calculates Chua's formula:

```
bondprice   1597.004
YTM             0.07
maturity          10
coupon           155
facevalue       1000


duration    6.554808


firstterm   34.73913
secndterm   5083.492
```

The formulas in the cells are the following (FIRSTTERM and
SECNDTERM refer to the terms in Chua's formula):

```
bondprice = @PV(COUPON,YTM,MATURITY)+FACEVALUE/(1+YTM)^MATURITY
duration  = (1/BONDPRICE)*(COUPON*FIRSTTERM+SECNDTERM)
firstterm = ((1+YTM)^(MATURITY+1)-(1+YTM)-YTM*MATURITY)/(YTM^2*(1+YTM)^MATURITY)
secndterm = +MATURITY*FACEVALUE/(1+YTM)^MATURITY
```

Now, add to this spreadsheet a column of interest rates and a column in
which we calculate the duration. Use /Data Table 1 to do the calculations
(see chapter 25). The final result looks like this:

```
                    Duration and the YTM
                    uses Chua's formula and /Data Table 1


bondprice  1597.004        ytm              <-- this cell (hidden here with /RFH) contains
YTM            0.07        0.005 7.215350        the formula "+duration"
maturity        10         0.01  7.165711
coupon         155         0.015 7.115808
facevalue     1000         0.02  7.065659
                           0.025 7.015282
duration   6.554808        0.03  6.964697
                           0.035 6.913922
firstterm  34.73913        0.04  6.862977
secndterm  5083.492        0.045 6.811880
                                  etc.
```

## 17.6 Calculating the IRR for Uneven Periods

A problem often encountered when dealing with duration is calculating the yield to maturity of a bond when the payments are not evenly spaced. This section gives a simple example of this problem and shows how a small trick can solve it.

Consider a bond that currently costs $100 and pays $5 in interest in 0.6 year, 1.6 years, 2.6 years, and 3.6 years. In 4.6 years the holder of the bond gets $105. What is the YTM of the bond? We are looking for an interest rate $r$ that solves

$$-100 + \sum_{t=0}^{3} \frac{5}{(1+r)^{t+0.6}} + \frac{105}{(1+r)^{4.6}} = 0.$$

It is difficult to solve this problem, as it stands, with Lotus. To solve the problem, divide through by $(1+r)^{0.4}$. This gives

$$0 = \frac{-100}{(1+r)^{0.4}} + \sum_{t=1}^{4} \frac{5}{(1+r)^{t}} + \frac{105}{(1+r)^{5}},$$

which is easily solved by Lotus provided we use a bit of trickery. Write the following spreadsheet:

```
time       0.6 <-- this is the time to the first payment

                        adjusted
         "period" cashflow cashflow
            0      -100      -100 <-- this cell contains the formula +COST/(1+IRR)^(1-TIME)
            1       5         5
            2       5         5
            3       5         5
            4       5         5
            5      105       105

         irr        0  cell formula:  @IF(MARKER<>0,0,@IRR(0,ADJ.CASHFLOW))
         marker     9
```

We need "marker" to start the iterations, and to make sure that we don't get caught in a loop of ERR's. When "marker" is not zero, the spreadsheet looks as it does above. However, when we put "marker" equal to zero, the spreadsheet starts to iterate. After the first iteration it looks as follows:

```
time      0.6
```

|        | "time" | cashflow | adjusted cashflow |
|--------|--------|----------|-------------------|
|        | 0      | -100     | -100              |
|        | 1      | 5        | 5                 |
|        | 2      | 5        | 5                 |
|        | 3      | 5        | 5                 |
|        | 4      | 5        | 5                 |
|        | 5      | 105      | 105               |
| irr    |        | 0.05     |                   |
| marker |        | 0        |                   |

From now on, each press of the F9 (CALC) key will produce an iteration of the spreadsheet. The next press on F9 will produce

```
time      0.6
```

|        | "time" | cashflow | adjusted cashflow |
|--------|--------|----------|-------------------|
|        | 0      | -100     | -98.0673          |
|        | 1      | 5        | 5                 |
|        | 2      | 5        | 5                 |
|        | 3      | 5        | 5                 |
|        | 4      | 5        | 5                 |
|        | 5      | 105      | 105               |
| irr    | 0.054519 |        |                   |
| marker |        | 0        |                   |

Hit F9 a few more times until the numbers on the screen stop changing, and you will get the answer:

time       0.6

|         | adjusted |          |
|---------|----------|----------|
| "time"  | cashflow | cashflow |
| 0       | -100     | -97.8827 |
| 1       | 5        | 5        |
| 2       | 5        | 5        |
| 3       | 5        | 5        |
| 4       | 5        | 5        |
| 5       | 105      | 105      |

|        |          |
|--------|----------|
| irr    | 0.054957 |
| marker | 0        |

## Exercises

1. What is the effect of *raising* the coupon payment on the duration of a bond? Assume that the bond's yield to maturity does not change. Use a numerical example and plot the answer.

2.
a. What is the effect on a bond's duration of increasing the bond's maturity? As in the previous example, use a numerical example and plot the answer. Note that as $N \to \infty$, the bond becomes a consol (a bond that has no repayment of principal but an infinite stream of coupon payments).
b. Analytically derive the duration of a consol.

3. "Duration can be viewed as a proxy for the riskiness of a bond. All other things being equal, the riskier of two bonds should have lower duration." Check this claim with an example. What is its economic logic?

4. A pure discount bond is a bond with only one payment of principal and interest at maturity. What is the duration of such a bond?

5. On January 23, 1987, the market price of a West Jefferson Development Bond was $1,122.32. The bond pays $59 in interest on March 1 and October 1 of each of the years 1987–1993. On October 1, 1993, the bond is redeemed at its face value of $1,000. Calculate the yield to maturity of the bond, then calculate its duration.

6. A sequence of bonds indexed by $i = 1, 2, 3, \ldots$ all have the same maturity, $N$, and the same yield to maturity, $r$, but each bond has a different coupon, $C_i$. Show (using Babcock's formula) that the duration of these bonds may be written as $D_i = N - KC_i$, where $K = N - (1 + r)$PVIF. Use Lotus to produce a graph of this curve for different values of $C_i$. (See Morrisey and Huang 1987.)

## References

Note: Some of the works listed at the end of chapter 18 are germane to chapter 17 as well.

Babcock, G. 1985. "Duration as a Weighted Average of Two Factors." *Financial Analysts Journal* (March–April): 75–76.

Brealey, R., and S. Myers. 1984. *Principles of Corporate Finance*. Second edition. New York: McGraw-Hill.

Chua, J. H. 1984. "A Closed-Form Formula for Calculating Bond Duration." *Financial Analysts Journal* (May–June): 76–78.

Morrissey, T. F., and C. Huang. 1987. "A Nomogram for Estimating Duration." *Financial Analysts Journal* (January–February): 65–67.

# 18 Immunization Strategies

## 18.1 Introduction

A bond portfolio's value in the future is subject to the interest-rate structure prevailing at the date at which the portfolio is liquidated. If a portfolio has the same payoff at some specified future date, no matter what interest-rate structure prevails at that date, then it is said to be *immunized*. This chapter discusses immunization strategies, which are an outgrowth of the portfolio's duration. Immunization strategies have been discussed for many concepts of duration, but this chapter is restricted to the simplest duration concept, that of Macauley.

## 18.2 Some Initial Formulas

Consider the following situation: A firm has a known future obligation $P$ (a good example would be an insurance firm, which knows that it has to make a payment in the future). The discounted value of this obligation is

$$V_0 = \frac{P}{(1 + r)^N},$$

where $r$ is the appropriate discount rate. The firm currently holds an asset, B, whose value, $V_B$, is equal to the discounted value of the future obligation, $V_0$. If $P_1, \ldots, P_M$ is the stream of anticipated payments made by asset B, then the net present value of the asset is given by

$$V_B = \sum_{t=1}^{M} \frac{P_t}{(1 + r)^t}.$$

Now suppose that the underlying interest rate, $r$, changes. Using a first-order linear approximation, we find that the new value of the future obligation is given by

$$V_0 + dV_0 = V_0 + \Delta r \left( \frac{-NP}{(1 + r)^{N+1}} \right).$$

On the other hand, the new value of the asset B is given by

$$V_B + dV_B = V_B + \Delta r \left( \sum_{1}^{M} \frac{-tP_t}{(1 + r)^{t+1}} \right).$$

If these two expressions are equal, a change in $r$ will not affect the hedging properties of the company's portfolio. Setting them equal gives us the condition

$$V_B + \Delta r \left( \sum_1^M \frac{-tP_t}{(1 + r)^{t+1}} \right) = V_0 + \Delta r \left( \frac{-NP}{(1 + r)^{N+1}} \right).$$

Recalling that

$$V_B = V_0 = \frac{P}{(1 + r)^N},$$

we can simplify this expression to get

$$\frac{1}{V_B} \sum_{t=1}^M \frac{-tP_t}{(1 + r)^t} = N.$$

This statement is worth restating as a formal proposition: Suppose that the term structure of interest rates is always flat (that is, the discount rate for a future cash flow occurring at time $m$ is equal to the discount rate for a future cash flow occurring at time $n$). Then a necessary and sufficient condition that the market value of an asset B be equal under all changes of the discount rate $r$ to the market value of a future obligation $P$ is that the duration of the asset equal the duration of the obligation. Here we understand the word *equal* to mean equal in the sense of a first-order approximation.

An obligation against which an asset of this type is held is said to be *immunized*.

The above statement has two critical limitations:

• The immunization discussed applies only to first-order approximations. When we get to a numerical example, we shall see that there is a big difference between first-order equality and "true" equality. In *Animal Farm*, George Orwell made the same observation about the barnyard: "All animals are equal, but some animals are more equal than others.")

• We have assumed that the yield curve is completely flat. At best, this might be considered to be a poor approximation of reality. In this chapter we shall retain this assumption. Alternative theories of the term structure lead, of course, to alternative definitions of duration and immunization (for alternatives, see Bierwag et al. 1981 and 1983 and Cox, Ingersoll, and Ross 1979). In an empirical investigation of these alternatives, Gultekin and Rogalski (1984) found that the simple concept of duration we use here works at least as well as any of the alternatives.

## 18.3   Example

You are trying to immunize a year-10 obligation whose present value is $1,000 (this means that, at the current yield to maturity of 6 percent, its future value is $1,790.85). You intend to do this by purchasing $1,000 worth of a bond or a combination of bonds.

You consider three bonds: one with 10 years remaining until maturity, a coupon rate of 6.7 percent, and a face value of $1,000; one with a coupon rate of 6.988 percent, a face value of $1,000, and 15 years until maturity; and one with a coupon rate of 5.9 percent, a face value of $1,000, and 30 years until maturity.

At the existing yield to maturity of 6 percent, the prices of the bonds differ. Since Bond 1 is worth $1,051.52, you have to purchase only $951 of face value of Bond 1 in order to acquire $1,000 of Bond 1. The amounts for the other bonds are given below:

|                | BOND 1   | BOND 2   | BOND 3  |
|----------------|----------|----------|---------|
| bondprice      | 1051.520 | 1095.957 | 986.235 |
| amount of bond | 0.951003 | 0.912444 | 1.01395 |
| YTM            | 0.06     | 0.06     | 0.06    |
| maturity       | 10       | 15       | 30      |
| coupon         | 67       | 69.88    | 59      |
| facevalue      | 1000     | 1000     | 1000    |
|                |          |          |         |
| duration       | 7.665    | 10.000   | 14.636  |

If the yield to maturity doesn't change, then you will be able to reinvest each coupon at 6 percent. Thus, Bond 2, for example, will give a terminal wealth, at the end of 10 years, of

$$\sum_{t=0}^{9} 69.88(1.06)^t + \left( \sum_{t=1}^{5} \frac{69.88}{(1.06)^t} + \frac{1,000}{(1.06)^5} \right) = 921.07 + 1,041.62$$

$$= 1,962.69.$$

The first term is the sum of the reinvested coupons. The second and third terms represent the market value of the bond in year 10, when the bond has five more years until maturity. Since we will be buying only $912.44 of face value of this bond, we have, at the end of 10 years, 0.91244 × $1,962.69 = $1,790.84. Except for a rounding error of $0.01, this is exactly what we wanted. The results of this calculation for all three bonds, provided there is no change in the yield to maturity, are given in the following:

| | BOND 1 | BOND 2 | BOND 3 |
|---|---|---|---|
| bond price | 1000 | 1041.618 | 988.5300 |
| reinvested coupons | 883.1132 | 921.0739 | 777.6669 |
| | | | |
| TOTAL | 1883.113 | 1962.692 | 1766.196 |
| total*proportion | 1790.847 | 1790.847 | 1790.847 |

The upshot of this table is that purchasing $1,000 of any of the three bonds will provide funding for your future obligation of $1,790.85 in 10 years, *if the yield to maturity doesn't change.*

Now suppose that, immediately after you purchase the bonds, the yield to maturity changes to some new value and stays there. This will obviously affect the calculation we did above. For example, if the yield to maturity falls to 5 percent, the table will now look as follows:

| | BOND 1 | BOND 2 | BOND 3 |
|---|---|---|---|
| bond price | 1000 | 1086.069 | 1112.159 |
| reinvested coupons | 842.7187 | 878.9431 | 742.0956 |
| | | | |
| TOTAL | 1842.718 | 1965.013 | 1854.255 |
| total*proportion | 1752.432 | 1792.965 | 1880.135 |

Thus, if the yield falls, Bond 1 will no longer fund our obligation, whereas Bond 3 will overfund it. Bond 2's ability to fund the obligation—not surprisingly, in view of the preceding section—hardly changes. We can repeat this calculation for any new yield to maturity. The results are shown in figure 18.1. As can be seen, the terminal value of Bond 2 is hardly affected by a change in the yield to maturity. This is what we want in an immunized obligation.

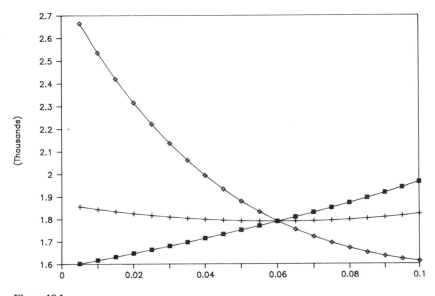

**Figure 18.1**
Immunization properties of three bonds (terminal value, reinvestment at new yield to
maturity). (■): 10-year bond; (+): 15-year bond; (◇): 20-year bond.

## 18.3  Not Only First Derivatives Are Bliss—A Continuation of Our Immunization Experiment

There is another way to get a bound investment with a duration of 10: If
we invest \$665.091 in Bond 1 and \$344.909 in Bond 3, we will have a bond
portfolio with that duration. You can verify this directly, or you can prove
that the duration of a portfolio is the weighted average duration of the
assets in the portfolio.

Suppose we repeat our experiment with this portfolio of bonds. As figure
18.2 shows, the portfolio's performance is very respectable. Changing the
scale on the graph (see figure 18.3) raises a new question: What causes the
difference between these two assets, each of which has a duration of 10?
Notice that while for both assets the terminal value is convex in the yield
to maturity, the terminal value of the portfolio of bonds is more convex
than that of the single bond. Redington (1952) thought this convexity very
desirable, and we can see why: No matter what the change in the yield
to maturity, the portfolio of bonds provides more overfunding of the
future obligation than the single bond. This is obviously a desirable prop-

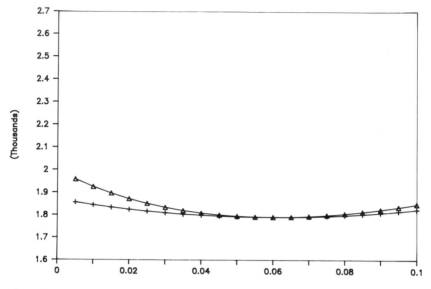

**Figure 18.2**
Comparison of immunization strategies (terminal value, reinvestment at new yield to maturity). (+): 15-year bond; (△): bond portfolio.

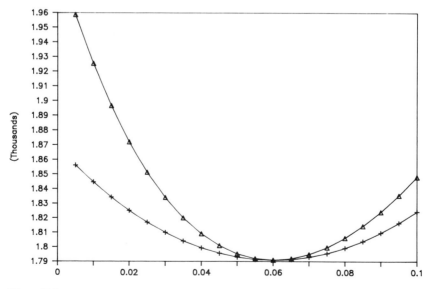

**Figure 18.3**
Comparison of immunization strategies (terminal value, reinvestment at new yield to muturity). (+): 15-year bond; (△): bond portfolio.

erty for an immunized portfolio. It leads us to formulate the following rule:

In a comparison between two immunized portfolios, the portfolio whose terminal value is more convex with respect to changes in the yield to maturity is preferable.

## 18.4   Building a Different Mousetrap

Despite what was said in the preceding section, there is some interest in deriving the characteristics of a bond portfolio whose terminal value is as insensitive to changes in the YTM as possible. One way of improving the performance of the bond portfolio (when so defined) is not only to match the first derivatives of the change in value (which, as we saw in section 18.2, leads to the duration concept), but also to match the second derivatives.

A direct extension of the analysis of the section 18.2 leads us to the conclusion that matching the second derivatives requires

$$N(N + 1) = \sum_1^M \frac{t(t + 1)P_t}{(1 + r)^t}.$$

The following example illustrates the kind of improvement that can be made in a portfolio where the second derivatives are also matched. Consider four bonds, one of which, Bond 2, is our old friend from the previous example, whose duration is exactly 10. The bonds are described in the following table:

| | BOND 1 | BOND 3 | BOND 4 | BOND 2 |
|---|---|---|---|---|
| bondprice | 827.9511 | 767.6254 | 1368.004 | 1095.957 |
| amount of bond | 1.207800 | 1.302718 | 0.730991 | 0.912444 |
| YTM | 0.06 | 0.06 | 0.06 | 0.06 |
| maturity | 20 | 14 | 10 | 15 |
| coupon | 45 | 35 | 110 | 69.88 |
| facevalue | 1000 | 1000 | 1000 | 1000 |
| | | | | |
| duration | 12.89642 | 10.84837 | 7.053934 | 10.00000 |
| secdur | 229.0872 | 148.7023 | 67.59801 | 136.4995 |

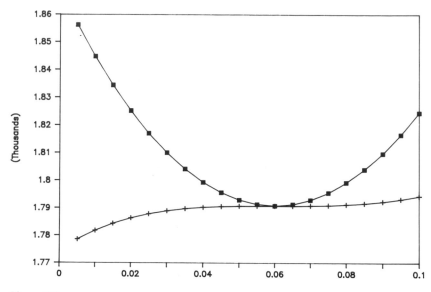

**Figure 18.4**
Comparison of immunization strategies (portfolio with two equal moments). (■): 15-year
bond; (+): bond portfolio.

The last line of this table, clumsily labeled "secdur," gives the new term
described in this section. We need three bonds in order to calculate a
portfolio of bonds whose duration and whose secdur are exactly equal to
those of the liability. The portfolio proportions are the following:

```
------------------------------
     bond 1     -0.56185
     bond 3      1.641528
     bond 4     -0.07967
------------------------------
```

As figure 18.4 shows, this portfolio provides a better hedge against the
terminal value than even Bond 2.

## Exercises

1. Prove that the duration of a portfolio is the weighted average duration
of the portfolio assets.

2. Set up a spreadsheet that enables you to duplicate the calculations of section 18.4.

3. The logic of section 18.4 can be extended: What are the characteristics of a portfolio whose first three derivatives match those of a "bullet liability" (i.e., a one-shot—pardon the pun—liability)? Can you set up a spreadsheet to do the calculations?

## References

Benninga, S., and A. Protopapadakis. 1986. "General Equilibrium Properties of the Term Structure of Interest Rates." *Journal of Financial Economics* 16 (July): 389–410.

Benninga, S., and M. Smirlock. 1985. "An Empirical Analysis of the Delivery Option, Marking to Market, and the Pricing of Treasury Bond Futures." *Journal of Futures Markets* 5 (fall): 361–374.

Bierwag, G. O. 1977. "Immunization, Duration and the Term Structure of Interest Rates." *Journal of Financial and Quantitative Analysis* (December): 725–741.

Bierwag, G. O. 1978. "Measures of Duration." *Economic Inquiry* 16 (October): 497–507.

Bierwag, G. O., G. C. Kaufman, and A. Toevs. 1983. "Duration: Its Development and Use in Bond Portfolio Management." *Financial Analysts Journal* (July–August): 15–35.

Bierwag, G. O., G. G. Kaufman, and A. Toevs. 1983. *Innovations in Bond Portfolio Management: Duration Analysis and Immunization.* Greenwich, Conn.: JAI.

Bierwag G. O., G. G. Kaufman, R. Schweitzer, and A. Toevs. 1981. "The Art of Risk Management in Bond Portfolios." *Journal of Portfolio Management* (spring): 27–36.

Billingham, C. J. 1983. "Strategies for Enhancing Bond Portfolio Returns." *Financial Analysts Journal* (May–June): 50–56.

Brealey, R., and S. Myers. 1984. *Principles of Corporate Finance.* Second edition. New York: McGraw-Hill.

Chance, D. 1983. "Floating Rate Notes and Immunization." *Journal of Financial and Quantitative Analysis* 18: 365–380.

Chua, J. H. 1984. "A Closed-Form Formula for Calculating Bond Duration." *Financial Analysts Journal* (May–June): 76–78.

Cooper, I. A. 1977. "Asset Values, Interest Rate Changes, and Duration." *Journal of Financial and Quantitative Analysis* (December): 701–723.

Cox, J., J. Ingersoll, and S. Ross. 1979. "Duration and the Measurement of Basis Risk." *Journal of Business* (January): 51–61.

Fisher, L., and R. L. Weill. 1971. "Coping with the Risk of Market-Rate Fluctuations: Returns to Bondholders from Naive and Optimal Strategies." *Journal of Business* (October): 408–431.

Gultekin, B., and R. J. Rogalski. 1984. "Alternative Duration Specifications and the Measurement of Basis Risk: Empirical Tests." *Journal of Business* (April): 241–264.

Gushee, C. H. 1981. "How to Immunize a Bond Investment." *Financial Analysts Journal* (March–April): 44–51.

Hicks, J. 1939. *Value and Capital.* Oxford: Clarendon.

Ingersoll, J. E., Jr., J. Skelton, and R. L. Weil. 1978. "Duration Forty Years Later." *Journal of Financial and Quantitative Analysis* (November): 627–650.

Joehnk, M. D., H. R. Fogler, and C. E. Bradley. 1978. "The Prince Elasticity of Discounted bonds: Some Empirical 'Evidence.'" *Journal of Financial and Quantitative Analysis* (September): 559–566.

Lanstein, R., and W. F. Sharpe. 1978. "Duration and Security Risk." *Journal of Financial and Quantitative Analysis* (November): 653–670.

Leibowitz, M. L., and A. Weinberger. 1981. "The Uses of Contingent Immunization." *Journal of Portfolio Management* (fall): 51–55.

Macauley, F. R. 1938. *The Movement of Interest Rates, Bonds, Yields, and Stock Prices in the United States Since 1865.* New York: Columbia University Press.

Morgan, G. E. 1986. "Floating Rate Securities and Immunization: Some Further Results." *Journal of Financial and Quantitative Analysis* 21: 87–94.

Morrissey, T. F., and C. Huang. 1987. "A Nomogram for Estimating Duration." *Financial Analysts Journal* (January–February): 65–67.

Nelson, J., and S. Schaefer. 1983. "The Dynamics of the Term Structure and Alternative Portfolio Immunization Strategies." In *Innovations in Bond Portfolio Management: Duration Analysis and Immunization,* ed. G. Kaufman, G. Bierwag, and A. Toevs (Greenwich, Conn.: JAI).

Ott, R. A., Jr. 1986. "The Duration of an Adjustable-Rate Mortgage and The Impact of the Index." *Journal of Finance* 41 (September): 923–934.

Redington, F. M. 1952. "Review of the Principle of Life-Office Valuations." *Journal of the Institute of Actuaries* 78: 286–340. Reprinted in *Bond Duration and Immunization: Early Developments and Recent Contributions,* ed. G. A. Hawawini (New York: Garland, 1972).

Samuelson, P. A. 1945. "The Effects of Interest Rate Increases on the Banking System." *American Economic Review* 35 (March): 16–27.

Weil, R. L. 1973. "Macauley's Duration: An Appreciation." *Journal of Business* (October): 589–592.

# V THE TECHNICAL BACKGROUND

# Overview

Chapters 19–25 address a number of technical topics that are pertinent to finance applications in the preceding chapters. Both mathematics and advanced Lotus applications are covered. However, You will not find a complete introduction to Lotus; it is assumed that you know the basics of setting up a spreadsheet.

*Chapter 19:    The Gauss-Seidel method.* This is a method for the recursive solution of simultaneous equations. It is used (implicitly) in the chapters on balance-sheet simulation.

*Chapter 20:    The Newton-Raphson method.* This is a method for finding roots of equations. We use it to find the implied variance in the options chapters. Insofar as theoretical finance tends to discuss the maximization of net present values or utility, the Newton-Raphson method may also be useful elsewhere (there is a classic example at the end of chapter 20).

*Chapter 21:    Matrices.* The chapters on portfolios use quite a bit of matrix manipulation. This chapter provides a brief survey of the necessary mathematics.

*Chapter 22:    Random-number generators.* Simulation gives a good feel for what is meant by sentences like "stock returns follow a lognormal process with mean $\mu$ and standard deviation $\sigma$." Lotus's @RAND function is used in chapter 14. Chapter 22 provides the necessary background to this function and other random-number generators.

*Chapter 23:    Lotus @ functions.* This chapter covers the @ functions that are used throughout the book, giving a brief explanation for each. If you look in the Lotus manual, you will see that the list given here is far from exhaustive.

*Chapter 24:    Macros in Lotus.* This chapter gives a brief introduction to programming with the Lotus macro language.

*Chapter 25:    Data Table commands.* These powerful commands can be used to generate useful tables from complicated models. This chapter shows how to use them.

# 19 The Gauss-Seidel Method

Many simultaneous linear equations can be solved by *recursive itera-tion* rather than by matrix inversion. One widely used method is the Gauss-Seidel method. To illustrate this method, consider the following equations:

$$2x + 3y = 10, \tag{1}$$

$$x - 4y = 2. \tag{2}$$

It follows from equation 1 that $x = (10 - 3y)/2$, and from equation 2 that $y = (x - 2)/4$.

The Gauss-Seidel method involves a loop: Set some initial value for $y$; for example, let $y = 0$. If $y = 0$, then (from equation 1) $x = 5$. But if $x = 5$, then (from equation 2) $y = 0.75$. Continuing this, we generate the following sequence of values:

| $y$ | $x$ |
| --- | --- |
| 0 | 5 |
| 0.75 | 3.875 |
| 0.46875 | 4.296875 |
| 0.574218 | 4.138671 |
| 0.534667 | 4.197998 |
| 0.549499 | 4.175750 |
| ⋮ | ⋮ |

As you can see, the values converge. It follows from the way we have con-structed the values that the limits of the two sequences are the solutions to the questions. (If this always worked, it would be a lot easier than inverting matrices!)

A neater way of solving the above problem is to set up the following spreadsheet (the second column indicates cell contents):

```
initial
marker
y            @IF(MARKER<>0,INITIAL,(X-2)/4)
x            (10-3*Y)/2
```

INITAL and MARKER are numbers. If MARKER $\neq$ 0, then $y$ is set to INITIAL; otherwise $y = (x - 2)/4$. This guarantees control of the iterative substitutions.

The Gauss-Seidel method is a somewhat untidy way of solving simultaneous equations. The solution may not always converge, and convergence may depend on whether $x$ or $y$ is solved for first. The advantage of this method is that it assures us that what we do in many financial models makes sense by allowing us to construct a model in which we set up the relations between the variables without asking how the equations are to be solved. If we observe convergence, then we have a solution. (See chapter 1 for a powerful example.)

## Exercise

Solve the following system using the Gauss-Seidel method:

$13x - 8y - 3z = 20,$

$-8x + 10y - z = -5,$

$-3x - y + 11z = 0.$

## References

Hildebrand, F. B. 1974. *Introduction to Numerical Analysis*. Second edition. New York: McGraw-Hill.

Johansson, J.-H. 1985. "Simultaneous Equations with Lotus 1-2-3." *Byte* (February): 399.

Miller, A. R. 1981. *Pascal Programs for Scientists and Engineers*. Berkeley: Sybex.

# 20 The Newton-Raphson Method

## 20.1 Introduction

The Newton-Raphson method, which solves for the zeros of equations by using successive approximations, is well suited for use with Lotus 1-2-3. To understand this method, suppose we want to find a root of the equation

$$f(x) = 3x^3 - 4x + 15$$

(that is, a value of $x$ for which $y = 0$). (In fact, this equation has several roots. We shall use Lotus graphs to identify each of these roots approximately. Precise roots can then be found by the Newton-Raphson method.)

The Newton-Raphson method uses successive approximations. Suppose that our first approximation is $x(0) = 0$. We find a second approximation by setting

$$x(1) = x(0) - \frac{f(x(0))}{f'(x(0))}$$

$$= 0 + \frac{15}{4}.$$

The next approximation is found similarly:

$$x(2) = x(1) - \frac{f(x(1))}{f'(x(1))}$$

$$= \frac{15}{4} - \frac{158.2031}{122.5625}$$

$$= 2.459204.$$

Subsequent values are given by

$$x(3) = 1.472064,$$

$$x(4) = 0.267019,$$

and so forth.

The process converges to give $x = -1.96818$. As figures 20.1 and 20.2 show, the process is not smooth. (Newton-Raphson methods don't always converge. Theorems on the convergence of the Newton-Raphson method can be found on pages 58ff of Saaty and Bram 1964. An example of non-convergence is given on page 86 of Gill, Murray, and Wright 1981.)

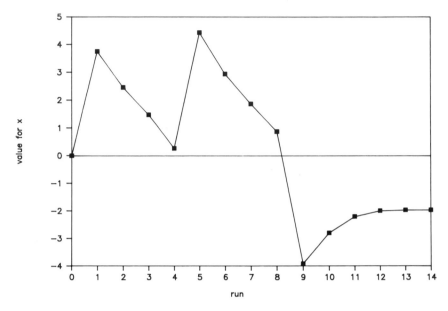

**Figure 20.1**
The Newton-Raphson method of finding a root, with $x = 0$ as the starting point.

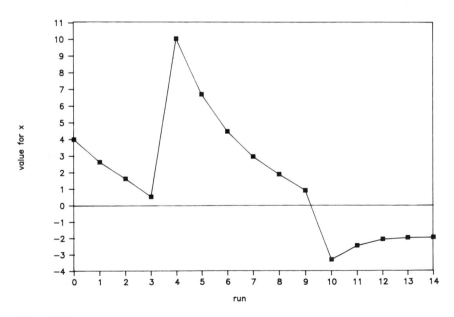

**Figure 20.2**
The Newton-Raphson method of finding a root, with $x = 4$ as the starting point.

## 20.2  Theory

What the Newton-Raphson method does is create a sequence of linear approximations to the function whose roots are being sought. Consider a function $f(x)$. When $x$ has a particular value $x_0$, the function's graph passes through the point $(x_0, f(x_0))$. A linear approximation to the function at this point is given by the line

$$y = f(x_0) + (x - x_0)f'(x_0).$$

Set $y = 0$ to find the root of this linear approximation. This gives

$$x_1 = x_0 - \frac{f(x_0)}{f'(x_0)},$$

which is, of course, the first step in the Newton-Raphson approximation.

Now repeat the process: At $x_1$ the function has a value $f(x_1)$ and is linearly approximated by

$$y = f(x_1) + (x - x_1)f'(x_1).$$

The root of this linear approximation gives

$$x_2 = x_1 - \frac{f(x_1)}{f'(x_1)}.$$

This process is illustrated in figure 20.3.

## 20.3  Finding Minima and Maxima

An extremum (i.e., a minimum or a maximum) of a function is a root of the function's first derivative. Thus, for example, to find the extremum of the function given in section 20.1, we have to find $x$ such that

$$f'(x) = 9x^2 - 4 = 0.$$

Disregarding for the moment the trivial nature of this calculation (see the exercises for a nontrivial example), we can use the Newton-Raphson method to find the maximum. To do this set

$$x(i) = x(i - 1) - \frac{f'(x(i - 1))}{f''(x(i - 1))}.$$

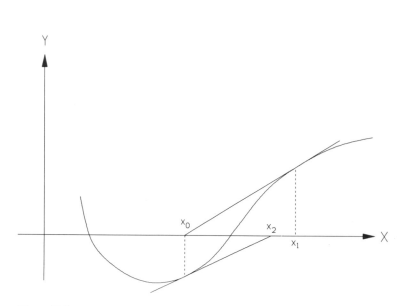

**Figure 20.3**

Now start with some initial value, say $x(0) = 0$. The solution will converge to $x = 0.6666$.

## 20.4  Using Lotus to Set Up the Newton-Raphson Method

Let us return to the example of section 20.1. The following formulas will generate the roots of $f(x) = 3x^3 - 4x + 15$:

```
marker
x                       aif(marker<>-1,marker,x-f(x)/f'(x))
f(x)                    3*x^3-4*x+15
f'(x)                   9*x^2-4
```

First, we use /Range Name Labels Right to give the cells to the right of the first column the proper names. We use the variable "marker" to control the starting value of the Newton-Raphson method. If we want to start from $x(0) = 0$, we set marker = 0. Setting marker = $-1$ starts the Newton-Raphson iterations. The F9 button is used to recalculate. When $x$ stops changing, we should have a root of the equation. Be sure to check that at this point $f(x)$ is close to zero; you should see something like $f(x) =$

2.5E – 15, which is close enough. (See chapter 24 for another way of implementing the Newton-Raphson method.)

## Exercises

1. Use the Newton-Raphson method to find all the roots of the function

$$f(x) = 3x^3 - 4x + 15.$$

Before doing this, locate the approximate roots by graphing the function using Lotus. Then use the Newton-Raphson method (starting in a neighborhood of the approximate root) to locate the roots to four-figure accuracy.

2. Use the Newton-Raphson method to find an extremum of the function

$$f(x) = [\ln(x)]^2 - 3x^2 + 12x.$$

3. A finance example: Consider the following application of the Hirschleifer model: A consumer has an initial endowment of $16,000. The consumer lives for only two periods, consuming $c_1$ in the first period and $c_2$ in the second. The consumer has a production function available to him, so that an investment of $z$ today provides him tomorrow with production of

$$f(z) = z + \sqrt{z}.$$

The consumer has a utility function over consumption in both periods given by

$$U(c_1, c_2) = h(c_1) + \delta h(c_2),$$

where

$$h(x) = \frac{x^{1-\gamma}}{1 - \gamma}.$$

Here $w$ is a *pure time preference factor*. The function $h(x)$ is called an *exponential utility function*, and is widely used in the economics and finance literature. Find an optimal $z$ when $\gamma = 2$ and $\delta = 0.95$. (Problems of this kind are considered throughout the economics and finance literature. For an introductory discussion, see chapter 4 of Levy and Sarnat 1986.)

# References

Gill, P. E., W. Murray, and M. H. Wright. 1981. *Practical Optimization.* London: Academic.

Levy, H., and M. Sarnat. 1986. *Capital Investment and Financial Decisions.* London: Prentice-Hall.

Saaty, T. L., and J. Bram. 1964. *Nonlinear Mathematics.* New York: Dover.

# 21 Matrices

## 21.1   Introduction

A matrix is a rectangular array of numbers. All of the following are matrices:

$$[2 \quad 3 \quad 4] \qquad \begin{vmatrix} 13 & -8 & -3 \\ -8 & 10 & -1 \\ -3 & -1 & 11 \end{vmatrix} \qquad \begin{vmatrix} 13 \\ -8 \\ -3 \end{vmatrix} \qquad \begin{vmatrix} 13 & -8 & -3 \\ -8 & 10 & -1 \\ -3 & -1 & 11 \\ 0 & 13 & 3 \end{vmatrix}$$

A matrix with only one row is called a *row vector*; a matrix with only one column is called a *column vector*. A matrix with the same number of rows and columns is called a *square matrix*.

A single letter is often used to denote a matrix or a vector. One may also write, for example, $A = [a_{ij}]$, where $a_{ij}$ stands for the entry in row $i$ and column $j$ of the matrix. For a vector, one might write $V = [v_i]$.

## 21.2   Matrix Operations

### Multiplication by a Scalar

Multiplying a matrix by a scalar multiples every entry in the matrix by the scalar. Thus,

$$6 \begin{vmatrix} 13 & -8 & -3 \\ -8 & 10 & -1 \\ -3 & -1 & 11 \\ 0 & 13 & 3 \end{vmatrix} = \begin{vmatrix} 78 & -48 & -18 \\ -48 & 60 & -6 \\ -18 & -6 & 66 \\ 0 & 68 & 18 \end{vmatrix}.$$

### Addition

Adding two vectors or matrices is accomplished by adding their corresponding entries. Thus, if $A = [a_{ij}]$ and $B = [b_{ij}]$,

$$A + B = [a_{ij} + b_{ij}].$$

For this to make any sense, the matrices being added must have the same dimensions.

### Transposition

Transposition is an operation by which the rows of a matrix are turned into its columns and vice versa. Thus, if

$$A = \begin{vmatrix} 13 & -8 & -3 \\ -8 & 10 & -1 \\ -3 & -1 & 11 \\ 0 & 13 & 3 \end{vmatrix},$$

then the transpose of $A$, denoted $A^T$, is the following matrix:

$$A^T = \begin{vmatrix} 13 & -8 & -3 & 0 \\ -8 & 10 & -1 & 13 \\ -3 & -1 & 11 & 3 \end{vmatrix}.$$

Formally, if $B = A^T$, then $b_{ij} = a_{ji}$.

Transposition turns row vectors into column vectors, and vice versa.

**Multiplication**

Suppose $X = [x_i]$ and $Y = [y_i]$ are both row vectors. Then

$$XY^T = [x_1, \ldots, x_n] \begin{vmatrix} y_1 \\ y_2 \\ \vdots \\ y_n \end{vmatrix} = \sum_i x_i y_i.$$

Now suppose that $A$ and $B$ are two matrices, and that $A$ has $n$ columns and $B$ has $n$ rows. Write $A$ as a collection of rows, and write $B$ as a collection of columns:

$$A = \begin{vmatrix} a_1 \\ a_2 \\ \vdots \\ a_n \end{vmatrix},$$

$$B = [b_1^T, \ldots, b_n^T].$$

Then the product of $A$ and $B$, written $AB$, is defined by the matrix

$$\begin{vmatrix} a_1 b_1^T & a_1 b_2^T & \cdots & a_1 b_n^T \\ a_2 b_1^T & a_2 b_2^T & \cdots & a_2 b_n^T \\ \vdots & & & \\ a_n b_1^T & a_n b_2^T & \cdots & a_n b_n^T \end{vmatrix}.$$

For example, if

$$A = \begin{vmatrix} 2 & -6 \\ -9 & 3 \end{vmatrix}$$

and

$$B = \begin{vmatrix} 6 & 9 & -12 \\ -5 & 2 & 4 \end{vmatrix},$$

then

$$AB = \begin{vmatrix} 42 & 6 & -48 \\ -69 & -75 & 120 \end{vmatrix}.$$

The order of multiplication is critical. Multiplication of matrices is *not* commutative; in general, $AB \neq BA$.

## 21.3   Matrix Inverses

A square matrix $I$ is called the *identity matrix* if all its off-diagonal entries are 0 and all its diagonal entries are 1. Thus,

$$I = \begin{vmatrix} 1 & 0 & \cdots & & 0 \\ 0 & 1 & \cdots & & 0 \\ \vdots & \vdots & \vdots & & \\ 0 & 0 & \cdots & 0 & 1 \end{vmatrix}.$$

It is easy to confirm that multiplying any other matrix by the identity matrix of the proper dimension leaves that matrix unchanged. Thus, if $I$ is an $n \times n$ identity matrix and $B$ is an $n \times m$ matrix, $IB = B$.

Now suppose we are given a *square* matrix $A$ of dimension $n$. The $n \times n$ matrix $A^{-1}$ is called the *inverse* of $A$ if

$$A^{-1}A = AA^{-1} = I.$$

Finding the inverse of a matrix can be a lot of work. Fortunately, Lotus does this for us.

A square matrix that has an inverse is called a *nonsingular matrix*.

The conditions for a matrix to be nonsingular are the following: Consider a square matrix $A$ of dimension $n$. It can be shown that $A = [a_{ij}]$ is nonsingular if and only if the only solution to the $n$ equations

$$\sum_i a_{ij}x_i = 0, \quad j = 1, \ldots, n$$

is $x_i = 0$, $i = 1, \ldots, n$.

Matrix inversion is a tricky business. If there exists a vector $X$ whose components are almost zero and which solves the above system, then the matrix is *ill-conditioned* and it may be very difficult to find an accurate inverse.

## 21.4   Solving Systems of Simultaneous Linear Equations

A system of $n$ linear equations in $m$ unknowns is written as

$$a_{11}x_1 + a_{12}x_2 + \cdots + a_{1n}x_n = y_1,$$

$$a_{21}x_1 + a_{22}x_2 + \cdots + a_{2n}x_n = y_2,$$

$$\cdots$$

$$a_{n1}x_1 + a_{n2}x_2 + \cdots + a_{nn}x_n = y_n.$$

Writing the matrix of coefficients as $A = [a_{ij}]$, the column vector of unknowns as $X = [x_j]$, and the column vector of constants as $Y = [y_j]$, we may write the above system in matrix notation as $AX = Y$.

Not every system of linear equations has a solution, and not every solution of such a system is unique. The system $AX = Y$ *always* has a unique solution if the matrix $A$ is square and nonsingular. In this case the solution is given by premultiplying both sides of the equation $AX = Y$ by the inverse of $A$:

$$A^{-1}AX = A^{-1}Y.$$

Since $A^{-1}A = I$ and $IX = X$, we get

$$X = A^{-1}Y.$$

## 21.5   Lotus and Matrices

Lotus will multiply matrices (we use the term broadly to include vectors). It will also invert square matrices and transpose matrices. The relevant commands are these:

```
/Data Matrix Invert.  Range to invert:  Output range:

/Data Matrix Multiply: First range to multiply: Second range to multiply:  Output range:

/Range Transpose:  Enter range to copy FROM:  Enter range to copy TO:
```

For all three of these commands, Lotus will write over anything you have written in the output range, so make sure that range is blank unless you truly intend to write over the material there.

## Exercises

1. Consider the following system of equations:

$$A = \begin{vmatrix} 13 & -8 & -3 \\ -8 & 10 & -1 \\ -3 & -1 & 11 \end{vmatrix},$$

$$Y = \begin{vmatrix} 20 \\ -5 \\ 0 \end{vmatrix}.$$

Solve $AX = Y$ using Lotus's matrix inversion.

2. Use /Range Transpose to transpose some matrics and vectors.

3. An ill-conditioned matrix is a matrix that "almost doesn't have" an inverse. An set of examples of such matrices are Hilbert matrices. An $n$-dimensional Hilbert matrix looks like this:

$$H_n = \begin{vmatrix} 1 & 1/2 & \cdots & 1/n \\ 1/2 & 1/3 & \cdots & 1/(n+1) \\ \vdots & & & \\ 1/n & 1/(n+1) & \cdots & 1/(2n-1) \end{vmatrix}.$$

a. Calculate the inverses of $H_2$, $H_3$, and $H_8$.
b. Consider the following problem:

$$H_n \begin{vmatrix} x_1 \\ x_2 \\ \cdots \\ x_n \end{vmatrix} = \begin{vmatrix} 1 + 1/2 + \cdots + 1/n \\ 1/2 + 1/3 + \cdots + 1/(n+1) \\ \vdots \\ 1/n + 1/(n+1) + \cdots + 1/(2n-1) \end{vmatrix}.$$

Find the answers to these problems by inspection. Now solve them in Lotus. How do you explain the differences?

4. Can you write a macro to calculate the determinant of a matrix?

5. A Bezier curve is a smooth curve determined by any four points on the plane. (For a reference see Enns 1986.) To draw such a curve, first determine any four points: $P_1 = (x_1, y_1)$, $P_2 = (x_2, y_2)$, $P_3 = (x_3, y_3)$, $P_4 = (x_4, y_4)$. Next plot the points

$$C(t) = [t^3 \quad t^2 \quad t \quad 1] B \begin{vmatrix} P_1 \\ P_2 \\ P_3 \\ P_4 \end{vmatrix}$$

where $t$ varies between 0 and 1 and $B$ is the matrix

$$B = \begin{vmatrix} -1 & 3 & -3 & 1 \\ 3 & -6 & 3 & 0 \\ -3 & 3 & 0 & 0 \\ 1 & 0 & 0 & 0 \end{vmatrix}.$$

a. Find the expression for $C(t)$ by multiplying the vector and matrix expressions above. Then pick four points and use Lotus to plot a Bezier curve.

b. Write a macro that takes different $t$'s and multiplies the vectors and matrices that make up $C(t)$ directly. Use this macro to plot a sequence of points which you can then graph to find a Bezier curve. (This is much harder than exercise 5a.)

## References

Dorfman, R., P. A. Samuelson, and R. M. Solow. 1958. *Linear Programming and Economic Analysis*. New York: McGraw-Hill.

Enns, S. 1986. "Free-Form Curves on Your Micro." *Byte* (December): 225–230.

Gill, P. E., W. Murray, and M. H. Wright. 1981. *Practical Optimization*. London: Academic.

Miller, A. R. 1983. *Pascal Programs for Scientists and Engineers*. Berkeley: Sybex.

Phipps, T. E., Jr. 1986. "The Inversion of Large Matrices." *Byte* (April): 181–190. See also the letter on this topic from Richard Branham on p. 340 of the August 1986 *Byte*.

# 22 Random-Number Generators

## 22.1 Introduction

What is a random number? Suppose we have an urn filled with 1,000 little balls, each numbered with a unique number from 1 to 1,000. Now we do the following: First, we draw one ball out of the urn and record the ball's number. Next, we put the ball back into the urn and shake the urn thoroughly so that the balls are mixed up again; then we repeat the procedure.

A *random-number generator* on a computer is a function that imitates this procedure. Lotus, for example, has a random-number generator that generates a number between 0 and 1. The function is @RAND, with no argument.

The random-number generators considered in this chapter are actually *pseudo-random-number generators*, since they are functions whose values are statistically indistinguishable from random numbers. All pseudo-random-number generators have cycles (that is, they eventually start to repeat themselves). The trick is to find a random-number generator with a long cycle. The Lotus @rand function has a cycle of over 1 million, which makes it a very good random-number generator for a microcomputer (see Modianos, Scott, and Cornwall 1987).

Try this function: Type @RAND in a cell, and hit ENTER. Notice that every time you hit ENTER, you get a new and different number in the cell.

Random numbers are useful in simulations, where we want to simulate the effect of uncertainty.

In this chapter we examine the Lotus random-number generator. In the next chapter we use that random-number generator to simulate the standard normal distribution.

## 22.2 Testing the Lotus Random-Number Generator

Suppose we want to generate a sequence of random numbers and record their frequencies to see if they are really distributed uniformly. To do this we shall write a macro. The macro does the following: First, it creates a random number (using @RAND) and puts it in a cell in the worksheet. Next, it determines in which of the intervals $[0, 0.1)$, $[0.1, 0.2)$, ..., $[0.9, 1)$ the number falls. (The notation $[a, b)$ denotes the *half-open* interval between $a$ and $b$; a number $x$ is in this interval if $a \leq x < b$.) Finally, we keep a running track of how many of the random numbers generated this way fall into each of the intervals.

The worksheet looks like this:

```
random    0.363273
group          4
                          \A          {blank freqline}
                                      {windowsoff}{paneloff}~
                                      {For counter,1,maxrun,1,\B}


FREQUENCY TABLE
                          \B          {let random,arand}
group      frequency                 {let group,aint(random*10)+1}
    1          95                     {put data,1,group,aindex(data,1,group)+1}
    2          93
    3          102
    4          121                    counter        1001
    5          97                     maxrun         1000
    6          97
    7          96
    8          103
    9          93
   10          104
```

Before you run the macro, you have to create ranges called GROUP, RANDOM, COUNTER, MAXRUN, DATA, and FREQLINE. GROUP, RANDOM, COUNTER, and MAXRUN are single cells, next to the appropriate labels. DATA consists of the two columns labeled "group" and "frequency." DATA *includes* the column headings of "group" and "frequency." (Inclusion of the headings is important only because Lotus numbers the first row and the first column of a range as 0. By including the column headings, we ensure that row *n* of the range DATA corresponds to the entry for group *n*. See the explanation of line 3 of \B below.) FREQLINE consists of the single column under the word *frequency*.

The macro consists of two parts. \A blanks the range FREQLINE to erase any previous data. {WINDOWSOFF} {PANELOFF} stops the screen display, so that the macro will run faster. The last command in \A is a loop instructing Lotus to run macro \B the number of times recorded in MAXRUN and to keep track of the current run number in COUNTER.

\B has three lines. Line 1 puts a value indicated by @RAND into the cell RANDOM. Line 2 of \B calculates the frequency group of the value in RANDOM. If RANDOM contains 0.363273 (as it does in this particular printout), the group is calculated by taking the integer portion of (0.363273)

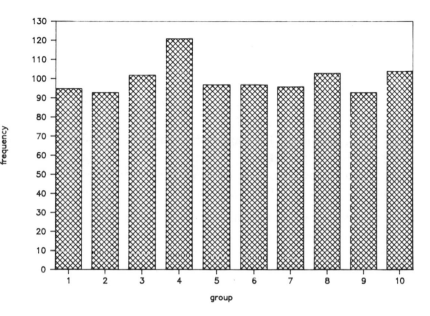

**Figure 22.1**
Frequency distribution of 1,000 random variables (@RAND).

(10) and adding 1. This guarantees that numbers between 0 and 0.0999999 will be in group 1, numbers between 0.1 and 0.1999999 will be in group 2, and so forth.

Line 3 of \B updates the record kept in the range DATA. It looks at column 1 of DATA and finds the row corresponding to the group of the current random number. It then takes the current entry of the cell thus found and adds 1 to it.

The time needed for this particular spreadsheet (1,000 random variables) was just over 2 minutes on an IBM-PC compatible with an 8087 numeric co-processor. A graph of the frequency is given as figure 22.1.

## Exercises

1. Here is a random-number generator you can make yourself: Start with some number, Seed. Let $X_1$ = Seed + $\pi$. Let $X_2 = e^{5+ln(X_1)}$. Let the random number be $X_2$ − Integer ($X_2$). Now let Seed = Random, and start all over again.

Implement this generator in a macro similar to the one given in the chapter. (This random-number generator is from Miller 1981.)

2. Define $A \bmod B$ as the *remainder* when $A$ is divided by $B$. For example, $36 \bmod 25 = 11$. Lotus has this function; it is written @MOD(A, B).

Now here is another random-number generator:

Let $X_{n+1} = (7X_n) \bmod 10^{10}$, where $X_0 = 1$.

Let $U_{n+1} = X_{n+1}/10^{10}$. These are the random numbers that are generated.

Implement this generator in a macro similar to the one given in the chapter. (This is one of the many random-number generators given in Abramowitz and Stegun 1972.)

3. Many states have daily lotteries, which are played as follows: Sometime during the day, you buy a lottery ticket, on which the seller inscribes a number you choose, between 000 and 999. That night there is a drawing on television in which three numbers are drawn. If your number matches the number drawn, you win and collect $500. If you lose, you get nothing.
a. Write a Lotus function that produces a random number between 000 and 999. (Hint: Use @INT and @RAND.)
b. Write a macro that reproduces 250 random draws of the daily lottery (about a year's worth, if there are no drawings on weekends). Assuming that a ticket costs $1, and assuming that you choose the same number each day, how much would you have won during the year?

## References

Abramowitz, M., and I. A. Stegun, eds. 1972. *Handbook of Mathematical Functions*. New York: Dover.

Knuth, D. E. 1981. *The Art of Computer Programming, Volume 2: Seminumerical Algorithms*. Reading, Mass.: Addison-Wesley.

Miller, A. R. 1981. *Pascal Programs for Scientists and Engineers*. Berkeley: Sybex.

Modianos, D. T., R. C. Scott, and L. W. Cornwall. 1987. "Testing Intrinsic Random-Number Generators." *Byte* (January): 175–178.

Wichmann, B., and D. Hill. 1987. "Building a Random-Number Generator." *Byte* (March): 127–128.

# 23 Lotus Functions

## 23.1 Introduction

The purpose of this chapter is to deal with the Lotus functions used in the book. In most cases the use of a function in Lotus is obvious, and elaborate explanations will not be necessary. However, some functions that appear to be obvious are not (@NPV is a good example), and the pitfalls will be explained here.

In general the syntax of a Lotus function is @FUNCTION (arguments). Occasionally the arguments are separated by commas; for example, @IF(condition, X, Y). The arguments are not present in all cases (@PI is a good example).

## 23.2 @NPV

Description: In the finance literature, the net present value of a sequence of cash flows $C_0, C_1, \ldots, C_N$ at a discount rate $r$ refers to the expression

$$\sum_{t=0}^{N} \frac{C_t}{(1 + r)^t}.$$

In Lotus, the function @NPV calculates the expression

$$\sum_{t=1}^{N} \frac{C_t}{(1 + r)^t}.$$

The user who wants the standard finance expression must therefore calculate $@NPV - C_0$.

Syntax: @NPV(interest rate, cash flows).

Example: Consider the following example.

| year | 1 | 2 | 3 | 4 | 5 |
|------|-----|-----|-----|-----|-----|
| cash flow | 156 | 23 | 33 | 234 | 44 |
| initial cost | 178 | | | | |
| interest | 0.1 | | | | |

When asked to calculate @NPV(0.1, cash flow), Lotus will answer with the following:

| npv | 372.7655 |
|-----|----------|

This expression represents

$$\frac{156}{1.1} + \frac{23}{(1.1)^2} + \frac{33}{(1.1)^3} + \frac{234}{(1.1)^4} + \frac{44}{(1.1)^5}.$$

The true net present value of 194.7655 is calculated by

@NPV(0.1, cash flow) − 178.

### 23.3  @IRR

Description: The internal rate of return is that interest rate $r$ for which the true net present value equals zero. If $C_0, C_1, \ldots, C_N$ is a series of cash flows, we are looking for $r$ such that the net present value is equal to

$$\sum_{t=0}^{N} \frac{C_t}{(1+r)^t} = 0.$$

The internal rate of return is usually difficult to calculate. It may not be unique; and it may not exist, since it is the root of an $n$th-degree polynomial equation.

The Lotus @IRR function does not have the same problem as the Lotus @NPV function. The cash flows put into the function start with the initial cash flow. Of course, at least one of the cash flows must be negative; otherwise the internal rate of return will not exist (it may not anyway).

Even in seemingly trivial problems, it may be worthwhile looking at the graph of the net present value of the cash flows under consideration to see what the meaning of the @IRR is.

Syntax: @IRR(guess, cash flows).

In most cases you can enter 0 as a guess and get a correct answer.

Example: Let us return to our @NPV example. However, this time we will write the spreadsheet as follows.

| year | 0 | 1 | 2 | 3 | 4 | 5 |
|------|------|-----|----|----|-----|----|
| cash flow | -178 | 156 | 23 | 33 | 234 | 44 |

The range CASH FLOW now refers to the series of numbers $-178, \ldots,$ 44. When we type @IRR(0, cash flow), Lotus gives

irr      -1.82351

However, this is a rather strange number ($-182.351$ percent) for the internal rate of return. Some calculations and a Lotus graph (figure 23.1) reveal

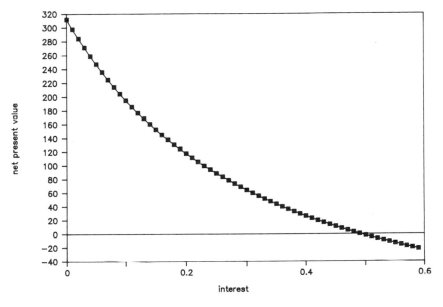

**Figure 23.1**
Calculating net present value.

that the internal rate of return we are looking for is closer to 50 percent. So we enter @NPV(0.5, cash flow), and indeed Lotus gives

irr       0.491994

A good way to make life easier is to create a range named GUESS. Write the formula as @IRR(guess, cash flow), and substitute in different values for a potential internal rate of return. When the GUESS is close, Lotus will come up with the correct answer:

irr       0.491994
guess          0.2

As you can see, the GUESS doesn't have to be very close.
By the way, the equation

$$-178 + \frac{156}{1+r} + \frac{23}{(1+r)^2} + \frac{33}{(1+r)^3} + \frac{234}{(1+r)^4} + \frac{44}{(1+r)^5} = 0$$

really does have a root at $r = -1.82351$. Thus is one of the difficulties associated with finding the internal rate of return.

## 23.4  @PV

Description: Calculates the present value of an annuity.

Syntax: @PV(payment, interest rate, number of years).

This function can generate the annuity tables contained in the back of every finance book.

## 23.5  @VLOOKUP

Syntax: @VLOOKUP(x, range, column).

Description: The best way to describe this useful function is through an example. Consider the following table.

| income | marginal<br>tax rate |
|---|---|
| 0.00 | 0.00 |
| 2479.00 | 0.11 |
| 3679.00 | 0.12 |
| 4749.00 | 0.14 |
| 7009.00 | 0.15 |
| 9169.00 | 0.16 |
| 11649.00 | 0.18 |
| 13919.00 | 0.20 |
| 16189.00 | 0.23 |
| 19639.00 | 0.26 |
| 25359.00 | 0.30 |
| 31079.00 | 0.34 |
| 36799.00 | 0.38 |
| 44779.00 | 0.42 |
| 59669.00 | 0.48 |
| 88269.00 | 0.50 |

The meaning of this table is as follows: For income $\leq \$2,479$, the marginal tax rate is 0 percent; for $\$2,479 < \text{income} \leq \$3,679$, the marginal tax rate is 11 percent; and so on.

We want to know what an individual's marginal tax rate is, given his income. The rule we use is the following: Given an individual's income, go down the "income" column of the table. When you get to the first number that is higher than the individual's income, go back one row. Then go over one column; this is the marginal tax rate.

For example, what is the marginal tax rate on $50,000 income? Going down the table, we stop at $59,669, the first number higher than $50,000. Then we go back one row (to $44,779) and over one column. The marginal tax rate is 42 percent.

VLOOKUP does this calculation for us. If we were to call the two-column range above TAX RATES, then the correct command would be @VLOOKUP(income, taxrates, 1). (Remember that Lotus numbers the first column as 0.)

Here is a slightly more dramatic use of the VLOOKUP function. Using the above information on marginal tax rates, we want to be able to calculate an individual's income tax, given his taxable income. First we rearrange the numbers as follows:

| BRACKETS | | | tax on previous | total tax on previous |
|---|---|---|---|---|
| low | high | tax rate | bracket | brackets |
| 0 | 2479 | 0 | | |
| 2479 | 3679 | 0.11 | 0.00 | |
| 3679 | 4749 | 0.12 | 132.00 | 132.00 |
| 4749 | 7009 | 0.14 | 128.40 | 260.40 |
| 7009 | 9169 | 0.15 | 316.40 | 576.80 |
| 9169 | 11649 | 0.16 | 324.00 | 900.80 |
| 11649 | 13919 | 0.18 | 396.80 | 1297.60 |
| 13919 | 16189 | 0.2 | 408.60 | 1706.20 |
| 16189 | 19639 | 0.23 | 454.00 | 2160.20 |
| 19639 | 25359 | 0.26 | 793.50 | 2953.70 |
| 25359 | 31079 | 0.3 | 1487.20 | 4440.90 |
| 31079 | 36799 | 0.34 | 1716.00 | 6156.90 |
| 36799 | 44779 | 0.38 | 1944.80 | 8101.70 |
| 44779 | 59669 | 0.42 | 3032.40 | 11134.10 |
| 59669 | 88269 | 0.48 | 6253.80 | 17387.90 |
| 88269 | | 0.5 | 13728.00 | 31115.90 |

The "low" and "high" income figures give the range to which the marginal tax rate applies. The column labeled "tax on previous bracket" gives the total tax on the bracket of the line above. For example, $128.40 is 12% × ($4,749 − $3,679). The column labeled "total tax on previous brackets" does exactly what it says. Thus, $260.40 = $128.40 + $132.00.

How do we calculate the total tax given the income? Here is where VLOOKUP comes in handy:

```
tax = aVLOOKUP(INCOME,TABLE,2)*(+INCOME-aVLOOKUP(INCOME,TABLE,0))+aVLOOKUP(INCOME,TABLE,4)
```

```
income      34789
tax         7418.30
```

Let's check this: If you have income of $34,789, your marginal tax bracket is 34 percent; this is given by @VLOOKUP(INCOME, TABLE,2). The total tax on previous brackets, @VLOOKUP(INCOME, TABLE, 4), is $6,156.90. The marginal tax rate applies only to the last part of your income, $34,789 − $31,079. Your total tax is therefore

$0.34 \times (34,789 − 31,079) + 6,156.90 = \$7,418.30$.

### 23.6 @INT

This function gives the integer portion of a number. Thus, for example, @INT(3.69782) = 3. In chapter 22 we used @INT(1000 ∗ @RAND) to give us a three-digit integer between 000 and 999.

### 23.7 @MOD(A, B)

This function gives the remainder of $A/B$. Thus, @MOD(3/2) = 1.

### 23.8 @PI

This function, which takes no arguments, produces the number $\pi$.

### 23.9 @ABS(x)

@ABS(x) gives the absolute value of $x$. For example, @ABS($-3.987$) = 3.987, and @ABS(4.01) = 4.01.

### 23.10 @SUM(range), @STD(range), @VAR(range), @COUNT(range)

The first three of these functions give the sum, the standard deviation, and the variance of an indicated range. @COUNT returns the number of non-blank cells in a range.

## 23.11   @NOW

This function returns a clock reading. If you do not format the cell in which you put @NOW, the number you get will look something like 32128.379444. The numbers to the left of the decimal place are the date (days since January 1, 1900), and the numbers to the right of the decimal place are the time. To get something more comprehensible, format the cell using /Range Format Date.

Some examples of the use of @NOW are the timing cells used throughout this book in complicated macros. These are composed of three macro commands, which relate to three cells:

starttime      {let starttime, @now}

stoptime      {let stoptime, @now}

elapsed        {let elapsed, starttime − stoptime}

When the commands are placed appropriately in the macro (i.e., the first command near the beginning of the macro and the last two commands at the end of the macro) and when the cells are formatted to show the time, these cells can show the amount of time it takes to run a macro. This is a must for good programming.

# 24 Macros in Lotus

## 24.1 Introduction

Macros in Lotus serve two main functions: They speed up certain kinds of operations by eliminating keystrokes, and they allow programming within the spreadsheet.

This chapter discusses both of these functions. It is not intended as a complete guide to Lotus macros; for this the reader is referred to the documentation provided by Lotus. Rather, the purpose of this chapter is to provide a brief introduction to macros, an explanation of the commands used in the book, and the distillation of some of the author's experience with the programming of macros.

## 24.2 A Simple Example

Suppose you are making up a list of names and telephone numbers. The list looks like

| NAME | TELEPHONE NUMBER |
|------|------------------|
| Doe, Mary | 721-8976 |
| Smith, John | 456-9087 |
| etc. | |

Of course, since you have a lot of friends and acquaintances, the list is very long!

Lotus is ideal for making and keeping such lists, since it can alphabetize them. However, typing such a list is not much fun. Here is what you have to do:

TYPE THE NAME
{cursor right}
TYPE AN APOSTROPHE, THEN THE PHONE NUMBER
{cursor down} {cursor left}
...
start all over again.

Why do you type an apostrophe before the telephone number? Because you want Lotus to regard the number as a label, so you can type in hyphens, parentheses, or spaces, as in the following:

718-5045
(215) 421-8976

There is another problem is typing in this list: When you type numbers on most IBM PC's or compatibles, you either have to use the top row of the keyboard (which is very cumbersome), or you have to keep pushing the [num lock] key in order to use the number pad both as arrows and as numbers.

This typing problem is solved by a Lotus macro. Go to a far-off corner of your worksheet (if you have about 100 names and numbers to enter, go to row 120, column 1, for example). Type in

{?}{RIGHT}'{?}{DOWN}{LEFT}

Now use /Range Name Create to give the cell a label. In order for a macro to work, the label must start with a backslash and be followed by one of the letters of the alphabet. (The only other possibility is \∅, a macro that operates as soon as the spreadsheet is called.) Let us call our macro \A.

To use the macro, put the cursor on the place where you want the first name to go. Now press [alt] A (both keys together). You will see CMD at the bottom of the screen. Type in your first names (Jones, Jim) and hit [enter]. Presto! The cursor goes right. Looking at the top left corner of the screen, you see that an apostrophe has already been placed in the cell for the telephone number. Now all you have to do is enter the number. Press [num lock] to make it easy to enter the number, type away (Jim's telephone number is 345-8976), and hit [enter] again. The number is entered (as a label, because of the apostrophe), and the cursor moves down a row and to the left, which is where you wanted it to go. CMD disappears from the bottom of the screen, because you have finished executing your first macro.

Now what? You could type [alt] A again and start over with the next name, but there is an easier way: Why not have the macro call itself, so that it keeps repeating? There is a command to do this. Go back to your macro, hit F2 for editing the cell, and add {BRANCH \a} to the end of what was already there. By now the cell will look like

{?}{RIGHT}'{?}{DOWN}{LEFT}{BRANCH \A}

What you have added to the macro is a "go to" command. {BRANCH \A} sends the macro back to \A, so now the macro says

{?}                            Wait for a keyboard entry
(Lotus will know you are finished when you hit [enter]
{RIGHT}            Move the cursor right

'{?}                    Put an apostrophe in the current cell, then wait for
                       further keyboard input
{DOWN}{LEFT}           Move the cursor down and then left
{BRANCH \A}            Go to the macro named A

The final step is to put the name of the macro in the worksheet. As we
have already seen, this is not strictly necessary for working the macro;
however, it is good programming practice, and it eliminates confusion. In
the cell to the left of the macro (or above it), type '\A. (Why the apostrophe?
Lotus will fill the whole cell with A's if you type only \A. The apostrophe
tells it that \A is a label, not a command.)

Now your worksheet area looks like

\A      {?}{RIGHT}'{?}{DOWN}{LEFT}{BRANCH \A}

### 24.3   Some Basic Macro Rules

1. All macro commands are either / commands or are enclosed in braces { }.

2. In most cases a macro will stop by itself. The macro

\A      {?}{RIGHT}{?}{LEFT}{DOWN}

will stop after two keyboard entries have been made. On the other hand,
the macro

\A      {?}{RIGHT}{?}{LEFT}{DOWN}{BRANCH \A}

will not stop of its own volition. To stop this macro, press [ctrl][break].
There will be a beep from the spreadsheet, and the top of the spreadsheet
will flash "error." Press [esc] and your problems are solved. (If you forget
{?}'s, you will be in trouble. The macro will then read

\A      {RIGHT}{LEFT}{DOWN}{BRANCH \A}

This will spin around the spreadsheet so fast that it will be impossible to
stop with [ctrl][break]. The only way to stop it will be to reset the
computer. Unless you saved your spreadsheet before you implemented the
bad macro, you will have to do all your work over again.)

3. A macro reads down a column, cell by cell, until it reaches the first empty
cell. When it reaches an empty cell, it stops. This means that there is nothing
to prevent you from making your macros neat and readable; just arrange

them neatly in cells down a column, making sure that the amount of information packed into a single cell does not exceed the amount a normal human being is capable of grasping.

4. Macros are indifferent to case: {let ...} and {LET ...} have the same effect.

## 24.4  An Advanced Macro

Let us implement the Newton-Raphson method for finding the maxima and minima of the function

$$f(x) = x^4 - 4x^3 - 6x^2 + 2$$

with a macro. Here is what we are going to do: In order to find the maximum of a function, we will enter the function's argument $x$, the function $f(x)$, its first derivative $f'(x)$, and its second derivative $f''(x)$ into the spreadsheet. We will also enter a cell named "marker," which will enable us to start the maximization at a given desired value of $x$, and a cell called "runnumber," which will enable us to see how many iterations of the procedure we have made. At this point the spreadsheet entries look as follows:

marker
runnumber
x
f(x)                    $+x^4 - 4x^3 - 6*x^2 + 2$
first der               $4*x^3 - 12*x^2 - 12*x$
second der              $12*x^2 - 24*x - 12$

Of course, before putting in the formulas, we will use /rnlr to attach the cell name to the cell to the right.

Now let us write the following macro, known as \B:

```
{if marker<>0}{let x,marker}{let runnumber,0}~{quit}
{let x,x-first der/second der}~
{let runnumber,runnumber+1}
{if runnumber>20}{calc}{quit}
{if aabs(first der)<0.00001}{calc}{quit}
{branch \b}
```

What this macro does is almost self-explanatory. Note the syntax of the {let   } statement and the {if   } statement. The macro quits operating if you have entered marker $\neq 0$ (which simply resets the values), or if you have made more than 20 runs, or if the absolute value of $f'$ is very small.

Two features of this macro are worth noting. The first is the tilde (˜) that is appended to certain of the commands. The tilde is a macro for [ENTER], and it is needed with certain macro commands to update the screen. When you first write a macro, don't spare the tildes; this way you will be able to see the macro in operation on the screen. Once you are sure that the macro works, start editing it and see how many tildes you can remove. (See exercise 3 at the end of this chapter.) The second notable feature of \B is the use of {CALC}. This command invokes the F9 key and causes the spreadsheet to recalculate before quitting. All the function keys can be used in macros if you simply put their names in curly brackets: {EDIT} (F2), {TABLE} (F8), {GOTO} (F5), and so on. In this particular case, if you leave off {CALC} the macro will terminate by leaving a CALC message on the bottom of the screen.

Running the macro \B, you find three extrema for the function in question: −0.79128, 0.00000, and 3.791288.

## 24.5   Macro Keywords

A full listing of macro keywords can be found in the Lotus manual (and the excellent on-screen help). The keywords used in this book are the following:

BEEP
BLANK
BRANCH
CONTENTS
FOR
GET
IF
LET
PUT
QUIT

## 24.6   Examples

This section gives some examples of how to use the macro keywords employed in the text.

## BEEP

Lotus can make the IPM PC and compatibles sound one of four "beeps." The beeps are labeled 0, ..., 3. (The speaker of the IBM PC can actually make a full range of sounds, from 37 to 32767 cycles per second. Lotus can access only 4 of these. Unless you want musical spreadsheets, this is not a severe limitation. To listen to the rest of the sounds, learn BASIC.)

The following macro (\A) sounds a beep of type TYPE:

```
type           2


\A        {BEEP type}
```

## LET

LET substitutes a value in a cell.

## FOR

FOR executes a subroutine a certain number of times. Here is an example:

```
\B        {FOR type,0,3,1,\C}~


\C        {BEEP type}~
```

The FOR statement sound a BEEP of type TYPE for TYPE = 0, 1, 2. The syntax of the FOR statement is:

{FOR counter location, start-number, stop-number, step-number, macro location}

Thus, the FOR statement in \B has start-number = 0, stop-number = 3, step-number = 1, and for each step runs the macro at \C.

## WINDOWOFF and PANELOFF

These two commands freeze the screen during macro execution. At first this can be quite irritating, since you have no idea what is going on. The only sign of macro operation you see if you use these commands is a CMD at the bottom of your screen. You should not use these commands until you are sure that your macro is working properly.

The panel referred to in PANELOFF is the top part of the screen. The rest of the screen is the window referred to in WINDOWOFF.

The advantage of WINDOWOFF and PANELOFF is that they speed up the operation of the macro considerably.

**WINDOWON and PANELON**

These may be inserted anywhere in the macro to reverse the effect of WINDOWOFF and PANELOFF. The effect will be to update the screen. Remember that QUIT automatically invokes WINDOWON and PANELON.

**GETLABEL and GETNUMBER**

These two commands put a message on the panel (the top of the screen) and wait for keyboard input. This input is then put into an appropriate cell. The following macro asks the user for his name and age:

```
name       Jonathan
age               6


\D        {GETLABEL What is your name?   ,name}~
          {GETNUMBER How old are you?    ,age}~
```

**PUT**

This command enters a number or a string into a specified location in a range. The syntax of the command is

{PUT range name, column number, row number, value or string}

**BLANK**

This command erases a cell or a range. For example,

{BLANK results}~

erases the contents of the range called RESULTS.

**IF**

This command continues the execution of the same macro line if the condition is true; otherwise, it goes on to the next line. Example:

{IF X(3) > 0}{LET Y(6), X(3)^2}
{IF X(3) <= 0}{LET Y(6), −X(3)}~

**BRANCH**

This command sends the macro to a different cell, where it continues execution.

## 24.7  Minimizing Macro Execution Time

Long macros, and macros that contain many loops (as do some of the simulation macros in this book), can take an extensive time to run. There are several ways to minimize the execution time of these macros:

1. Use {WINDOWSOFF}{PANELOFF} to prevent the macro from updating the screen. This can save up to 40 percent of the execution time. Do this only when you are sure that the macro works.

2. Turn the spreadsheet to manual recalculation. This prevents the spreadsheet from recalculating (often a time-consuming process) except as you direct it to be recalculated. Once you have done this, you will need to use {CALC} to recalculate the spreadsheet.

3. Minimize the number of formulas in cells. It is less time-consuming to place data in cells through a macro than to put data in cells via a formula. The formula will recalculate with every spreadsheet recalculation, whereas data placed in the cells via a macro will change only when the macro tells them to change.

4. Economize on tildes. A tilde is the macro equivalent of [ENTER]. Some macro commands need a tilde in order to execute. Examples of such commands are {BLANK}, {GETLABEL}, {GETNUMBER}, and {LET}. Other commands (notably {BRANCH}) need no tilde. Often several tildes can be replaced by one.

5. Try to avoid putting cursor movements into your macros. When you first learn macros, you may be inclined to use commands that mimic the actual movement of the cursor on the spreadsheet. For example, both of the following macros generate a random number and put it in a cell, but the second macro (which calls the range of cells into which the number DATA can be put) is much more efficient:

```
'\A
 '@rand/rv~~
 {down}

'\B
 {put data,0,runnumber,@rand}
```

6. Use efficient programming. This is the hardest technique, and poten-
tially the most useful. After your macro works, go back and look to see if
there is a better and simpler way you can get the same tasks accomplished.

## Exercises

1. Write a macro to find the roots of the function

$$f(x) = x^3 + 6.6x^2 - 29.05x + 22.64.$$

2. The Newton-Raphson example given in this chapter has two separate
conditions for quitting the macro. Use the #or# logical argument to
combine these two conditions.

3. Reconsider the Newton-Raphson macro in the text. What happens if
you take out all the tildes? What happens if you take out the {calc}
commands? Put in a timing loop (see chapter 22 for an example). Is there
a difference in execution time between a macro with no tildes and a macro
with tildes that uses {windowsoff} {paneloff}?

# 25 Data Table Commands

## Introduction

Lotus's Data Table commands are powerful commands that make it possible to build tables. There are two such commands: /DT1, which makes it possible to build a table that depends on only one variable, and /DT2, in which a single formula varies with changes in two parameters.

## 25.2 An Example

A project has an initial cost of $1,150, and seven subsequent cash flows. The cash flows in years 1–7 grow at a rate $g$, so that the cash flow in year $t$ is

$CF(0) \times (1 + g)^t$.

Given a discount rate $r$, the net present value (NPV) of the project is

$$NPV = -1,150 + \sum_{t=1}^{7} \frac{CF(0) \times (1 + g)^t}{(1 + r)^t}.$$

The internal rate of return (IRR), $i$, is the rate at which the NPV equals zero:

$$-1,150 + \sum_{t=1}^{7} \frac{CF(0) \times (1 + g)^t}{(1 + i)^t} = 0.$$

These calculations are easily done in Lotus:

| year | 0 | 1 | 2 | 3 | 4 | 5 | 6 | 7 |
|---|---|---|---|---|---|---|---|---|
| cashflow | -1150 | 234 | 257.4 | 283.14 | 311.454 | 342.5994 | 376.8593 | 414.5452 |
| growth | 0.1 | | | | | | | |
| discount | 0.15 | | | | | | | |
| irr | 0.176025 | | | | | | | |
| npv | 101.4556 | | | | | | | |

## 25.3 Setting Up /Data Table 1

We want to know how the NPV and the IRR are affected by a change in the growth rate. /Data Table 1 allows us to do this simply.

First, set up a formula. Put the formulas for NPV and IRR on the top row, and put the variable you wish to vary on the first column. Leave the upper left corner blank.

In the example below, the cell below the text "npv" contains the formula for the net present value:

$(-1150 + @npv(\text{discount, cash flow}))$.

Similarly, the cell below the text "irr" contains the formula for the internal rate of return. "Discount" and "cash flow" are range names that refer to the spreadsheet of the preceding section.

|              | npv      | irr      |
|--------------|----------|----------|
|              | 101.4556 | 0.176025 |
|              | 0.1 101.4556 | 0.176025 |
| growth rate  | 0.15 274.3478 | 0.215019 |
|              | 0.2 474.1957 | 0.253736 |

Now press /DT1. You are first asked for the appropriate range. This is the rectangle whose upper left corner is the blank cell and which includes the growth rates and the formulas (but *not* the titles "npv" and "irr"). Next you are asked to indicate the variable on which both formulas depend. Go back to the spreadsheet of the preceding section and put the cursor on the growth rate (0.10). When you strike [enter], Lotus will calculate the table.

With /Data Table 1 you can put multiple formulas on the top row, as long as the dependence is on the same variable.

## 25.4   Using /Data Table 2

/Data Table 1 allows you to vary *many* formulas while changing one parameter. /Data Table 2 allows you vary *one* formula while changing *two* parameters.

As an example, we will calculate the NPV's of the cash flows for different growth rates and discount rates, using the example above. We create a new rectangular range. Down the left column we put values of the first variable we wish to vary, and across the top row of the range we put values of the second variable. The upper left corner (the one left blank in /DT1) now contains the formula whose value we wish to calculate for different combinations of the two variables—in this case,

$(-1150 + @NPV(\text{discount, cash flow}))$.

If you have done another Data Table in the same spreadsheet, first do /Data Table Reset. Now hit /DT2. As before, you first indicate the range—in this case, the rectangle that starts with the formula in the upper left corner. Lotus now asks you for the first variable; indicate 0.1 in the original spreadsheet (the growth rate). The second variable is 0.15 in the original spreadsheet. Wait a few seconds and the whole table will appear as follows:

| | discount rate | | | |
|---|---|---|---|---|
| 101.4556 | 0 | 0.1 | 0.15 | 0.2 |
| 0.1 | 1069.998 | 339.0909 | 101.4556 | -82.6117 |
| growth rate 0.15 | 1439.631 | 558.2505 | 274.3478 | 55.74242 |
| 0.2 | 1872.321 | 812.6476 | 474.1957 | 215 |

## 25.5  An Aesthetic Note: Hiding Unnecessary Cells

Data Tables tend to look rather strange, because the formula being calculated shows up either on the top row (in the case of /DT1) or in the top left corner (in the case of /DT2). You can make the table look nice by *hiding* the formulas. Put the cursor on the formula, and hit /Range Format Hidden. Presto! The cells in question appear blank. They are not really blank, however, as you can tell from looking at the upper left corner of the screen. Lotus will still calculate their values. You just can't see them in the spreadsheet, and their contents won't print.

# Index

Order Form for diskettes to be used with
*Numerical Techniques in Finance*
by Simon Benninga

These diskettes contain the Lotus 1–2–3 spreadsheets that illustrate examples
from *Numerical Techniques in Finance*.
Permission is granted for users to make as many copies as needed.

You must have Lotus 1–2–3 or a compatible spreadsheet program to use
these disks.

Please send the following:

| Qty | Version | Code | unit price | Total |
|-----|---------|------|-----------|-------|
| _____ | IBM 5.25 in. (360K, 3 disks) | BENDI5 | $19.95 | _____ |
| _____ | IBM 3.5 in. (1.44MB, 1 disk) | BENDI3 | $19.95 | _____ |
| | | postage | | $2.50 |
| | | Grand Total | | _____ |

All prices in U.S. dollars.  Checks must be drawn on a U.S. bank.

_____ Check enclosed payable to The MIT Press.

_____ Bill my MasterCard        _____ Bill my Visa

Credit Card No. _____ Signature _____

Ship to    Name_____

           Address _____

           City _____ State_____ Zip_____

Special Instructions_____

_____

Send Order to:  The MIT Press, 55 Hayward Street, Cambridge, MA 02142